Alvin Rosenbaum 9/83 NYC

MAN ABOUT TOWN

THE MIT PRESS, CAMBRIDGE, MASSACHUSETTS, AND LONDON, ENGLAND

MAN ABOUT TOWN

FRANK LLOYD WRIGHT IN NEW YORK CITY

Herbert Muschamp

© 1983 by
The Massachusetts Institute of Technology

This book was set in Melior
by The MIT Press Computergraphics Department
and printed and bound by Halliday Lithograph
in the United States of America.

Library of Congress Cataloging in Publication Data

Muschamp, Herbert.
  Man about town.

  Bibliography: p.
  1. Wright, Frank Lloyd, 1867–1959. 2. New York
(N.Y.)—Buildings. I. Title.
NA737.W7M87 1983   720′.92′4   83–9840
ISBN 0-262-13192-7

To a Sublime Quartet
Amy, Dick, and Tucker Ashworth, and James Baxter

C O N T E N T S

ACKNOWLEDGMENTS

This project was begun with support from the National Endowment for the Arts and continued with a grant from the Architectural Fellowships Program of Educational Facilities Laboratories. I am especially grateful to Nancy Ambler of EFL for her interest and support throughout the term of the fellowship. For assistance with illustrations, I would like to thank Edgar Tafel, Bruce Brooks Pfeiffer of the Frank Lloyd Wright Memorial Foundation, Thomas Grischowsky of the Museum of Modern Art, Pamela Sharpless of New York University's Department of Fine Arts, Suzanne O'Keefe, Max Protetch, William Goidell, Muriel Muschamp, and especially Pedro Guerrero, whose pictures are each worth a thousand words of thanks. Though they may find my de Tocqueville excerpt less pertinent to Wright's Utopian planning than to my interpretation of it, I am much indebted to Robert Twombly and William Allin Storrer for reading the manuscript and offering helpful suggestions for improvement. My special gratitude also goes to Everard Ashworth, Marc Balet, Randy Bourscheidt, Henry Geldzahler, Ethan Geto, Kenneth Halpern, Bernard Hanson, Andrew MacNair, Alexandra Morphett, Diane Peterson, Bosa Raditsa, Molly Snyder, Michele Turre, and Victoria Woodhull. I am much indebted to Robin Bledsoe for her careful attention to the text and to Eric Ashworth for his generous attention to me.

I N T R O D U C T I O N

The Guggenheim Museum is Frank Lloyd Wright's most famous building and one of New York City's most distinguished landmarks. At the same time the Guggenheim's fame and distinction have obscured the fact that Wright's work in New York was not limited to this singular, memorable design.

The Guggenheim's flamboyant formal eccentricity, its deficiencies as a museum of art and its defiance of Fifth Avenue's bland architectural manners, the proverbial invitation of its spiral ramp to roller skates as well as controversy—all lead easily to the popular assumption that the museum is, indeed, "Wright's joke on New York," a city he was known to despise. However, the Guggenheim is but one in a series of New York buildings, projects, and interiors, spanning a major segment and defining a major theme of Wright's long career. That series is the subject of this book.

If you're a writer and you live in New York, you naturally want to write about it. If you're an American and you write about architecture, you want to write about Frank Lloyd Wright, and I am fortunate that my subject has enabled me to focus my interest in these two large fields in one small book. But I had a quite different subject in mind when I began to write it. Originally, Wright was one subject in a study I planned to make of New York architecture as captured in images and words by contemporary artists and writers during the city's rise to dominance in twentieth-century culture.

In addition to Wright, my subjects included Fritz Lang, Colette, Henry James, Georgia O'Keeffe, F. Scott Fitzgerald, Christopher Isherwood, Le Corbusier, Berenice Abbott, Mondrian, Duchamp—artists who had helped to shape our image of the city by writing, painting, photographing, or drawing images of its buildings.

What these figures have in common, apart from being artists, is that they were, initially had been, or in some cases chose to see themselves as, outsiders—visitors, tourists, immigrants, pilgrims, authentic or self-styled aliens to the city and its culture. How had these cultural out-of-towners variously oriented themselves toward New York as the city approached its apogee of cultural influence? My objective was to document the wide diversity of their responses, an emotional and intellectual spectrum ranging from rapture and enthusiasm, through brief, intense flirtations and abiding affection, mild intimidation and sensible criticism, to abject fear and obsessive loathing. It was not easy to select who among this group had fashioned images that best captured the infrared of ardor, but at the ultraviolet end of extreme antipathy Frank Lloyd Wright had little competition. As Morton and Lucia White observed in their 1962 survey, *The Intellectual versus the City*:

With Wright [the] tale of more than a century and a half of intellectual anti-urbanism reached a climax. . . . He stands out among American architects as the irascible, bombastic critic of the American city. . . . He was a Wisconsin farm boy who seems never to have changed his mind about cities from the day he first came to "dazzling," "brutal" Chicago in 1887, when he reacted much as Dreiser's Carrie did.

Actually, Wright did change his mind about Chicago. In 1939, speaking before a group of British architects, he praised Chicago's "generous park system, the greatest on earth." He paid tribute to the fact that

thanks to an architect, Dan Burnham, Chicago seems to be the only great city in our States to have discovered its own waterfront. Moreover, to a greater extent than any other city, it has a life of its own. Chicago takes pride in building things in a big broad substantial way. . . . Eventually, I think that Chicago will be the most beautiful great city left in the modern world.

But Wright seems never to have changed his mind about New York from the time he journeyed there in 1926—a fugitive from justice under the Mann Act—to get his "worm's eye view" of society. New York remained for him a place that reduced its citizens to the life of insects. "Streams of more and more insignificant facades and dead walls rise and pour out of hard faced masses behind and above human beings all crawling on hard pavements like ants to hole in somewhere or find their way to this or that

2

cubicle." In 1958, the future Wright saw for such a city was oblivion, "by way of the atom bomb."

Traces of my original plan remain in the first two chapters of this book. That I did not complete it as planned was the result of two factors.

The first was a matter of timing. As I write this introduction in 1982, New York City is experiencing a building boom surpassing any I have witnessed, and many New Yorkers have, for the time being at least, suppressed the memory of the fiscal crisis that monopolized the headlines six or seven years ago. Happy days are here again. The lights are back on the bridges. The city fathers of Houston have not, after all, persuaded the Museum of Modern Art to move its collection to the Sun Belt. And so it seems somewhat spoilsport and un-civic-minded to bring up the bad days; to recall, for example, how the appearance in New York harbor on Independence Day 1976 of a flotilla of tall-masted schooners was seized upon as a desperate symbol of imminent salvation. At the time, New York seemed headed for oblivion not with the bang of an atom bomb but with the whimper of wounded pride.

I returned to New York in the mid-70s after a time in California, where doom was typically imagined in the form of an earthquake. Here the specter was bankruptcy, a tidal wave of bad bonds on its way to inundate the city, dissolve its remaining assets, topple its towers like sandcastles. This was not an abnormal fear. Even those of subtler mind who rephrased the big question—"Will New York survive?"—along intellectually more engaging lines—"In what form?"—could not dismiss the evidence of daily headlines charting the deepening crisis; the spectacle of corporation pullouts and department store closings; the disturbing silence of jackhammers not hammering far into the night.

I greatly admired my more unflappable friends who managed to keep the whole thing in calm perspective, who saw no reason to panic, or who found it all vastly entertaining, thinking that there were after all far worse ways to spend one's life than rearranging the deck chairs on so stylish a sinking ship. But I suspect there was also a lot of whistling in the dark—and a lot of dark to whistle in, as the energy crisis descended, casting an additional pall. Even Frank Lloyd Wright had singled out for rare praise the glittering look of New York at night; now, in accordance with federal energy guidelines, New York had put away its nighttime jewels, or, as seemed more likely, pawned them.

I recall those depressing days not for the sake of nostalgia—although, come to think of it, there was something stirring, in a paranoid way, about feeling so embattled, and the silence of the jackhammers made a nice change—but to explain my dissatisfaction with the concept of my project.

I had been drawn to the idea because, after a period of traveling, my fresh impression of the city made me want to explore the impressions of others. But in the mid-70s such an approach seemed not only trivial but morbid. It was a time for passions rather than impressions, and my concentration on the artists of an earlier era seemed only to confirm the claims of the city's detractors: that the best years were over, nothing left now but the memories, pictures, and words that I was assembling for my arty scrapbook.

The triumph of the I-told-you-so's, at least to me, rankled even more than the grubby streets, the shredded pavements, the subway's pan-sensory assault. I hadn't been back long enough to build up a thick skin; and with the overcompensating chauvinism of a prodigal returned, took it all somewhat personally. I found myself drawn increasingly to the Wright chapter as though it offered a chance to rebut symbolically those critics who applauded the decline Wright had so self-righteously predicted.

But the second factor that contributed to my change of subject is that, as the Wright segment began to monopolize my time and interest, I began to realize that Wright was not, in fact, the ideal antagonist in my imaginary agon. In the course of research, it became clear that Wright's true attitude toward the city was not all congruent with the tone of his many published outbursts against it, that his feelings were complicated by an ambivalence not entirely dissimilar from the love-hate stance of the average New Yorker. In a series of projects, in his essays and autobiographical writings, I discerned a more than casual connection between Wright and New York, a connection which, formed in Wright's middle years and continuing to influence a significant area of his work thereafter, represented an unwritten chapter in the story of his later years. Finally, it appeared to me that, quite apart from the curiosity value attached to many unbuilt projects and lesser-known works by major designers, the fruits of this connection illuminated Wright's thought on issues of continuing philosophical pertinence to American architecture at the present time.

Because I take issue with the popular assumption that Wright was anti-city, perhaps I should emphasize strongly that I am not claiming the opposite. What I do claim is that the city provoked in Wright an ambivalent reaction that exercised a sizable influence upon his life and art in later years. The major architectural projects discussed here—the steel and glass cathedral, the St. Mark's towers, the Guggenheim—can each be read as either anti-urban or pro-urban. I believe they must be read both ways. And I ask the reader to indulge the occasionally abrupt compass sweeps of my argument as the result of my efforts to keep reasonable pace with the zigzags of Wright's tirelessly inventive intuition.

4

To describe the ambivalence the city engaged in Wright's personal life is more properly a biographer's task. Though this is not a biography, I have included some biographical material in the opening chapter to support my interpretation of the ambivalent element in Wright's later work. Wright explicitly offered up his life along with his work for critical appraisal, insisting that neither could be adequately understood without the other. I have taken up his offer to the extent necessary to show how the conflicts that brought his work to a halt at the beginning of the middle years (1910–1935) helped to shape the development of the work he undertook when he resumed more active practice.

Ambivalence in one's emotional life is perhaps a defect. I will argue that in Wright's creative life it emerged, after much personal hardship, as a decided asset in carrying out the task of his later years with which I am principally concerned: his philosophical exploration of the architect's role in American culture. No American architect was more acutely conscious of the divided nature of his medium, of architecture's dualistic fidelity to the social and artistic programs set forth by American culture. No one was more painfully aware of how often the expectations with which America burdens its architects—to create masterpieces and to serve high-minded democratic and social ideals—are brought into conflict by the very medium, the building, in which the architect seeks their harmonious resolution. It is in the field of urban design that Wright looked for ways to resolve these conflicts, and it was here that he succeeded in transcending his personal ambivalence by equating it with contradictions inherent in the American architect's cultural role.

The book is in three parts. In the first, I have traced the dotted line of Wright's middle years against the cultural backdrop of early-twentieth-century America to highlight some of the reasons that his contact with New York in the 1920s marked a change in the direction of his career. In the second part, New York's role in the development of Wright's later career is emphasized in an analysis of buildings, projects, and writings that illustrate aspects of his work and thought in the field of urban design.

In the concluding part, which can be read almost as a separate essay, I have tried to locate this area of Wright's work within the wider context of American twentieth-century architecture and urbanism. New York's value to Wright lay primarily in enabling him to realize more perfectly his Romantic conception of self and art, and the primary value of the work reflecting his connection to New York lies, in turn, in illustrating the impact on American architecture of the Romantic tradition in art, an influence that in my view has been underestimated in surveys of the Modern period.

The reasons for this oversight are partly semantic, arising from confusion about what the term "Romantic" means—a movement, a period, a sensibility—and from the suspicion that the term may in fact be so imprecise as to have no meaningful application except to those artists who have applied it to themselves. Here I shall use it to mean what I understand Frank Lloyd Wright to have meant by it in connection with himself: individualistic, nonconformist, heroic, emphasizing emotional authenticity over objective reason, self-validated experience over social consensus, inspiration over common sense—all that is implied by the panache with which he flourished his family motto, "Truth Against the World."

This conception of Romanticism as a form of embattled antinomianism grew more pronounced in Wright's middle and later years, as he set himself in strategic opposition to the comparative solidarity of the Modern Movement. And his use of the term thus to define himself was not inappropriate to the circumstances. At midcentury, and to a diminishing extent until quite recently, the tendency of architectural historians was to endorse the supposition advanced in the name of Modernism that Romanticism in architecture—as exemplified by Gothic Revival or picturesque buildings in the nineteenth century, by pre-Bauhaus European Expressionist movements in the early twentieth—had been securely interred by an international consensus among the world's leading architects. Historians of Modernism were in fact markedly slower to abandon this belief than many of these leaders themselves proved to be. Thus, when in *Pioneers of Modern Architecture* Nikolaus Pevsner is moved to condemn the "irrational" backsliding of Le Corbusier in his later work, his attempts to satisfy the public's craving for a "surprising and fantastic . . . escape out of reality into a fairy world," he sought to perpetuate an article of propaganda that the architects whose works he purported to chronicle were themselves no longer able to sustain.

Like late Le Corbusier, late Wright provides a lavish illustration of the persistence of Romanticism into the Modern period. But it is, perhaps, the widespread refusal of the Post-Modern generation to mount the anti-Romantic Modern platform that makes the persistence of Romanticism more than an academic exercise in art historical dating. Wright complained that the Modernists had learned from his forms but ignored or misunderstood his ideas. He would find among architects of the Post-Modern generation a far warmer appreciation for ideas Modernists chose to ignore or reject; and they, in turn, may find in Wright (who unlike Le Corbusier simply carried through in later life the implications of a philosophy he had openly espoused throughout his career) a sound defense, should one still be needed, against the charge that their departures from orthodox Modernism represent an irrational aberration.

This is hardly to say that Wright would have looked with favor upon the eclectic forms and ideas of "Post-Modernism," whatever one takes that term to mean. Indeed, he was careful to point out that his own ideal of Organic Architecture, while conceived in "Romance—the Free Philosophy" was "no mere license for doing the thing that you do as you please to do it in order to hold up the strange thing when done with the 'see what I have made' of childish pride." Nonetheless, just as his "pre-Modern" architecture was a major influence on the development of Modernist forms, so the conceptual orientation of his later work may guide receptive Post-Modern architects to legitimately claim for themselves a philosophical heritage from which Modernism was itself, in respect to its ideology, an often surprising and fantastic aberration. Which is simply to say that Wright's Romanticism, once so charmingly out of date, was his response to cultural conditions with which today's architects must still contend.

"Follow the zigs and zags of any given intellectual," William Barrett recently observed, "and you may turn out to be reading the fever chart of the next generation." With the imagination of a world's fair Futurama designer and the inspiration of a preacher possessed, Wright in later years cut some of his most impressive—and most Romantic—zigzags through the field of urban design; and I conclude the book with an attempt to show why a study of Wright's work in this field is not only critical to an assessment of his later career, but of singular value in appraising the sometimes feverish cultural behavior of American architects in the decades following his death.

I would like to clarify two final points. First, there may be readers who would prefer to be warned at the outset that I am concerned at least as much with architectural rhetoric as with architecture itself. I do not mean to imply by this emphasis that Wright's rhetoric—his books, essays, lectures, and remarks—are as important as his buildings. What Wright wrote is unquestionably less valuable—and less eloquent, even as rhetoric—than what he built.

But Wright was rarely content to let his buildings speak for themselves. Acutely aware of Victor Hugo's theory that the printing press had murdered architecture, he did not hesitate to use the press to give his works more life. Books by Wright, prominently displayed atop Wright-designed furniture, are occasionally to be seen in the photographs of interiors used to illustrate other books by Wright. It was not sufficient for Wright to design the house, design and arrange the furniture, select the fabrics, and choose the art work for the walls: like Buckminster Fuller for a later, less gracious generation, he produced "operating manuals" for those who regarded a house not merely as a place to live, but as an opportunity to participate in a way of life imbued with cosmic significance. Wright's printed texts augmented his dwellings in literally bringing home the message (as the blurb for one volume put it) "of architecture not merely as one phase of our life concerned with shelter and comfort, but as a basic, organic necessity for a true democracy."

Yet even critics determined to resist the sometimes cultlike softness of mind indulged in by Wright's most devoted admirers have occasionally been persuaded by Wright's rhetoric to accept the most fanciful interpretations of his buildings. For example, a recent appraisal of the Price Tower by a generally sober authority on Wright states, "refusing to design highrises in city centers, he placed his only one in tiny Bartlesville—population 27,000 in 1960—where it would stand freely like sculpture in a park."

Not quite. Wright originally designed the tower in 1929 for New York City (population 7,000,000), and subsequently sought to interest builders in Chicago (1930) and Washington, D.C. (1940). In none of these "city center" proposals would the tower have stood "freely like sculpture in a park"; in each case Wright prepared drawings depicting the project in groups of closely spaced towers (the Chicago scheme, especially, is a contextualist's delight). That Wright's one skyscraper came eventually to stand in its single Oklahoma version ("an idea that had to wait over thirty years for full realization," as Wright observed) was, of course, a decision made by the client he finally found to build it.

Yet the writer's tribute to Wright's powers of persuasion, while inadvertent, was not misplaced, for to Wright himself, the tower symbolized his Romantic quest for precisely that autonomy the writer credits him with having attained. Of course, an architect almost never has the chance to "place" any building where he will, and seldom such choice over what kind of building he will design—or will "refuse." Like other architects, Wright was subject to H. H. Richardson's First Law of Architecture: "Get the Job." To a degree rarely matched by other architects, Wright made each job an opportunity to prove he was a law unto himself.

In several sections of this book I have tried to analyze Wright's opportunism in action. I rely upon the sophistication of the reader to understand that the word "opportunist" cannot be applied to any architect in a pejorative sense. An architect, Wright said, must have a thorough understanding of his self, his tools, and his opportunities. Long before John Cage inflicted his aleatory music upon the public, Wright had practiced the art of bringing order out of inspired accident. Just as a choreographer like George Balanchine creates, as he says, "on union time," so an architect creates on a borrowed bit of space, on real estate parcels of unforeseen dimension owned by clients with unforeseeable demands. How Wright was able to sustain the coherence, organic development, and unity of his work in a profession governed by fragmentation and fortuitousness was not the least of his many accomplishments. How he added writing to his other tools to achieve these goals is a major theme of this book. By adding writing to the tools of the architect's trade, Wright made the most of each opportunity he had to build; writing was the cementing agent that bound the aggregate of his projects into a carefully formed unity.

Then, too, what Wright wrote was very often a substitute for what he would have liked to build had his society granted him the power of eminent domain that he occasionally considered his due. And when he ventured into the field of urban design, an area in which the instruments of design are customarily held by politicans and bureaucrats rather than architects, his rhetoric often had to carry the full burden of his intentions. Since urban design is the area of his work with which I am primarily concerned, my objective is to show how Wright's writings and his architectural designs were both essential elements in the structure of the whole.

The second point I would like to clarify is whether or to what extent this account of Wright's later work significantly contradicts previous interpretations. Because the bearing of New York City on this work, great or small, has not previously been the subject of critical speculation, this book may strike some readers as an exercise in historical revisionism. I do not consider it so, if only because there are no prior interpretations of this subject to contradict. What I mean by this tautology is that the emphasis I have placed on New York's influence on Wright is meant not to displace but to augment influences discerned by previous observers.

Obviously my account touches on many areas previously written about by others, and occasionally there are areas of disagreement. In focusing on a specific chapter in an artist's life, one's point of view is necessarily different from that adopted in more comprehensive surveys, and one can reasonably expect to reach conclusions different from, though not necessarily incompatible with, the conclusions drawn in full-length treatments.

Wright's "middle period," for example, has been particularly resistant to adequate treatment in full-length studies, in part because, judged against the productivity of his earlier and later years, he appeared to accomplish so little for so long a time. My account judges this period according to different criteria. In my judgment twenty-five years is not too long for a middle-aged man of genius to reinvent himself. And I find the process by which a genius reinvents himself interesting in itself, not simply as a warm-up for his eventually renewed productivity. On the whole, however, I view the first two sections of this book as a kind of pendant to the major large-scale portraits by Henry-Russell Hitchcock, Norris Kelly Smith, and Robert Twombly, and not as an attempt to repaint them. On the contrary, I acknowledge my debt to these writers for assembling the full narrative without which my "unwritten chapter" in Wright's career could not have been written.

"In conclusion," wrote Hitchcock shortly after Wright's death in 1959,

it should be noted that Wright was not a silent creator. Difficult as it may be sometimes to see precisely how, in detail, his ambitions for a universal "organic architecture" of the 20th century reached the particular expression that they did in his own works, his career owed much to what he said and wrote. Posterity will have more material concerning Wright than can be readily digested for a long time in a tremendous oeuvre, a vast volume of intrinsically fascinating drawings, and a written gospel, on which to base a later judgement on this great architect, who was also perhaps the greatest American of his generation.

Here I am trying to account for the particular form of expression reached by Wright in the buildings, drawings, and writings that derived from his connection to New York. Though the account is based on facts, my interpretation is speculative. And while I would be pleased if the reader is persuaded to accept the accuracy of my interpretation, I would be scarcely less gratified if the visitor to the Guggenheim finds his experience of that work enriched by my speculations.

Once you learn to look upon architecture not merely as an art more or less well or more or less badly done, but as a social manifestation, the critical eye becomes clairvoyant, and obscure, unnoted phenomena become illumined.
—Louis Sullivan

1 9 1 0 – 1 9 2 5

TOWARD THE WRONG PLACE AND TIME

In 1915 the English architect William Lethaby defined architecture as "a developing structural art which has as its main purpose the better ordering of town life." A decade later Frank Lloyd Wright had reached the opposite conclusion: his architecture, in many ways reminiscent of Lethaby's Romantic mixture of mythology and morality, began to take as its openly avowed objective the destruction of "town life" as we know it. At the precise moment of America's transformation from an agrarian to a predominantly urban culture, the hardy American strain of antipathy toward the big city found in Wright its most zealous representative since Thomas Jefferson; and, as the capital city of that culture, New York was inevitably to become a major target of his zeal.

To consult Wright on the subject of cities, particularly New York, might seem therefore as perverse an idea as to consult a Visigoth on Rome. Yet while Wright is widely regarded as the most outspoken city hater in American architectural history, one might say that each of the three distinct periods in his seventy-year career was centered upon a different American city.

Chicago, the city with which he is most often associated, provided the setting for most of his early work (1893–1910); he built nothing there after 1914. In the middle years (1910–1935), Wright's most distinctive buildings were the ornate concrete "textile-block" houses of Los Angeles, a city of nomads and scandal sheets that most suitably accommodated the strained life of rootlessness and notoriety that Wright himself led in those years. This book is about the correlation between a third city—New York—and the final period of Wright's work (1935–1959), and about New York's impact on the development of his architecture throughout this culminating phase of his career.

With Wright's early years, the Chicago years in which he perfected the form of the Prairie House that was to remain in the view of many his greatest contribution to modern architecture, this book is only incidentally concerned. Wright's contact with New York was minimal before his departure from Chicago in 1910, though his first New York design is dated that year: a sales booth for the Universal Portland Cement Company, designed for a trade fair at Madison Square Garden.

The design was no more than a trifle, and the city itself seems to have made no overwhelming impression upon him at the time. It was not until 1925, more than halfway through the calamitous middle years of his career, that the city played a significant part in his affairs as other than a place to buy and sell Japanese prints. The major designs considered here are late Wright, artifacts of the period in which the architect's major creation was arguably himself: the Frank Lloyd Wright of popular legend, "the Fujiyama of Architecture," in Lewis Mumford's phrase, an architect whose public persona overshadowed all but a handful of his buildings. It was partially in pursuit of this goal, a dubious one in the opinion of most students of his work, that Wright stumbled into the field of town planning, a youthful profession whose special blend of private self-interest and public relations was itself formulated during this period. He had undertaken a few small-scale projects in community planning, but it was not until the mid-1920s that his interest in urban issues began to emerge as a major theme, culminating in plans for the Utopian "Broadacre City" that preoccupied him from the 1930s forward.

In the past Wright's theoretical work in urban planning has been the subject of thoughtful analysis and harsh criticism, as well as outright rejection by those for whom such visionary projects are at best irrelevant to architecture's fundamental nature as the most practical and down-to-earth among the arts. Yet no one has traced this work back to its specific source in place and time: New York City in the decade 1925–1935. Nor has anyone described how this theme was renewed, developed, and partially fulfilled by Wright's continual contact with New York and New Yorkers throughout his career. For this reason much of the meaning of Broadacre City has eluded the efforts of writers to reconcile Wright's theories, and his insatiable appetite for them, with his more solid achievements in the traditional materials of his medium. It has long been a commonplace to say of Wright's architecture that each building derived "organically" from the nature of the site for which it was designed; Wright's New York designs, and his writings about the city, affirm that his Utopian visions possess this quality as completely as any house he ever built on solid earth. The difference is that his theoretical forms derived not from the natural landscape of divine creation but from the cityscape made by man.

One reason that the nature of Wright's connection to New York has been overlooked is that it was so easily taken for granted; self-evident, one would have thought, from the tone of his well-publicized remarks:

A place fit for banking and prostitution and not much else . . . a crime of crimes . . . a vast prison . . . triumph of the herd instinct . . . outgrown as overgrown . . . the greatest mouth in the world . . . humanity preying upon humanity . . . carcass . . . parasite . . . fibrous tumor . . . pig-pile . . . Incongruous mantrap of monstrous dimensions! Enormity devouring manhood, confusing personality by frustration of individuality. Is this not Anti-Christ? The Moloch that knows no God but *more*?

In light of such outbursts, what is there to add? Of course, an observer might note a discrepancy between the tenor of these remarks and the frequent New York jaunts of their author; but then the very provocation of the insults—New York's position as the nation's capital of culture—was itself a reason to attach no special significance to this apparent betrayal of Wright's principles. What American artist of the twentieth century, even the most fanatic Regionalist painter, did not have to deal with the Moloch of Manhattan? The New York apartment that Wright maintained in the 1950s could be explained by his work on the Guggenheim and other East Coast projects throughout this period. Why subject his business trips to aesthetic interpretation?

True, a psychologist might suspect that both the intensity and the imagery of Wright's epithets were inspired by an object of unusual attraction. If so, he would find that Wright was unusually attracted to a number of people, places, and things besides New York City: Le Corbusier, the Bauhaus, Harvard, abstract painting, Pittsburgh, Washington, D.C., his home state of Wisconsin, the restoration of Colonial Williamsburg, St. Peter's in Rome, and Skidmore, Owings, and Merrill were just a few among Wright's many un-favorites, and one does not readily discern any special strategy to his New York attacks amid the indiscriminate abuse he showered upon everything that threatened to cast the slightest shadow on his turf.

The barbed automatic reflex was integral to Wright's public image; a useful prop, like his cape and malacca cane; even part of his charm. But a review of his published diatribes—sections of his books are scarcely more than that—shows that of all his many adversaries, personal and professional, real and imagined, the city cast by far the longest shadow. He devoted three entire books, and considerable portions of several others, to the city and its place in American culture. The first book he ever wrote (as distinct from portfolios of drawings) dealt with this subject; so did the last one published in his lifetime.

But these books were all published in New York, and American cultural history was itself for the most part written there. Historians have attached no great importance to Wright's attacks because their hometown could afford to overlook what myopia did not already blur: noblesse oblige in the face of lèse majesté, so to speak. Since Wright's dependence upon New York publishers in itself refuted his published "proof" of the city's insignificance, there was no cause for alarm, much less for rebuttal. A city that could go blithely about its business while being dismantled by Robert Moses hardly had sufficient time or reason to ponder the tantrums of an incurable curmudgeon.

But the most obvious reason that the city's importance to Wright has been overlooked is, of course, the absence of important architecture to indicate otherwise. In Oak Park, Chicago can claim a complete outdoor museum of Wright's finest early work. Los Angeles still has its six textile-block houses of the 1920s, the most distinguished works Wright created in this genre. The cities of Buffalo, Kalamazoo, Phoenix, Madison, Racine, and half a dozen more American towns each possess more Wright buildings than New York.

And New York has the Guggenheim, and even the Guggenheim was not completed until after Wright's death. Without concrete evidence to suggest otherwise, why should Wright's Manhattan visitations warrant closer scrutiny? Why search for the origins of a line of work that never came to practical fulfillment?

The answer is that the value of New York was not in providing a congenial setting for Wright's buildings, like Chicago, Los Angeles, and many expensive American suburbs; indeed, the reverse was true. Half the projects Wright designed for New York never left the drawing board; had they done so, New York could not have served him half so well. For Wright's essential New York design was antithesis, a principle that governed his later work as it has the work of many Romantic artists. The city's function, simply put, was to provide him with a reliable means of acting in accordance with this principle.

In the event of nuclear attack, Wright once claimed, the Guggenheim would survive alone, triumphantly intact amid the city's rubble rather as though Wright himself had dropped the bomb. Whether or not the Guggenheim was truly intended as an architectural rendition of his verbal abuse, the notion that Wright hated New York is not, then, a distortion of the position he worked hard to establish. My contention is that this position was itself a distortion, a half-truth, for it was upon the city—more accurately, upon the Utopian anti-city it inspired—that Wright built up the conceptual superstructure of his later work.

Wright's New York designs illustrate the odyssey of a drifter, a has-been who, in late middle age, locates in aggressiveness and anger the means to transform his failure into triumph. They reflect the ambivalence of a man dependent upon the object of his contempt; of one who recognizes in that object a creative challenge he can afford neither to reject nor to relinquish once accepted.

If this pattern is clearer now than it was twenty years ago, it is partly because the object itself has changed. Perhaps only after the focus of Wright's hell-fire sermons had suffered a reverse in fortune comparable to his own at the moment he began to preach could both the pattern and historical pertinence of these designs, and of Wright's urban work in general, be discerned.

Because an architect has far less liberty than other modern artists in determining how, when, where, and on what projects to exercise his talent, much of the "meaning" of his work may often be laid to chance; and it is true that the connection between Wright and New York owed as much to circumstance as to design. New York challenged his imagination because, like Everest, it was there. And it is perhaps because it is no longer quite so solidly "there" as formerly that the connection has acquired in historical meaning what it failed to produce in the form of finished buildings.

This "failure" was, as I have suggested, part of the design. A third of Wright's projects were exhibition structures designed not to last—achievements almost more literary than architectural, given that their function was to generate copy. These ambivalent structures, palpable but not permanent, suited Wright's purposes well, exploiting the city's cultural resources far more efficiently as special events than they could as lasting buildings.

Indeed, the significance of Wright's connection to New York is more apparent now than before primarily because we are culturally more receptive to the forms in which that connection made itself felt: for an architect to base a career on writings and drawings has become almost the rule rather than the exception. More important, we are far more attuned than twenty years ago to the content of Wright's forms. Issues worth barely more than passing mention in the history of architecture assume a higher profile in the context of urbanism, a frame of reference whose cultural significance has increased dramatically since Wright's death. The phenomenon of an architect's public persona, the relation of his philosophical intentions to the built results, his use of the tools of mass communication to project a private vision, the question of his social motivations, are all speculative areas of limited value in objectively assessing the formal achievement of an individual building. At the same time, as indicators of the way an architect conceives and structures his relation to society, these issues are highly pertinent to urbanism, itself a field primarily given to theoretical speculation on architectural intentions.

The Guggenheim Museum, for example, offers a classic illustration of the contrast between architectural and urbanist values. To judge the building's architectural merit one needs no knowledge of Wright's opinions on urban civilization, his view of that civilization's future, his conception of the architect's role in the task of bringing that future about; to appreciate the spatial grandeur of the Guggenheim's rotunda one needs good eyes and a stout neck, not intellectual data. But to assess its worth in the social context of the changing urban environment it is valuable to take into account the philosophical objectives with which the building's design was intentionally saturated.

18

Wright liked to insist that the art of architecture was "even more abstract" than music, and in later years his own architecture tended in fact to become so. He used the exhibition structure, as he used his personal exhibitionism, his books, his speeches, and above all his urban concepts, to convey ideas that could not be so forcibly expressed in more conventional architectural forms: to conduct what amounted to a public twenty-five-year seminar on the architect's role in American culture. That these metaphysical objectives contributed to nothing on the order of the Prairie House may be readily admitted. But to the development of urbanism they contributed much that has yet to be assessed.

Why was New York City Wright's Everest, and why did he wish to scale it? What are the reasons—artistic, social, personal—that America's greatest architect, at a particular moment in his career, took as an adversary America's greatest city at a particular moment in its history? What is the legacy of this connection to urban culture more than twenty years after Wright's death? Is there a discernible connection between Wright's views and the decline of the central city? Do architecture and urbanism constitute in some sense a polarity in our culture? And what, after all, is the specific meaning of "urbanism"?

Although the questions raised by Wright's New York designs are important, some of the designs themselves are from his bottom drawer and might have been better off in his wastebasket, and I do not wish to overestimate their value or indeed that of his urban work in general. Wright's contribution in the field of urban planning, I believe, is far more significant as historical fact than it ever was as practicable theory. And the value in restoring the theory to its proper historical context rests in large part on the importance of history to architecture at the present time. I concur with Vincent Scully that, in the present age of urbanization, "history is essential for architecture, because the architect, who must now deal with everything urban, will therefore always be dealing with historical problems—with the past and, a function of the past, with the future."

Wright's New York designs are the work of the American architect who most strenuously resisted the need to deal with anything urban. In his view the city had no future at all to speak of—only an ignominious "pig-piled" past best buried and forgotten. By his own admission, he would have gladly destroyed all cities rather than compromise his art by cultivating an architectural etiquette of aesthetic self-restraint, harmony with neighbors, sacrifice of self-assertion to an environment ordered by consensus— all the civic virtues the Guggenheim so proudly flouts. And yet, in the very extremity of the symbolic destruction he was compelled to advocate in order to preserve his artistic integrity, Wright ironically anticipated the increasing influence of urbanism on architecture in the years since the Guggenheim went up on Fifth Avenue, coiled for attack.

History has thus far neither proved nor disproved Wright's prophecy that the central city has no future except as the museum of a lost way of life. But in his own time, his inability to resist the city forecast an uncertain future for the solitary masterpiece conceived in flagrant disregard for the urban environment from which, as Wright's own work demonstrated, there was no real escape.

Because Frank Lloyd Wright so loudly broadcast his determination to live a life of Emersonian nonconformity and self-reliance, it is easy to underestimate how obediently that life conformed to Emerson's equally stern contention that "no man can quite emancipate himself from his age and country. . . . Above his will and out of his sight he is necessitated by the air he breathes and the idea on which he and his contemporaries live and toil, to share the manner of his times."

The task of clarifying Wright's position among his contemporaries is challenging, partly because his creative life spanned so many generations (at his death in 1959 his age was more than half his country's), and partly because he was temperamentally incapable of acknowledging a contemporary as a peer. Evidently his age and temperament were logarithmically linked: as he grew older, the larger his figure loomed in his culture, the more vehemently he appeared to shrink from contact with it. At the end of his Oak Park career in 1910, his reputation in Europe outranked that of any other living American artist; by the time he reached middle age—and New York—Europe had lockstepped into the Modern Movement, and Wright chose to stand alone.

In later years he did his best to place himself above competition with his colleagues. Unwilling to lend himself to an "International Style," he sought a universal one, a style of being as much as art, designed to invite comparison to such figures as Moses, Lao-Tse, and Buddha. It is almost easier to concede that his was an intelligence caught in a historical time warp, a divine emanation of gnostic proportions. And yet his determination to break the bonds of history befitted an age in which the American imagination had been captured by Houdini.

Wright's customary classification with Europeans as one of the three or four giants of modern architecture, his frequent characterization as "an American exponent of Modernism," while not entirely inaccurate, increases the difficulty of evaluating his position in American culture by mistakenly implying that, in his middle years, he had more in common with the Bauhaus than with the Boosters, more in common with Walter Gropius, Mies van der Rohe, and Le Corbusier than with, say, Batton, Barton, Durstine & Osborne, or any number of Americans with whom, individually or collectively, more accurate parallels could be drawn: Henry Ford, Hemingway, Lindbergh, Mencken, Darrow, Chaplin, O'Neill, Hecht and MacArthur, Gertrude Stein, Sinclair Lewis, George Gershwin, Jimmy Walker, Hearst, Ring Lardner, Walt Disney, Ziegfeld, Jack Dempsey, Gertrude Ederle, Aimee Semple McPherson, Fatty Arbuckle, Al Capone, Leopold and Loeb—these last not mentioned casually, for in the era of love nests, flappers, and front-page exposés, Wright was better known across America for scandal than for art.

The almost impudent incongruousness of placing these names alongside Wright's reflects an art historical fallacy. Since Wright was an artist, it is appropriate to group him with other artists and, though his own philistinism was not the least American aspect of his creative life, inevitable to look to Europe for contemporary architects of comparable stature. But the result is to make him look a bit ridiculous—an Arts and Crafts bumpkin wheeling about in a maze of modern steel and glass. As Vincent Scully tactfully put it:

Wright's long life's work spanned two vastly different cultural periods, and it did more than a little to bring the second of them, that of the mid-twentieth century, into being. Yet, throughout all the unique invention, it continued to recall the objectives of the first. Wright's "time, his day, his age" was that of late nineteenth-century America.

But if it is misleading to consign Wright to Modernism, it is scarcely better to reduce him to anachronism, a nineteenth-century Romantic adrift in the twentieth, a Rip van Winkle oblivious to the flashing lights of Times Square. To be sure, alienation from his time is one aspect of Wright's later years—part of the myth he intentionally exploited. But it does nothing to explain the resurgence of his career after 1925, when he began once again to participate in the cultural transformation of his time with a vigor at least as potent, and no less impetuous, than that of figures more commonly associated with Jazz Age New York, gangland Chicago, Hollywood, and Detroit. Even if Wright's later architecture were purely an appeal to latent nostalgia, which it was not, the response to that appeal—his unprecedented fame—still says more about America in the 1930s, 40s, and 50s than about any preceding era.

Wright's exile from twentieth-century America, even if initially self-imposed, expresses the dominance of the International Style at midcentury. The waning of that style, its obsolescence as both a cultural gauge and an architectural style, demands the repatriation and chronological adjustment of the climate from which Wright's later architecture emerged. Though it is unlikely that Wright himself would have agreed to the reconciliation gracefully, in retrospect it should be clear that his later work was not conducted in a vacuum, that at every turn he drew upon his cultural environment, if only in an effort to repudiate it. If his emancipation from his age and country has been exaggerated, it is largely because the contempt he showered freely on his surroundings has been taken at face value, not as the expression of an ambivalence that prevailed upon him to remain in America in the teens and twenties, at a time when Europe offered him the chance to escape the shambles of his career at home.

The New York designs are testimony to that ambivalence. Begun at a time when the New York skyline was expanding toward the outer regions of the modern metropolis, when the city itself was advancing toward its midcentury cultural supremacy, these designs are evidence of Wright's commitment to participate in the most dramatic architectural event of his country and time, even when—perhaps especially when—he appeared to turn his back in a huff, or reappeared to whirl a wrecking ball of rhetoric.

To some extent Wright's allegiance to the nineteenth century was overstated by his own attempt to portray himself as a Transcendentalist, using Emersonian language to mask the plain bad manners of his personal quirks and professional quixotries. In fact, two generations stood between Wright and Concord; his prose, his clothes, his mannerisms evoked Brook Farm much the way a suburban drive-in bank evokes the colonial mansion— spuriously. His own life in the late nineteenth century was gregariously urbane. His isolation—ascendent only after his flight from marriage and suburbia in 1910—was as much a symptom of modern "alienation" as an homage to Thoreau; and by 1925 alienation had become his most habitual mode of participation in the events of his time. Of course, Wright's "Transcendentalism" and his "alienation" were both primarily manifestations of the Romantic core of his being, and the characterization of him as "our greatest nineteenth-century architect" reflected the views of critics and historians who—falsely, as one of the most prominent, Philip Johnson, later admitted—prided themselves in thinking that twentieth-century architects had broken decisively with the Romantic tradition Wright himself was proud to carry on.

But a Romantic needs a conventional culture to set himself in opposition to, and if Wright felt that to be American was to be Romantic, then he was never more American than in New York, his admonition that "the real America begins west of Buffalo" notwithstanding. The city renewed his impulse to transcend America only because transcendence expressed America best, because America's purpose was to reach forever, beyond time and place, for perpetual renewal. And in its own intoxicated way the city was the most impressive incarnation of the same impulse, the figment of an ambitious imagination as fully "nineteenth century" as Wright's.

In its thrust toward the sky, New York was as dedicated as Wright to the proposition that a cloud continent could be attained through the medium of architecture, not just invoked through silent meditation. Though he took the city on as adversary, Wright's New York designs are the consequence of an affinity between the city and Wright's view of America at a time when, in Fitzgerald's view, "New York had all the iridescence of the beginning of the world."

New York in 1925 was New York without tears; not a year to set before the sentimental New Yorker half a century later, when the proudest avenues began to darken into so many *vias dolorosas*. New York in 1925 was extravagantly unsentimental; with scarcely a murmur of civic protest, down came Stanford White's Madison Square Garden, up went the New York Life Insurance Tower. The city needed no landmarks: who in the world didn't know where and what it was? In the year 1925 New York captured the cultural vortex; a quickening pull of centripetal and centrifugal forces drew the world into its harbor, cast its energy around the globe like so many Van Allen belts. Trains and steamships arrived; radio waves, newsreels, and ticker tapes rippled outward. *The New Yorker* appeared; so did Rodgers and Hart's "Manhattan," Dos Passos's *Manhattan Transfer*, Fitzgerald's *The Great Gatsby*, and Janet Flanner's *The Cubical City*. But it is Paul Rosenfeld's *Port of New York*, published the year before, that evokes most radiantly the city's rise to cultural supremacy:

The steamers no longer descend from one plane onto another when they come into New York. The port is not the inferior situation, depressive to every spiritual excellence and every impulse to life, which once it was. . . . The port of New York lies on a single plane with all the world today. A single plane unites it with every other port and seacoast and point of the whole world. Out of the American hinterland, out of the depths of the inarticulate American unconsciousness, a spring has come, a push and a resilience; and here where Europe meets America we have come to sit at the focal point where two upspringing forces balance. The sun is rising overhead, the sun which once shown brightly on Europe alone and threw slanting rays merely upon New York. The sun has moved across the Atlantic.

By 1925 the sun had long since set on Frank Lloyd Wright's career. The year's high spot for him was the publication, in Holland, of a sumptuously illustrated monograph, *The Life Work of the American Architect Frank Lloyd Wright*, but even this singular honor had a double edge, for its title appeared to acknowledge what critics had been saying for some years: Wright's life work was over.

Fifteen years had passed since Wright's abrupt departure from Oak Park, his home in the "Golden Age" when, as Louis Sullivan's most gifted disciple, he had made his name as a leader of the Chicago School, inventor of the Prairie House, an internationally respected architect whose early designs helped set the course of European Modernism. Wright had built several major works since his departure from Chicago, but the number of his commissions had steadily declined.

In the prosperous years before the Depression, America was enjoying a building boom; architecture was the Great Prosperity made visible. But Wright's career showed no sign of revival. He was fifty-eight years old in 1925, and already it was time for him to retire to architectural history, time to celebrate his influence, to honor his contribution to an art now advancing into the modern age in the hands of a younger generation. But if his career lay dormant, his personal life was far from inactive. In the past fifteen years he had energetically paved his passage through several legal and not-quite-marriages with a series of highly publicized scandals, as though notoriety were his destination; a defunct architectural practice telegraphed his safe arrival.

Wright stayed in New York in December 1925, and again the following November. He came to the city not to seek his destiny but to escape it, his destiny at that point being a welter of exposé headlines, mortgage foreclosures, suits, countersuits, bankruptcy sales, searches and seizures, his house twice burned down, twice rebuilt, the birth of an illegitimate child, a month in hiding on Lake Minnetonka, a night in the Hennepin County Jail, and no immediate prospects for anything better. His first visit to New York followed the birth of the child, his second the Minnesota arrest.

Wright went to live in New York partly because of circumstance—relatives lived there—but mostly because the city provided a respite, an escape, a place where he could find anonymity to "roam the streets ... alone," to avoid "the newspapers' pursuit of news." His hiding out in the Minnesota woods had been unsuccessful; he hoped the city might absorb him.

He considered traveling to Mexico, then decided upon Puerto Rico—Atlantis, he called it, ingenuously projecting his fear of imminent submersion—and later fled to California. But for now he sought sanctuary on a raft of urban clichés: faceless crowds, winter sidewalks, and a week-old infant tucked into a bureau drawer in an anonymous midtown hotel. The degree and nature of his desperation were reflected in the scale and content of his first significant design for New York: a "Steel Cathedral including Minor Cathedrals for a Million People."

Dubbed "a sort of religious Empire State Building" by Henry-Russell Hitchcock, Wright's cathedral would have been taller than any building then standing—an updated, New World Chartres. While Wright's putative patron, the Reverend William Norman Guthrie, was Episcopalian, both Wright's Unitarian background and his showmanship are unmistakably expressed in the six "minor cathedrals," consecrated to as many faiths and lashed together in a glass-tented, six-ring double-Barnum & Bailey House of God.

Though not in any usual sense an example of Gothic Revival architecture, Wright's cathedral was his most explicit homage to the Gothic tradition that he had been consciously pursuing since his exposure to European architecture in 1910. An inflated glass version of the wooden tepee-style bungalows Wright designed for a Lake Tahoe resort project in 1923, the cathedral bears little formal resemblance to subsequent Wright designs. Its dramatic use of glass anticipates his visionary scheme for the 1933 Chicago Century of Progress Exposition; its elephantine metropolitan scale can be discerned in the atomic-powered "Mile-High Illinois" office-tower project of 1956; finally, a miniature version of the cathedral's tentlike glass pyramid was eventually realized in the suburban Beth Sholom Synagogue of 1959.

But if its contribution to Wright's formal development is slight, the cathedral's place in his philosophical development is momentous. Wright's undercover New York visits were a turning point of his middle years, an experience in which the unfocused aims of the past fifteen years began to crystallize into coherent purpose. New York failed to provide him with the physical and emotional sanctuary he sought so desperately in 1925, but it gave him something more valuable: a viable architectural motif on which to build his second great creative phase.

"After 1910," wrote Hitchcock, "with the wide acceptance of his early work by the European world as the basis of a new architecture, he was conscious of his fame and responsive to a more universal destiny."

But twenty-five years would pass before destiny in turn was responsive to Wright. These years are often described as a hiatus, yet the word hardly seems appropriate to summarize a period half again as long as that in which Wright first made his name. Indeed, the period between Wright's "two careers" was a career in itself of sorts, a time in which he pursued misfortune with the thoroughness and dedication befitting a profession.

Historians of Wright's work have focused on the few but showy architectural achievements of those years (Midway Gardens, the Imperial Hotel, Hollyhock House) and on the personal scandals that limited Wright's output to those few. They have tended to step quickly and gingerly through this troublesome interlude, pointing out this building or that wife but generally not pausing long enough to consider the possibility that this interminable hiatus had an inner consistency, a logic and a development comparable in achievement to the first Golden Age in Oak Park. Accurate enough as an indication of the paucity of buildings constructed, the term "hiatus" misleads by implying that the construction of buildings was, or at least ought to have been, the primary objective of Wright's middle years.

In an essay written in 1910, the period's outset, Wright defined the architect as "a man disciplined from within by a conception of the organic Nature of his task: knowing well his tools, his opportunity and—most important—himself. An Individual working out his problems with what sense of Beauty the gods gave to him." But by 1910 Wright's problem was precisely that he had grown bored with himself, lost interest in his tools. As he recalled in his autobiography, "This absorbing, consuming phase of my experience as an architect ended about 1909. . . . I was losing grip on my work and even interest in it. . . . I could see no way out. Because I did not know what I wanted, I wanted to go away."

Evidently the problems to be worked out now did not lend themselves to treatment in wood, brick, and stone, but in the "organic" material of some internal mechanism but dimly discerned. Wright had misplaced his tools, lost acquaintance with his self, but, in the invitation to travel to Europe to supervise the German publication of a volume of his work in 1910, he at least had opportunity, a chance to go away, perhaps to recover the other two prerequisites for creative discipline. Thus his European success formed "the basis of a new architecture" essentially by giving him the chance—and the courage—to obliterate the old.

But why did success impell him toward so many years of failure? Why was he unable to add success to success and emerge with triumph? Why was an act of self-obliteration essential to his recovery of self-esteem? What was it about his Oak Park life that oppressed him, that stood between him and "the organic Nature of his task?"

Wright's autobiography alludes to the pressures of conventional suburban life, the distractions of his five children at play around and about the studio that ajoined his house, a gradual estrangement from his wife. But the vehemence of the break suggests that these irritants were symptoms of a deeper dissatisfaction that could not be assuaged simply by seeking a divorce, lining his workrooms with cork, moving his office back to downtown Chicago. Instead he left town, left the country at first, and soon after his return proceeded to alienate his professional colleagues more irrevocably than he broke from his family.

Unless one takes as accident that the break occurred at the moment of his widest recognition, then the impulse to go away must be traced to the earliest days of Wright's training, to his formulation of the goals he had now, in large part, achieved. If "the organic Nature of his task" now eluded him, it was perhaps because the task was completed; and the self and tools he had shaped to achieve it were of no further use.

The Chicago School of Architecture was a consequence of the Great Fire of 1871, the cultural flower of twenty years of rebuilding Chicago from rubble into the second largest city in America. Arriving as a young man in the final, culminating years of this period, when the city seemed visibly to promise more future than past, Wright saw Chicago's vitality as a parallel to his own potential, its fresh, many-storied forms as so many stepping-stones to the architectural glory his youthful ambition projected. Although his first impressions of the city were negative, he had no doubt that he had come at the right time to the right place. Years later, in the charac-teristically messianic terms of *A Testament*, he retroactively set the stage for his arrival:

Victor Hugo, in the most illuminating essay on architecture yet written, declared European Renaissance "the setting sun all Europe mistook for dawn." During 500 years of elaborate reiteration of restatements by classic column, entablature and pediment—all finally became moribund. Victor Hugo, greatest modern of his time, went on to prophesy: the great mother-art, architecture, so long formalized, pictorialized by way of man's intellect could and would come spiritually alive again. In the latter days of the nineteenth or early in the twentieth century man would see architecture revive. The soul of man would by then, due to the changes wrought upon him, be awakened by his own critical necessity.

I was fourteen years old when this usually expurgated chapter in *Notre Dame* profoundly affected my sense of the art I was born to live with—life-long; architecture. His story of the tragic decline of the great mother-art never left my mind.

The University of Wisconsin had no course in architecture. As civil-engineer, therefore, several months before I was to receive a degree, I ran away from school (1888) to go to work in some real architect's office in Chicago. I did not want to be an engineer. A visit to the pawnbroker's— "old man Perry"—made exodus possible. My father's Gibbon's *Rome* and Plutarch's *Lives* (see Alcibiades) and the mink cape collar my mother had sewed to my overcoat financed the enterprise.

There, in Chicago, so many years after Victor Hugo's remarkable prophecy, I found Naissance had already begun. The sun—architecture—was rising!

The rhetoric is inflated, but the sense of expectation was neither singular nor unjustified, for by 1888 Chicago had produced Louis Sullivan, and Sullivan had already begun to shape commercial architecture toward ends no less glorified than those Wright claimed that Hugo had prophesied. Steel cage, Otis elevator, railroad bridge, grain elevator, steam engine, stockyard— from the vitality signified by these mundane manifestations Sullivan was molding the tall office building into an idea, "a proud and soaring thing, rising in sheer exultation."

Sullivan brought to the task a vision no less heroic than Wright's, a will no less firm than Wright's would become. In his quest for an architectural principle "so broad as to admit of no exception" (eventually to crystallize into his well-known dictum, "form follows function"), Sullivan tried to invest the meaning of an entire culture in the design of a single building. With him, as with Wright, determination begat determinism: "We are at that dramatic moment in our national life wherein we tremble evenly between decay and evolution, and our architecture, with strange fidelity, reflects this equipoise."

And ambition caused Wright to tremble in even rhythm with his mentor's do-or-die depiction of American culture, as a preparation for the moment of his own arrival. If, as Lewis Mumford wrote, "Sullivan was the first American architect to think consciously of his relations with civilization," and if, as Wright supposed, the rebuilding of Chicago was nothing less than the moment of "critical necessity" by which man would see architecture revive, then Wright was entirely correct to regard Sullivan as an awakening of the modern soul, from Hugo by way of Viollet-le-Duc. And, in joining Sullivan's firm during its most brilliantly creative phase, five years before the Chicago World's Fair put a stop to Sullivan's rise, Wright was in a position to declare himself heir to the impulse Sullivan had first brought forth in architectural form.

As the passage on Hugo shows, Wright not only recognized the historical opportunity at hand, but identified its dawning with the rise of his own ambitions. Perhaps, with luck, he himself was to be the "sun," his the destiny foretold, with such uncanny accuracy, yet with such a conveniently wide margin for Wright to establish himself, "in the latter days of the nineteenth or early in the twentieth century."

And there it was: the future spreading out before him, boundless as the prairie. No matter that in 1893 Sullivan fired him for moonlighting on his own commissions; he was through with being an apprentice, and the World's Fair was about to terminate Sullivan's future anyhow. His mentor's fall might only add a note of patricidal glee to the confidence with which Wright pursued his own destiny. He had by now opened his own practice, married, and moved to Oak Park; and destiny did not intrude upon fantasy for the next fifteen years.

But Wright's abiding sense of cultural determinism, so encouraging in 1888, so reassuring throughout his Oak Park years, ceased to be so fortuitous when the rising sun of American architecture was eclipsed by cultural upheaval and artistic advance abroad. Did not the eclipse of American architecture signify Wright's also, as its rise had foretold his own? This was one element in the dilemma that Wright's European recognition presented in 1910.

Gratifying on the one hand, his success abroad was also deeply disturbing, for, as Wright himself was well aware, it marked the passage of authority in modern architecture from Chicago to Berlin—and with it the eastward transit of the sun that had illuminated the Golden Age in Oak Park. Where once a historical premise had given him confidence, he now reaped the disadvantages of having attributed any measure of his success to being in the right place and time.

In retrospect it now appeared that the flurry of activity constituting Wright's "Naissance" was not the cosmic fulfillment of Hugo's "remarkable prophecy," but the outcome of the more prosaic circumstance that Chicago had burned down and needed buildings in a hurry. That these buildings were new and tall, "proud and soaring" things owed perhaps less to aesthetic conviction than to the destruction by fire of over 17,000 of the old ones, and the wider profit margin in tall ones.

As Wright had once been secure in casting himself as messiah to Hugo's prophet, so another of Hugo's declarations might now return to shatter that confidence: if nothing is more powerful than an idea whose time has come, can anything be feebler than one whose time has come—and gone? Was "Naissance" nothing more than the Chicago Fire that Frank Lloyd Wright mistook for dawn? Or was the eclipse only temporary, a moment's darkness that he could scare away with loud noises, with cries of betrayal and rage, with the trumpet-blowing egocentricity that now began to figure so prominently in his relations with the world?

The ascent of European Modernism robbed Wright of the rationale with which he had carried on Sullivan's cause since the setback of the World's Fair. Since modern architecture was clearly neither dead nor defeated, but alive and flourishing in Berlin, his conception of the Modern as a native American social phenomenon was deflated. His recognition abroad signified that both he and Sullivan had at least tentatively been assigned their places in the past, that the future of architecture lay not with the honored but with those now in a position to offer the acclaim—indeed to advise Wright to move to Germany if he wished to have a future. In Berlin, Peter Behrens now occupied the role Wright had assigned to Sullivan: mentor to the generation of architects—Mies, Gropius, Le Corbusier—who would make Modernism an international destiny.

The conflict caused by Wright's success in Europe is one germ of truth at the heart of his generally groundless complaint of early neglect in America. In 1893 Sullivan could with some honesty blame his culture for his defeat by pointing to the imported plaster casts at the World's Fair. In 1910 Wright could blame no one, for he had suffered no defeat at all. He, personally, was a success; yet his warm reception abroad undermined the security he had felt as an artist borne aloft by the tide of cultural history.

This was an ironic twist on Sullivan's position seventeen years before. Though he held the World's Fair responsible for his decline, Sullivan was the only architect at the Fair to receive the Gold Medal from the visiting Beaux-Arts committee from Paris. The Fair may have driven him out of business, but by then he had already made his name as the most innovative architect of his generation. Wright's European recognition, on the other hand, came at a time when he had not fully emerged from Sullivan's shadow. While his genius was acknowledged, he was still widely regarded as a member of the School whose aims Sullivan had done the most to shape. Wright's reputation abroad did not dispel this image at home, any more than Sullivan's Gold Medal had improved his image in the eyes of the patrons of the ascendent American Beaux-Arts style.

Wright's European acclaim marked the beginning of his "more universal destiny," then, by aborting the "Naissance" that had sustained him throughout his Oak Park years. His reading of history had led him to view himself as the mother-art's messiah; apparently now he was to become no more than another of its prophets. Was it all a nefarious plot? Who was responsible for "expurgating" Hugo's prophecy from the pages of Notre Dame? Wright now had to choose between confronting his betrayal or accepting tenure as one of Modernism's many sources, a tributary rather than the fountainhead.

Just as Wright's identification with his culture's direction had become inconvenient by 1910, so too he found himself increasingly encumbered by the role he had fashioned for himself to take advantage of his earlier opportunity. He had designed his "tools," his "self," to exploit possibilities that no longer existed. As the opportunity dimmed, turned to ashes in the light of European development, so the role itself became as obsolete as the American lead in architectural design.

The collector of Japanese prints, the sponsor of matinee musicales, the opera-goer, the lawn-mower, the man who boasted erudition like a boy trying to impress a schoolmaster with the titles of books read last summer, the devotee of Ruskin and Morris, the advocate of Arts and Crafts, the perpetrator of subtle suburban indiscretions (long hair and floppy cravats)— in later years, after most of his property had been seized by his creditors for public auction, Wright would shower contempt on such people, claim he had never been—of all things—a collector; but such was the life he had led in those years. A model turn-of-the-century suburban host worthy of Veblen, Wright cultivated himself and his clients simultaneously, and so reaped his early success.

The role had been something of a sham. Not that Wright lacked culture; he simply liked to perform, and by 1910 he had begun to suspect that a self might not be the same thing as a role, might not after all be a thing chosen, selected as from a rack; and felt, rightly or not, that his Oak Park persona had become an obstacle between himself and something finer, more elemental, in his nature, an essence he needed to draw upon to continue. There was now no incentive for him to retain this role. It no longer suited circumstances at home, and in any case he had now been certified by Europe, the ultimate source of the cultivated principle.

Wright directed his dissatisfactions toward the petty nuisances of marriage and suburbia, but evidently the most galling aspect of his Oak Park life was that he had chosen it himself, custom designed it with as much care as his Oak Park house and studio, selected his wife primarily on the basis of her to-the-manner-born ability to help him perfect and refine the role of the cultivated gentleman. By 1910 he had not only outgrown her teaching; he had outgrown the role itself. Thus the break from family and colleagues was almost incidental to the overwhelming need to break from self.

Perhaps the buildings that actually were built in the middle years provide the most compelling argument that Wright's major task in this period was not the construction of buildings. Not that they show signs of indifference; on the contrary, with one exception, the most important of them (Midway Gardens, the Imperial Hotel, the Los Angeles textile-block houses) display a sense of fussiness, an overworked attention to detail in marked contrast to the calm mastery of architectural volume that distinguished his earlier work. These buidings were wonderful performances, more art direction than architecture, perhaps, with a period-piece monumentality worthy of de Mille. Still, while not inappropriate to Hollywood in the twenties, their impressive theatricality seemed a substitute for the confidence Wright lacked in their execution.

While individually the buildings show the passion for unity characteristic of Wright at his best, the effect is of order triumphing heroically and at great cost over confusion, not the unity that in earlier works seemed the natural emanation of building matched harmoniously to site. Apart from the textile-block houses, moreover, the buildings as a group are linked by little stylistic unity save the ubiquitous imprint of Wright's determination to find one.

The exception was Taliesin, the Wisconsin estate Wright built for himself at the period's outset, and rebuilt twice before the period was over. His preoccupation with this, the greatest work of the middle years, suggests his intuitive awareness that his path toward the "more universal destiny" of his future was a psychological journey above all. To undertake it was to attempt to reform not the environment but the self—though a reluctance to distinguish between the two helps explain both Taliesin's success and Wright's refusal to abandon building as his primary means of expression, however uneven the results elsewhere. And indeed his facility of self-expression was unimpaired; it was the self he wanted to express that needed reappraisal.

The break was ragged. After running off to Berlin in 1909 with the wife of a client, Wright returned after a year abroad to live again with his family in Oak Park. Yet for much of this period of attempted reconciliation, he was occupied with the design and construction of the house he would be sharing with his mistress fourteen months later. His behavior was bewildered, perhaps deceitful; certainly it displayed an ambivalence that made his crisis all the more difficult to resolve.

Although he wrote that "because I did not know what I wanted I wanted to go away," the move to Taliesin indicated that, on the contrary, what he wanted was to go home; not back to Oak Park but farther back, to childhood. The house overlooked property owned by his mother's family, a farm that had provided occasional seasons of stability thoroughout the fly-by-night childhood imposed by the interminable wanderings of his intinerant preacher father. He built Taliesin ostensibly for himself and his mistress, but eventually invited his mother to share it, as if to restore and make permanent the temporary refuge of those earlier Wisconsin summers.

Wright had fulfilled the ambitions of the runaway of twenty; now, aged forty-four, he reverted to the even more ambitious expectations of the boy he'd left behind, to his mother's vicarious longings. It was Anna Wright, after all, in the hagiography that now began to take shape, who had decided her son's profession before he was born, she who had given him the Froebel blocks to play with (regressing him to kindergarten exercises at the age of nine), hung Timothy Cole's prints of the great cathedrals on his nursery walls. If the Chicago Naissance had failed, there appeared to be endless comfort in the ritual of his own nativity.

Naissance, nativity, mother-art, mother, childhood, ritual: the words are garishly mythopoetic, yet of gossamer subtlety compared to the inscriptions in which Wright chiseled his experience from this point forward. To announce his decision to move to Taliesin, for example, he called a press conference on Christmas Day 1911.

If Taliesin solved Wright's personal crisis, his artistic crisis continued. Secure for the time being in a retreat of his own design, his confusion flared up whenever the spell of introspection was broken by the opportunity to design for others. Though he naturally sought commissions, they seemed to compromise his creativity rather than to extend his creative range. Nowhere was this more apparent than in the first major commission of the middle years, a block-long, $350,000 restaurant-cafe-entertainment complex for downtown Chicago.

As Hitchcock says, Midway Gardens was Wright's "last great Chicago work," but in fact and in spirit he had already left Chicago. The building itself was a remarkable triumph, considering that it represented a tribute to the urbane pastimes he had by then repudiated, an exuberantly Florentine celebration of the cultivated arts from an artist already embarked on a pilgrimage to the Gothic. The result was a sprawling experiment in ambivalence—how to go forward, whether to go back, in the end an ambitious attempt to erect a crowning glory to a spent creative vein.

But the opportunity was irresistible; the very site had resonance. To receive so important a commission in Chicago was a chance for Wright to thumb his nose at those who assumed that scandal had wrecked his career. Nor was the potential for vindication purely personal; designed to occupy a portion of the former site of the 1893 Fair, Midway Gardens may have inspired Wright with the hope of vindicating Sullivan also, at least of cutting short by several decades Sullivan's curse that the World's Fair would set American architecture back by fifty years. Most important of all, the project gave Wright the opportunity to convince himself that recognition abroad had been an artistic as well as personal triumph, not the creative setback he feared it might become. As such, Midway Gardens was to his Chicago years a glorious sunset that he himself mistook, albeit briefly, for a new dawn.

A vaguely midwesternized *Gesamtkunstwerk* in Tivoli drag, featuring highbrow entertainment at beer-garden prices, the building was Wright's memento of continental culture, brought back from his travels like a satchel of souvenirs for the children. The sounds and sights of prewar Europe all seemed to clamor for a place in his design, from Miss Cranston's tea rooms to Viennese Jugendstil, from Beyreuth to Diaghilev, all rolled up into a monumental overestimate of the taste of the American people. In less than two years the venture was broke, the property purchased and put to less ethereal use by the Edelweiss Brewing Company.

While the scheme's impracticality was more its promoters' fault than Wright's, their insensitivity to public taste was matched by their architect's inability to take stock of his own post-European position. He had visualized the Gardens as "a synthesis of all the Arts"; but *urbanity*, the one art required to animate the whole (as Daniel Burnham had understood so well in organizing the Fair's White City) was the one art Wright, now a semi-recluse in rural Wisconsin, was unable to master. For all their wealth of ornamental detail, the Gardens were a bleak prototype of those drawing-board fantasies that in fifty years' time would fill American cities with empty stretches of unwanted amenities.

The design of Midway Gardens coincided with the publication of the essay in which Wright first complained of his alleged neglect in America; the building itself suggests that a probable basis of his demand for greater recognition was his own failure to recognize how success had changed him. He designed the Gardens as though he could go home again, not only back to his family but back to his beliefs, back to impulses already worked out in his Oak Park architecture. He could no longer design a building from the inside out, for success had lifted him out of the problem. The Gardens were synthetic not only of "the Arts," but of creative motivations no longer organic to Wright's experience. The alternative was braggadocio; but even this was undermined by his dependence upon a public unwilling to support his homecoming celebration. The building eventually found public favor as a parking lot before its demolition in 1929.

Because there was a second act in the life of Frank Lloyd Wright, complete with happy ending, it is possible to underestimate the hardships he faced in the long intermission, particularly since so many of them were of his own making. On the other hand, Wright all too often trivialized the obstacles he encountered by exploiting them to avoid responsibility for the ones he had created. Just as his overreliance on history may have undermined his confidence in his own talent, so reliance on fate undermined confidence in his character, turning life into a drama that responded somewhat cynically to crisis.

In mid-August 1914, while Wright was in Chicago supervising the construction of Midway Gardens, a deranged servant set Taliesin on fire after murdering six of its inhabitants, among them Wright's mistress and two of her children. Without question, the episode was the most painful of Wright's life; and because it is hard to conceive that such an atrocity could be less than devastating, it is reasonable to consider it a primary cause of Wright's instability in these years. Wright himself encouraged this interpretation; so do biographical tidiness and sympathy for the bereaved. But Wright's account of the tragedy also suggests another interpretation: that he used the incident to mask his failure to deal with a more formidable adversity—the crippling bewilderment that had afflicted him five years before disaster struck. The question is not whether the event was shattering, but what was shattered—his confidence, or his capacity to bluff it. That he made a public spectacle of his grief, then proceeded to find a new companion in a matter of weeks, showed poor taste if not hypocrisy. But Wright's ethics are not an issue except as they shed light on the tragedy's impact.

Wright himself, however, was very preoccupied with the matter of personal ethics, for his account of the disaster turned on whether or not the "immorality" of his conjugal relations had provoked divine retribution. He protested too much that the destruction was not the work of Yahweh, for he jumped at the chance to escalate his defiance: "Not a chastened Taliesin. No, up in arms now, declining to take the popular Mosaic-Isaian idea of punishment as worthy the sacrifice demanded and taken at Taliesin." But "free love" was a red herring; if there was a sin Wright thought worthy of punishment, it was the confusion that had plagued him since 1910.

Something was coming clearer, now, through all the brutalizing Taliesin had received. Something—no, not rebellion. Conviction. Purpose now lifted the crown of the head higher. . . . The tread that faltered for a moment in weakness and confusion became elastic and more sure as Work came alive again.

Running off with the wife of a friend, abandoning his family, hurling insults at colleagues—this was all in a day's work. But to falter for even a moment in confusion—in weakness!—was almost to beg to be cast down.

Wright composed this account of his reaction to the disaster more than a decade later, when there was some truth to the claim that "something was coming clearer"; but conviction was as elusive after the fire as it had been before. Purpose and conviction sustained him as ideals, but "Work" did not truly come alive again for another twenty years—when he had withdrawn even farther from the world.

At most, the destruction of Taliesin brought to the surface qualities that had motivated Wright at least since his escape to Europe five years earlier. His life at Taliesin belied the notion that the move from Oak Park was undertaken to pursue a course independent of community approval. Wright wanted his new neighbors in rural Wisconsin not just to tolerate his unconventional life but to applaud it as a noble experiment. His community relations transcended tact, revealing a concern for appearances not easily reconciled with his claim to "individual sovereignty." The move to Spring Green was a return not to a simpler life but to a place that offered even less resistance to his tendency toward the pretentious. From the very start Taliesin had been an attempt to establish a lost sense of security. Wright's prescription for regaining his confidence was to indulge his taste for the grandiose, the Gothic, the grotesquely overstated; in short, his talent for show.

If Midway Gardens was the showplace, Taliensin was the show. However genuine the emotion and legitimate the pretext, Wright's performance reduced the affair to melodrama, setting an unfortunate pattern for the miserable years ahead. Aiming for a dramatic range somewhere between *Götterdämmerung* and the Flood, he devised a scenario more suitable to *The Perils of Pauline*, one of the year's top box-office attractions. The heroine was lost, but the house could be, and was, rebuilt—and paid for by the new chatelaine. If something was coming clearer, it was manifested at Taliesin alone, expressed with singular authority in Wright's determination to banish perplexity from his own house.

An artist trying to begin his art anew, as Wright was in the years after 1910, might be expected to strip away ornament, discarding the inessential to emphasize formal purity. But Wright's buildings throughout this period became more heavily ornamented, the spatial clarity of the Prairie House became obscured by his pursuit of new forms to convey an expanded sense of development. The wide-ranging repertory of these forms (Mayan and Navajo motifs, clunky orientalia, Sullivanesque vegetable variations, cubist images, "machine-art" details) attest not to conviction but to Wright's inability to sustain it beyond a single performance.

One reason for the direction he took may have been that the Europeans, especially the Dutch De Stijl group, had already begun to create an architecture of pure, pared-down geometry, going beyond Wright's own precedent toward the imminent International Style. Possibly Wright wished to accentuate their derivation from him by making his buildings more decorative, as if to boast that he had long ago mastered the theme; now he could perform the variations.

But a more important reason is that, for all his determination to break from the past, Wright was simply not ready for a new beginning in architecture, and would not be so for another two decades. He had cut himself off from the past, and he now stood alone and vulnerable. Commissions gave him the opportunity not to enlarge his conception of architecture in any significant way, but to thicken his protective mantle while a new conception took gradual shape within. The carved stone embellishments of Midway Gardens, the crystallized lava forms of the Imperial Hotel, the perforated concrete blocks of the inward-facing Los Angeles houses: these resembled the encrusted forms of a private chrysalis, from which Wright would not emerge, transformed into Wright the cultural icon, until the 1930s.

During the middle years, the concept that Wright termed "Organic Architecture" shifted from an approach to the design of buildings (outlined in articles and speeches before 1910) into an account of his personal experience. Gradually it ceased even to masquerade as an aesthetic method and offered itself frankly as a list of events—some provoked by Wright's actions, others circumstantial—and his responses to them. Eventually, as architecture became indistinguishable from autobiography, the trend culminated in his sitting down to write his memoirs in 1925.

Of the events that came to constitute Organic Architecture, some were buildings. But even when nominally the main attraction, a building's interest—to Wright—was often derived from elements extraneous to the design itself. Thus the physical form of Midway Gardens was subordinate to the historical nature of the opportunity it offered; and Wright got as much mileage from the venture's failure as from his design, proud that two demolition companies went bankrupt trying to tear the building down. Thus the Imperial Hotel (1916–1922) was not simply an opportunity to erect a large public facility amid a culture Wright had long admired, but a chance to "help Japan . . . to her feet." Thus the design of La Miniatura (1923), a two-bedroom bungalow in Pasadena (the emphasis on the building's small scale was Wright's), became the occasion to create "nothing more or less than a distinctly genuine expression of California in terms of modern industry and American life—that was all."

Superficially Sullivanesque, the approach was uniquely Wright's and in some ways the opposite of Sullivan's. Wright diverged from his mentor in theory, exalting the architect above the society he sought to express; and, in practice, giving form to a lot of exuberantly idiosyncratic, often second-rate architecture, as though the architect must hold his ground on a plane of experience superior even to his own achievements. His sense of proportion between the nature of the task and his part in it was as lopsided as the client permitted. Of La Miniatura, he wrote:

that house represented about as much studious labor over a drawing board and attention to getting construction started as the Cathedral of St. John the Divine in New York City, certainly more trouble to me than any the architect had with the Woolworth Building. . . . The house was by now, to me, far more than a mere house. . . . And I might as well admit it—I quite forgot this little building belonged to Alice Millard at all.

When a project offered no opportunity for such labors, as in the case of the prairie houses he still occasionally designed, the results were uninspired. Only in the various incarnations of Taliesin did he strike a balance between the project and his interests, for there they were one and the same.

Perhaps the most telling illustration of Wright's conception of Organic Architecture in the middle years was his response to the Japanese earthquake of 1923, an event made memorable by the fact that the Imperial Hotel, whose design and construction had consumed almost seven years of Wright's life, did not fall down. No feature of the Imperial's design had more meaning than its capacity to withstand the calamity.

Contrary to Wright's claim, the structural technique that insured the building's survival was neither innovative ("He sunk piles," his foreman declared), nor installed on Wright's initiative (if Rudolph Schindler's account is accurate), but rather over his protests. Even so, while the victory may not have been entirely honest, it served Wright well as a tangible, publicly visible symbol of his powers. He had devoted almost a quarter of his professional life to this one building, and his personal identification with its survival was explicit.

For once in a lifetime good news was newpaper news and the Baron's cablegram flashed around the world to herald what? To herald the triumph of good sense in the head of an architect tough enough to stick to it through thick and thin. Yes, that. But it was really a new approach to building, the ideal of an organic architecture at work, that really saved the Imperial Hotel. . . . But for the quality of thought that built it, the ideal of an organic architecture, it would surely have been just "another one of those things" and have been swept away.

In this account, the disaster itself was barely more than a pretext for the "good news" of the building's survival. Hundreds die, thousands go homeless, as the world awaits a signal to break into applause. As for the Japanese vernacular, so long admired: that was just one of those things.

Actually, Wright suspected that the Imperial was perhaps not one of his masterpieces; was, if not quite the eyesore some have claimed, then a "transition building," as he euphemistically termed its fussy, oppressive sprawl. "The New Imperial only partially realized the ideal of an organic architecture," he confessed; "were I to build it again it would be entirely different." But here, as at Midway Gardens and Taliesin a decade earlier, the building was less important than the emotion it symbolized. Wright's buildings had ceased to be discrete works of art, nor were they systematic elements in an overall strategy. In the middle years they remained fragmented episodes in a vigorous campaign toward an objective that remained obscure even to Wright himself.

"Are really good buildings all transition buildings?" he demanded, as if to insist that his sprawling personal development could be comprehended only in the grandest terms and phrases of world architectural history. Certainly the idea must have been reassuring to one in the midst of a particularly choppy transition.

Stylistically, as Robert Twombly observed, the Imperial Hotel was "a monumental dead end . . . contributing little to the overall development of [Wright's] architecture." But conceptually it contributed much, elevating to a major theme Wright's inclination to approach each project as an intense emotional struggle.

In shifting the emphasis from designs to the emotional climate he wrapped around them, Wright groped for a mental equivalent to the historical circumstances that had once formed the basis of his confidence. It was as though he wished to see history and psychology transposed, to endow his mental activities with the significance of historical events, and to hold history to blame for its failure to correspond to his mental imperatives. When thought and event appeared to coincide, as in the Imperial's survival, it was time for congratulations all around. To paraphrase Emerson, for Wright there was no history, only autobiography.

The strain was not new, but the emphasis was. In Oak Park days, Wright had addressed the more ambitious themes of culture, habitually departing from conventional wisdom in his view, but then his dissent had been tempered with reason, dictated to a degree by fashion. As Sullivan's apprentice, his views were a legitimate inheritance. As a rising young architect, he chose enemies with care and did not hesitate to make allies, in the Chicago School, the Arts and Crafts Movement, even with Daniel Burnham. But now his dissent became indiscriminate, his irascibility automatic. In the eight-year interval (1908–1914) between editions I and II of "In the Cause of Architecture" (Wright's running commentary on his art), that cause had become synonymous with his own; "Truth Against the World," his mother's family motto, had become the mother-art's slogan; and the central nervous system of Frank Lloyd Wright had become the one and only organ of Organic Architecture.

In the decade following 1914, Wright continued to transform himself into a walking antithesis without a specific thesis, without a means to focus his frustrations and in the process perhaps convert them into the articles of a constructive architectural philosophy. He reacted against Europe; he reacted against his American colleagues; he reacted against contemporary art in general ("mere 'artistic activity,' " he called it, when he noticed it at all), against American taste in particular; against manners, against morals, against fate. Above all he reacted against the passage of time, retreating from its advance by absenting himself to Wisconsin, to Tokyo, to Los Angeles. When the return to childhood Wisconsin went up in flames, he sought refuge in the arrested time of Japanese culture, the prehistoric time of pre-Columbian culture, the tabula rasa of 1920s West Coast no-culture. But the periphery offered no escape from the sense of loss he felt at no longer occupying the center of culture; it merely reinforced his bitterness at being on the sidelines.

Toward the end of the middle years, Wright had, it is true, carved out quite a territory for himself with his vituperations; he could claim a continent of void between the ideas and forms of others. In the years of the Great Prosperity, he parlayed his great neglect into one of America's largest architectural projects. What he lacked was a means of investing his property with a value independent of the scattered objects of his contempt, a catalyst that might enable him to fuse his myriad reactions coherently into a Grand Design. Such an incentive was not immediately forthcoming. With a fanfare that barely concealed his discontent, Wright announced his intention to return to Chicago in 1925 and devote his practice exclusively to commercial architecture.

Wright's mother died in February 1923. In November Wright went through a formal marriage ceremony with Miriam Noel, his companion for the past nine years. In April 1924 Louis Sullivan died, a personal wreck and a professional failure, alone in a fleabag hotel. That same month Wright's second wife left him after five months of marriage. He announced his plans to return to Chicago shortly thereafter.

The plan appeared to be born of resignation, of disgust with fifteen years of willful aliention from the world. The decision to devote his practice to commercial architecture spoke of an eagerness to be done with emotional complications, to erase from memory his domestic worries, to reconstitute his life by absorbing himself in the mechanics of a commercial operation as a kind of self-prescribed occupational therapy. More an act of renunciation than of affirmation, his return to the scene of his former success seemed an effort to break with the daemon–muse that had brought grief in the intervening years.

But if the objective was to sell out, he never had the chance to find a buyer, for the Chicago comeback was abandoned when, the following April, Taliesin burned down once again, and Wright was forced to sell his Oak Park house to finance the reconstruction. Worse, within a few months his life was again overtaken by scandal.

In July 1925 Wright's divorce action against his second wife, coupled with the promptness with which he had enlisted her replacement, set off a chain reaction of legal complications that lasted three years, brought him to financial ruin and imprisonment, his name to the front page and to wanted posters (with a $500 reward), his practice and mobility to a halt. Instead of settling down to a normal life in 1925 as planned, he found that his years of self-imposed exile terminated in involuntary incarceration, renewed social ostracism, and a court injunction against leaving the state of Minnesota.

If these events were traumatic for Wright, they are no less trying for a biographer trying to discern the precise point in his fortunes at which the tragic gave way to the risible. Hadn't Sinclair Lewis already written this novel? Hadn't Mack Sennett already filmed the special effects? "I suspect tragedy in the American countryside," Fitzgerald wrote in 1925, "because all the people capable of it move to the big towns at twenty. All the rest is pathos." Whether tragic, pathetic, satirical, or slapstick, Wright's tribulations were not yet over. But a sign of imminent salvation was about to descend from the machine and hit the stage with an impressive thud.

In April 1925, several hours before the second fire at Taliesin, Alexander Woollcott came to lunch. The men had never met, but Wright's troubles had given him considerable press, and, on an afternoon off from a lecture tour in nearby Madison, Woollcott decided to go "see with my own eyes the home that such a man would build for himself." Although his curiosity had been aroused more by his host's notoriety than by his architectural achievements, evidently the meeting was mutually rewarding, for the two became good friends.

They spent two hours rambling around Taliesin, and Woollcott's account of the meeting, published in *The New Yorker* several years later, explains what at first glance seems an unlikely association. What appealed to Woollcott most, at least initially, was Wright's failure, his evident readiness to lend himself as a Cause, a crusade to right a cultural wrong. As Wolcott Gibbs wrote in a profile of his *New Yorker* colleague,

The truth is probably that he prefers to dig up his own crusades, finding no especial satisfaction in getting excited about something that excites everybody else. So, while most commentators have been busy with anti-Fascist demonstrations, labor disputes and other community activities, Mr. Woollcott has found his own causes and stood up for them, vocal and alone.

In short, Woollcott practiced a cosmopolitan version of Wright's "Truth Against the World." And so, ceremoniously bestowing the title only one living American genius upon an architect others had by then dismissed as hopelessly passé, Woollcott took up the cause of Frank Lloyd Wright.

As he saw it, Wright's professional demise had been callously engineered by the more disreputable element of Woollcott's own profession, by the witless and vindictive indictments and all the ugly hoodlumism which the yellow newspapers can invoke when once an outstanding and inevitably spectacular man gives them half a chance. Wright gave them a chance and a half. The reporter pack, in full cry, followed his every naïve move, creating an atmosphere in which no artist could work well, and no architect could work at all.

What Wright gave Woollcott, to his delight, was a chance and a half to perform a selection of his most cherished public roles: champion of the underdog, connoisseur of the arts, foe of the philistine, sentimental milkman of human kindness. What did Woollcott offer Wright? Support both public and private, financial and moral, in a campaign that survived his own death in 1943. (Woollcott's last byline, a posthumously published Broadway review, compared Thornton Wilder's work to Wright's as the highest compliment he could tender; but by then Wright's reputation was in good repair.)

It would be a gross exaggeration to call Woollcott Wright's mentor, in any sense resembling the position Sullivan had held. But now, at fifty-eight, Wright had no use for a mentor in architecture. What he needed was someone in another sphere completely, a friend sufficiently worldly to sponsor his return to the world, someone to help him return not with the resignation in which he had conceived his Chicago comeback, but on his own demanding terms, lest his years of defiance be wasted.

Noting the bind that Wright was in as an architect who tried to behave like a Romantic artist, Woollcott wrote: "When a Samson Agonistes has made sport for the Philistines, he can, if he be a sculptor, say, or a poet, or a painter, retreat to the wilderness and fulfill his destiny. Your architect, on the other hand, must work in and with a community."

"The Man Who Came to Dinner," the "New Jersey Nero who mistook his pinafore for a toga": Alexander Woollcott's image is of an overweight lightweight, a prototypal talk-show host with vain pretensions to intellectual substance, certainly not a writer of whom one would expect a profound understanding of an artist of Wright's caliber. And yet, in comparing Wright to the trite convention of the Romantic artist, he put his pudgy finger more accurately than most observers on precisely the problem that had caused Wright's break with Oak Park in 1910 and kept him firmly on the route to failure for the next fifteen years.

For to Wright the image of the Romantic artist was not a trite convention. It was his standard of excellence, a standard not all the commissions of his successful Oak Park practice brought him any nearer to attaining. Quite the reverse, for the architect's success is a worldly, public success to a degree no Romantic artist's success is supposed to be; hence by his own standards Wright was no less a failure before his 1910 break than in the difficult years that followed.

An architect longing to be a Romantic artist walked a tightrope between commercial and artistic failure; he must find a way to "work with" but be definitely not of the community. And assuming it was possible for Wright to establish such a paradoxical relationship to the world, surely no one was more qualified than Alexander Woollcott to guide him. For who knew better than Woollcott that the age had indeed produced a community where the insult was an asset, where convention could be flouted to acclaim, where "Hello, repulsive," was considered an acceptable form of greeting? As a critic who had achieved his first byline by getting himself banned from the Shubert theaters, who was more able to show Wright how to use his irascibility to open doors rather than close them, to employ contempt as a social tool instead of a provocation to exile? Woollcott had made a career of it, and in lending Wright his support he indicated how he might go about reconstructing his own. He could also show him where.

About now Wright began to devote most of his time to writing, but it was not with the intention of joining Woollcott at the Algonquin Round Table that he traveled to New York in December 1925 and again the following November. His literary pursuits did not lead immediately to wisecracks, and his need was for the opposite of limelight.

Wright had been to New York several times on business and had passed through on his way to Europe. Most recently, he had gone there to persuade his future third wife, Oglivanna, whom he had met in Chicago several months earlier, to return with him to Taliesin (as his "housekeeper") after his second marriage had fallen apart. Now, with Taliesin again in ashes, Wright joined her in New York a week after the birth of their child. The city was still a peripheral place to him; that was its advantage. Under court order not to leave the country (he had thought at first to find respite south of the border), he wanted an unlikely place to hide. He sought for himself what he felt he had provided for the citizens of Tokyo two years earlier, shelter from the disaster that engulfed him, that every move seemed to intensify.

What he looked for in New York were qualities just the opposite of those that had drawn him to Chicago almost forty years before, and he found the city well equipped to serve him. New York offered him no genuine refuge—his visits each time amounted to no more than several weeks— yet this very precariousness suited his needs better than any sanctuary.

In its lack of solace, its lack of promise, its impressive declaration of his insignificance, the city accommodated Wright's need to draw together the disparate, fragmented elements of Organic Architecture into a coherent point of view. What Chicago had been for him in 1888, New York was for him now in negative: the supremely wrong place for him to be. As such it was exactly what he had been seeking for fifteen years: an anti-place from which to begin again as a genuine Romantic artist, authentically antipathetic to the cultural conventions of the age.

Time, building, commerce, power, fame, money, success, European gateway, cultural supremacy, the future: all these were concentrated in New York in 1925 as never before or since. In a masterstroke of artistic economy, Wright recognized the advantage of narrowing his range of infinite reactions to focus upon one physically compact, culturally cohesive nerve center, a symbolic source of everything that had plagued him for the past fifteen years, everything that had eluded, defeated, contradicted, mocked or ignored him.

Five years before, with no more entrée than Wright's ("half a dozen unmarried college friends and a few new literary acquaintances"), and a first novel postmarked St. Paul, Minnesota, Scott Fitzgerald had been appointed New York's spokesman. Now, at the height of the Jazz Age, Frank Lloyd Wright saw an opening as the city's opponent. Of the climate he was held to personify, Fitzgerald wrote, "We thought we were apart from all that; perhaps everyone thinks they are apart from their milieu." But only a Romantic knows how to exploit this feeling for the maximum artistic advantage.

"But you see I am cast by nature for the part of the iconoclast," Wright had written to Charles Ashbee in 1911. "I must strike—tear down, before I can build—my very act of building destroys an order." It takes no great psychological insight to see how Wright had struck against himself in 1910, tearing down the order of his life and career with remarkable thoroughness. Now, in 1925, at last it was time for him to rebuild.

1   9   2   6   –   1   9   5   9

T   W   O   C   I   T   I   E   S

In democratic communities, each citizen is habitually engaged in the contemplation of a very puny object: namely, himself. If he ever raises his looks higher, he perceives only the immense form of society at large or the still more imposing aspect of mankind. His ideas are all either extremely minute and clear or extremely general and vague; what lies between is a void. When he has been drawn out of his own sphere, therefore, he always expects that some amazing object will be offered to his attention; and it is on these terms alone that he consents to tear himself for a moment from the petty, complicated cares that form the charm and excitement of his life.

This appears to me sufficiently to explain why men in democracies, whose concerns are in general so paltry, call upon their poets for conceptions so vast and descriptions so unlimited.

The authors, on their part, do not fail to obey a propensity of which they themselves partake; they perpetually inflate their imaginations, and, expanding them beyond all bounds, they not infrequently abandon the great in order to reach the gigantic. By these means they hope to attract the observation of the multitude and to fix it easily upon themselves; nor are their hopes disappointed, for as the multitude seeks for nothing in poetry but objects of vast dimensions, it has neither the time to measure with accuracy the proportions of all the objects set before it nor a taste sufficiently correct to perceive at once what respect they are out of proportion. The author and the public at once vitiate one another.

We have also seen that among democratic nations the sources of poetry are grand, but not abundant. They are soon exhausted; and poets, not finding the elements of the ideal in what is real and true, abandon them entirely and create monsters. I do not fear that the poetry of democratic nations will prove insipid or that it will fly too near the ground; I rather apprehend that it will be forever losing itself in the clouds and that it will range at last to purely imaginary regions. I fear that the productions of democratic poets may often be surcharged with immense and incoherent imagery, with exaggerated descriptions and strange creations; and that the fantastic beings of their brain may sometimes make us regret the world of reality.
—Alexis de Tocqueville

■ SUNDAY IN NEW YORK

I would go back to town . . . in the morning, to roam the streets of New York alone. I didn't care to see anyone at the time for fear of revealing our whereabouts to the newpapers' pursuit of news.

It was then I began to write. I tried to write some impressions of the big city. "In Bondage" was one. "The Usonian City" another; later to begin this work.

Wright's assertion in An Autobiography that he "began to write" on his 1925 visit to New York is significant, for by that year he had already written and published several books and a number of influential articles and speeches. Presumably the beginning was symbolic; what he "began" that year in New York was not writing per se, but an approach to his art in which writing would begin to serve a new function. Formerly no more than an adjunct to his career, at most an ethically acceptable form of advertising, writing now came alive to him as a creative medium. "Knowing well his tools," to the pencil he added the pen, a tool whose potential he had barely begun to exploit.

"Architecture and eloquence are mixed arts," wrote Emerson, "whose end is sometimes beauty and sometimes use." And for the next ten years Wright's art would itself be mixed, a hybrid in which architecture supplied the beauty, eloquence the use. He employed the two with equal zest if not skill, moving back and forth between writing and designing with increasing fluidity, as though they were parts of a unified composition.

The Disappearing City, Wright's major statement on cities in general, abstracted from his view of New York in particular, was published in 1932 (the same year his autobiography appeared); but the book's main theme— the replacement of the obsolete central city by a more spiritually advanced alternative—had been anticipated six years before by his project for a "Steel Cathedral including Minor Cathedrals for a Million People."

Taller than any building then standing in New York or anywhere else, almost as wide in plan as it was high in elevation, the cathedral's implicit intention was to obliterate by its scale whatever portions of the city had not been razed in the preparation of its site. As Wright's first design for an American urban public facility since Midway Gardens, the cathedral showed the direction his progress had taken; now he would not attempt to reform urban culture from within but would blast it from without.

But what did Wright have against New York? What had the city done to warrant his wrath? The city's sin, simply put, was to be seen in the eyes of the world as the fountainhead of an American culture grown sufficiently strong and distinct to rival that of the Old World. As Rosenfeld wrote, "perhaps the tradition of life imported over the Atlantic has commenced expressing itself in terms of the new environment, giving the Port of New York a sense at last, and the entire land the sense of the Port of New York."

To compound this sin, the city had given this new sense a distinct and explicit architectural form. As José Clemente Orozco wrote in 1929:

The new races that have appeared upon the lands of the New World have the unavoidable duty to produce a New Art in a new spiritual and physical medium. Already, the architecture of Manhattan is a new value, something that has nothing to do with Egyptian pyramids, or with Saint Sofia, any more than it has to the Maya palaces of Chichen-Itza or with the pueblos of Arizona.

The architecture of Manhattan is the first step. Painting and sculpture must certainly follow as inevitable second steps.

As an architect who felt, not without justification, that it was he who had taken that first step, Wright could hardly help but resent the aplomb with which Manhattan accepted the honor. No matter that a German professor years before had awarded that honor to Wright; to everyone else, as Rosenfeld wrote, "it was the towers of Manhattan one wanted to see garlanded with loveliness."

Ironically, Wright at this moment was at the height of his pre-Columbian phase, producing designs for buildings that had quite a bit to do with Mayan palaces and Arizona pueblos. His steel and glass cathedral, for that matter, resembled nothing so much as an enormous ceremonial tepee, perhaps expressing Wright's belief that the best plan for Manhattan was to give it back to the Indians.

Although the design inaugurated Wright's campaign against the city, like many other buildings by him the cathedral was agreeably matched to its setting. It complied perfectly with the local code of manic hyperbole that a few decades earlier had not just imagined, but had actually begun to build, "the world's largest Gothic cathedral," St. John the Divine (a structure whose ecumenical ambulatory chapels prefigure the "minor cathedrals" housed within Wright's project). It reaffirmed the affinity between Gothic style and skyscraper scale that Cass Gilbert had already explored in the Woolworth Building, a connection also suggested by the compromise plan put forward by Hugh Ferriss: a real church lodged in the pinnacle of a commercial skyscraper.

Nor was the cathedral's catastrophic obliteration of New York at all out of place in a city already long accustomed to seeing itself as "the disappearing city," a city whose insatiable appetite for change (advertised with pride in the teens and twenties on thousands of "Building Coming Down" signboards) had long been as celebrated a local attraction as London's Changing of the Guard.

Wright's cathedral coincided with his attempt at a first draft for *The Disappearing City*, and in a sense the design is the frontispiece to the published work, an uplifting image comparable in spirit to Lyonel Feininger's *Crystal Cathedral*, the woodblock design that adorned the cover of the first Bauhaus manifesto in 1919. But while Feininger's semiabstract cathedral was no more than an image, Wright presented his design as a feasible project, complete with plans, dimensions, scale drawings, estimated costs, an ostensible client (the Reverend William Norman Guthrie of St. Marks-in-the-Bouwerie), and, most important of all, a specific location: New York City.

Feasible but impossible, the project was more than a little reminiscent of Le Corbusier's Voisin Plan for Paris, whose public exhibition preceded Wright's scheme by one year. Both projects were designed for the cultural capitals of their architects' countries, both called for (directly or by implication) the destruction of most of the features that made these cities capitals, or even cities. But while Le Corbusier's clinically "Cartesian" plan resembled a surgical operation, an attempt to replace "diseased" urban tissue with a set of industrially produced artificial parts, Wright's project more nearly resembled a rite of exorcism. If, as Wright maintained, New York was "a place fit for banking and prostitution and not much else," how better to banish Mammon and Venus than to consecrate their real estate holdings to the Lord?

This somewhat literal architectural rendering of the Augustinian admonition of "no salvation outside the church" echoed the claims made in the previous century on behalf of Gothic architecture by A. W. Pugin's book *Contrasts* (1836). But while Pugin sought to cleanse the soul of industrial society by encouraging restoration of an architectural style historically associated with piety, Wright's New York purification ceremony consisted of imposing a single monumental work derived from his own imagination.

Although by 1926 Wright had distanced himself theoretically from the younger generation in Europe, the cathedral alludes both in style and iconography more to European than to American precedent. By 1926 the phrase "steel and glass" had already become virtually synonymous with modern architecture in Europe. And the cathedral's blend of cataclysm, religiosity, and monomania recalls a number of projects conceived in the Romantic climate of early Modernism, before its more eccentric expressions had been absorbed and tamed by the programmatic dictates of the Modern Movement.

In 1919 Bruno Taut's *Alpine Architektur* specified not only buildings but worshippers, their vestments, and a map of their pilgrimage up Alpine trails past chrysanthemum-shaped mountain temples toward The Rock

Cathedral. "The purpose of the cathedral? None—if prayer in the midst of beauty is not sufficient." Tony Garnier's *Cité Industrielle* emphasized the spiritual function of architecture by embracing every type of urban building—except churches. Impassioned students pulled a model of Tatlin's *Monument to the Third International* through the streets of Moscow as a kind of sacred effigy in the conviction that the designer should serve as spiritual counsel to the State, a hope briefly shared by the Italian Futurists in the early days of Fascism, before Mussolini built the Via della Conciliazone for the Pope. In its most active phase (1904–1914), Futurism was conducted as an evangelical sect: Marinetti provoked mock-ecclesiastical debate with several theologians on the probable diet in the hereafter, accepting one suggested entrée—*vermicelli al pomodoro*—as proof of "the monotony of Paradise and of the life led by the angels."

After the Bauhaus had consolidated Modernism into a Movement, Wright scorned the German influence on architecture; but two German artists—neither of them architects—provided the most striking parallels to Wright's project. Had he taken up film instead of writing, the result could not have been dissimilar to Fritz Lang's *Metropolis*. Inspired by Lang's first glimpse of Manhattan in 1924 and completed two years later, the film seethes with the tortured Manichaean imagery that Wright was struggling to express in prose. The saintly True Maria, the demonic False Maria, the demoralized worker-slaves held in bondage to the evil industrialists, the Armageddon narrowly averted before the vast cathedral of Metropolis: all have their counterparts in the theme and tenor of Wright's tract. Indeed, had Wright's cathedral not anticipated the release of Lang's film by several months, it would be easy to conclude that he went into town every morning not "to roam the streets of New York alone" but to go to the movies.

Another German, Paul Scheerbart, was a poet whose depiction of glass architecture as a secular religion was largely responsible for the talismanic quality that glass was to assume throughout the Modern Movement. Scheerbart's book *Glasarchitektur*, published in 1914, not only forecasts Wright's 1926 design but is written in a style that anticipates Wright's most deadening hortatory. Compare Scheerbart:

The face of the earth would be much altered if brick architecture was ousted everywhere by glass architecture. It would be as if the earth were adorned with sparkling jewels and enamels. Such glory is unimaginable. All over the world it would be as splendid as in the gardens of the Arabian Nights. We should have a paradise on earth, and no need to watch in longing expectation for the paradise in heaven.

to Wright fourteen years later:

Imagine a city iridescent by day, luminous by night, imperishable! Buildings, shimmering fabrics, woven of rich glass; glass all clear or part opaque and part clear, patterned in color or stamped to harmonize with the metal tracery that is to hold all together. . . . Such a city would clean itself in the rain, would know no fire alarms; no, nor any glooms.

Wright's cathedral affirmed Scheerbart's claim that "the whole of glass architecture stems from the Gothic cathedral" and renewed his prophecy that "the free churches of America may well be the first to build glass temples." But Wright and Scheerbart had more in common than a passion for the metaphysical properties of glass; both indulged joyously in the Romantic ability to distinguish between the visionary and the realistic. Scheerbart's contention that "so many ideas constantly sound to us like a fairy-tale, when really they are not fantastic at all" anticipates Wright's belief that to equip his vision with blueprints was sufficient to endow his fantasy with all the essential qualities of a tangible object. Of his iridescent metropolis, Wright wrote, "I dream of such a city. I have worked enough on such a building to see definitely its desirability and its practicability." But doing away with window washers and firemen was not the only practical advantage of the dream, for the problem most in need of remedy was Wright's own obsolescence.

Wright's "obsolescence" in the twenties owed at least as much to his Romanticism as to his scandalous romances. His personal life merely flouted Mrs. Grundy; his artistic convictions appeared to defy the course of cultural history, as, under the supervision of Gropius, modern architecture set a course toward the neoclassical mode typified in the end by the bronze and travertine towers of Mies, the CIAM grids and Cartesian towers of Le Corbusier.

Feininger's *Crystal Cathedral* and Gropius's depiction of the building of the future as "the crystal symbol of a new faith" both alluded to the rapturous Scheerbartian climate from which the Bauhaus had emerged. But under Gropius the expressionist mannerisms of early Modernism were curbed in the search for objective principles; the secular religion of glass gave way to the pseudoscience of good design. Scheerbart himself sought "to resist most vehemently the undecorated 'functional style,' for it is inartistic," but to no avail, for the Bauhaus architects sought to go beyond art into the realm of social engineering, and to prove themselves good citizens in the bargain.

Though it more nearly approximated the Gothic model Wright himself esteemed, the Bauhaus ideal of the building as a collective work prohibited the posture of Romantic individualism expressed in Wright's cathedral. Where Gropius believed that his "crystal symbol" would "one day rise toward heaven from the hands of a million workers," Wright's cathedral was the proud handiwork of two hands only, dispensed magnanimously to the one million worshippers specified in the title of his shrine.

In any other setting the cathedral would have been an intolerable affront to the *Zeitgeist*; but here Wright's atavism seemed justified, for New York was a city that appeared to many, above all to Europeans, at once a vision of the future and an evocation of the purest Gothic romance. Like Modernism itself, the city recalled the cathedral epoch even as it repudiated the past.

Viewed from his arriving ocean liner at night, Manhattan inspired Fritz Lang with a morality play in which the industrial society of the year 2000 bows in the end to the greater power of faith, symbolized by Metropolis's forsaken Gothic cathedral. "Like a cluster of unlit candles at the foot of an absent saint," was Luigi Barzini's impression of the skyscrapers upon his arrival in 1925. To Colette, on board the *Normandie*'s maiden voyage, they resembled a "grove of churches, a Gothic bouquet, and remind us of that Catholic art that hurled its tapered arrow toward heaven, the steeple stretching up in aspiration." In Le Corbusier's famous phrase, they composed a vision of "when the cathedrals were white," of a youthful vigor that European cultures had buried under centuries of grime and manners. Though "not tall enough" to satisfy him, the skyscrapers were nonetheless palpable enough to be the harbinger Modernism required. Though disordered to a degree objectionable to Modern theory, the city was a welcome fact, lending its visible energy to the momentum Modernism hoped to harness as a Movement.

But if New York seemed from afar to promise the eventual fulfillment of Modern European forecasts, to Wright it offered a more immediate vindication. For if Wright's Romanticism flew in the face of history, New York's certainly did not. And if, in his ambivalence toward the city, antagonism predominated, the city gained his attachment by neutralizing much of his waywardness in the years of Modernism's rise.

Here was an opportunity for Wright to dust off the old deterministic notions of his Chicago days, for it was here in New York that "American architecture confirmed the prophecy of Victor Hugo by becoming action; beginning to feel sinews anew, take on vital flesh, lift its head high for new vision. New forms were born—forms natural to freedom!" Chicago's boom had been only a fluke—the creation of Mrs. O'Leary's cow. It was here in New York that architecture had become action, to all appearances for its own sake, in the most Romantic architectural experiment ever witnessed. As Paul Rosenfeld wrote, "It seems a misty architectural shape is taking up into itself like individual building stones the skyscrapers, tenements, thoroughfares, and people; and with the mass of them erecting a tower higher than any of them, even the highest, toward the sky."

Wright shared with Rosenfeld and the Europeans the Romantic perception that New York was not really a city at all but rather a single work of monumental proportions, the imaginative projection of a collective intelligence. And while he deplored the form its vitality took—a form not of his own design, a projection not of his own individual intelligence—he approached the city in the spirit of profound if jealous kinship; he saw that, as the most tangible representation of the Modern spirit, the city's arising shapes gave his Romanticism the weight of fact and history, his individualism an edge over more sensible European conceptions of technology tamed, the future planned according to principles of good design.

Romanticism, moreover, evoked a field on which an individual might easily defeat an entire city single-handed—precisely because he *was* single-handed, an individual set in opposition to cultural convention. Years before, Wright had looked out over Chicago at night and exclaimed, "If this power must be uprooted that civilization may live, then civilization is already doomed." But now, looking up at New York from his "worm's eye view," he was prepared to consign both city and civilization to history's dustheap. Where once he had identified his own ambitions with the "Naissance" of Chicago's skyscrapers, he now opposed himself to the even more impressive spectacle of New York's. As an unemployed architect, Wright had little to lose by refusing to compromise with the most powerful architectural expression of his culture. And as a Romantic he had quite a bit to gain.

Just as the Guggenheim is notoriously the showplace of its own design, often to the detriment of the paintings it was nominally designed to display, so Wright's cathedral expresses a more fervent devotion to the spirit of architecture than to any of the six faiths it purported to house. Wright did not have to import the idea of architecture-as-religion from Europe; it was another part of his inheritance from Sullivan, who once wrote, "With me architecture is not an art but a religion, and that religion but part of the greater religion of Democracy."

Wright turned this hierarchy upside down. He rejected what he considered Sullivan's "sentimentality" about democracy, chiding the softness of his attitude toward "the mobocracy," ridiculing his efforts to educate "them asses." With Wright, the religion of architecture was but a part of the greater religion of Wright. Where Sullivan's identification was idealistic, Wright's was pragmatic. To Sullivan religion had meant humility, to Wright a license for self-righteousness.

Wright felt that Sullivan's conception weakened the architect's already feeble position within his culture; his own was intended to strengthen it, to extend the latent power of the artist's transcendental grip, *urbi* if not *orbi*, by emulating the institution best skilled in the arts of spiritual manipulation. If Wright's friend Bruce Barton could enlist Christ to advertise Big Business, and could turn the idea into *The Man Nobody Knows*—a national best-seller for two years running (1925–1926)—why couldn't Wright use Him to sell architecture? If an advertising man could interpret parables to mean that "*all* business is his Father's business," couldn't an enterprising architect find some use for "in my Father's house there are many mansions"? The city was the perfect meeting ground for such a merger; architecture and religion were the two things paradoxically excluded from this cluster of candles, this Gothic bouquet. Unity of faith, unity of form: the skyline evoked these images even as it priced them out of town.

Henry James had earlier observed with some distaste how the spires of lower Manhattan's churches had been overtowered by skyscrapers erected by the elders of these same churches. But what to James was irony was to Wright a provocation to Luther-like frenzy. Branding the established church "The Light That Failed," he harangued: "Why does the Church no longer lead man out of merchantdom into realms of the poetic principle? Why should it attempt to follow the merchant and so become itself a merchant?" And: "The failure to see God and Man as one has disaffected all art for it has betrayed architecture. . . . With Christianity as tenant today, architecture is a parasite, content with an imitation of an imitation, like the spurious St. John the Divine in New York City."

Those who assumed that medieval masons had served the church had got it backward. As the spiritual landlord of humanity, the architect had both the right and the duty to insist that tenants respect the premises or forfeit the lease. But only with architecture as tenant could architecture be truly safe from betrayal and the Light again be lit. No one could deny that a cathedral is an advantage to one preparing to speak ex cathedra, and Wright's looks forward to the time a decade hence when, having reconstructed his architectural practice in the form of a sacred calling to the mother-art, he would literally deliver Sunday sermons from his private chapel's pulpit to the Taliesin Fellowship, his private cult. But for now he had the even more expansive vision of the unemployed.

While the proposed materials were steel and glass, the cathedral's actual medium was, of course, paper and pencil, and the project's form expressed the nature of these materials as honestly as any Wright structure built of wood and stone. Just as he inflated the Gothic cathedral's scale to the proportions of the modern city, so he translated the Gothic aim of structural lightness into contemporary terms, obtaining a symbolic equivalent to medieval aspiration not in the material lightness afforded by steel and glass, but in the transcendent weightlessness of the unbuilt, unbuildable concept.

To the extent that any cathedral built since the Renaissance cannot escape comparison with those built before, the modern cathedral is inherently atavistic, more a reminder of unity lost than a prospectus for future catholicity. Where Gaudí pushed the Sagrada Familia to the practicable limits of fantasy, Wright went farther, advancing his cathedral into a state as unattainable as the cultural consensus its medieval model once expressed. His was a monument to the lack of consensus in the center of worldliness. His steeple did not aspire to be the city's glory, but the mark of its shame, a token of divine wrath against a city whose most notable liturgical event of the year was the riot of 30,000 bereaved Valentino fans outside Frank E. Campbell's funeral chapel.

As a "serious" proposal, Wright's cathedral was redundant: the city was choking with buttresses and spires, and in commerce already had a state religion. But even if God did exist, it would be necessary to create Him— or what's a cathedral for? To express aspiration beyond the worldly, Wright made the paper concept analogous to the Gothic arch. To build higher in fact was merely to escalate the mundane; to remain a paper concept was to surpass even Cass Gilbert's scale with unsurpassable structural integrity. Paper is cheap, words are cheap, but in 1926 so were buildings. As Fitzgerald wrote of the year, "a new expression 'Oh Yeah?' summed up all the enthusiasm evoked by the announcement of the last super-skyscrapers." And to judge from Ralph Adams Cram's performance at St. John's, perhaps it was better to be invisible than to be hollow, better not to build at all than to achieve the dubious celebrity of being forever unfinished. God himself did not need to erect a new temple when his purpose was to inscribe writing on the wall.

The unbuilt building had an even more ingenious advantage over the built. Throughout the middle years Wright had shown, in the contrast between the various Taliesins and his other works, that his genius was brought to bear only on his own buildings, that his artistic confusion emerged only when he turned to architecture not for his personal use. The unbuilt building was thus a practical means of regaining the confidence that had evaded him since 1909, for, despite what patron's name might be affixed to the drawings, all such buildings were designed for Wright's personal use, blatantly so, without compromise or apology.

It mattered that the cathedral be feasible, not that it be built. It was useful to him either way—if not as a physical monument, then as evidence of his neglect, testament to his irrepressible spirit. "We have to get people, states and buildings *thought-built!*" he later declared. Here, he erected his most ambitious mental edifice so far, opening an approach to architecture that insured him against wasted effort while more conventional avenues of expression remained closed.

It goes without saying that at any time in his career Frank Lloyd Wright would have preferred to build; that at this point he turned his inability to build to his artistic advantage is what the cathedral signified. The transformation was to shape the course of his career even after his capacity to build had been restored; indeed, it was instrumental in bringing about the restoration.

Architecture is dethroned. . . .
The book is about to kill the edifice.
The invention of printing was the greatest event in history.
It was the first great machine, after the great city.

Wright first paraphrased Hugo's theory in 1901, but it took him another quarter-century to rearrange the sequence, to add printing to edifice and so kill off the city. It is ironic that the time and place of Wright's "discovery" of writing should be commemorated by his most explicit homage to the Gothic tradition, for his Romantic rebelliousness derived from an era in which the press was perceived as the cathedral's replacement as a vehicle of memory and thought. It was to print that Wright turned to bring his own architecture back to life. Hugo's idea originated with Michelet, the nineteenth-century historian for whom, as Edmund Wilson wrote, "the press was to become the great symbol of the advance of modern thought, and printing a veritable religion." Now Wright took up the printed medium to spread the word of his own religion of architecture.

Wright's choice of the cathedral as instrument of the city's annihilation was an additional irony of which he was possibly unaware; for his impulse of Romantic destruction sprang directly from a tradition that a century earlier had set out to systematically annihilate the cathedral and Gothic architecture in general as symbols of social oppression. The Gothic affinities of Michelet (1798–1874), Hugo (1802–1885), and Viollet-le-Duc (1814–1879) were a reaction against the immediately preceding epoch, when engineers had published manuals describing the most efficient techniques for demolishing Gothic churches; when, in the words of one historian, "cathedrals suffered execution, like kings, in symbolic punishment for ancient crimes."

In his writings Wright was repeatedly to characterize New York as a collection of crimes both social and artistic. Though he conceded that, unlike the doctor, "the architect cannot bury his mistakes," the cathedral's function was clearly to transform the city into a vast churchyard of his culture's most conspicuous errors. "We go occasionally to the graveyards of our ancestors, so why not to the remains of their cities?"

The cathedral's prismatic form refracted the negativity of Wright's middle years into a range of values culturally acceptable within the established tradition of anti-urbanism. Against the city's power he matched his refusal to submit to obscurity, against the city's physicality the evanescence of his art, against its density his passion, against its skyline his aspiration, against its self-destructive vitality his hope for creative renewal. The effect of the pairing off was chemical, a reaction in which Organic Architecture's heretofore negative and disordered gestures were fused into a constructive and coherent point of view. With an opponent as formidable as New York, no outburst on Wright's part was too overblown to pass as an artistic principle, too trivial to be dismissed as peevishness. With a focus so sharply defined, Wright's art ceased to be at the mercy of random disappointments and imaginary persecutions.

The cathedral was an initial response to a problem not immediately analyzed, a seed crystal that gave a pervading structure to Wright's art in the years ahead. Just as it had taken him several years from his arrival in Chicago to recognize the nature of his opportunity there, so several years would elapse before he could state the new problem concretely, and a decade had passed by the time he returned to New York to unveil his solution. For now, he approached the problem through writing, revisiting the city chiefly to renew his ire, to affirm the city's worth as an adversary.

Although it is doubtful that writing would have become so important to him had he been flooded with commissions, Wright did not turn to it in despair, as Louis Sullivan had done in *Kindergarten Chats* when his career had ended. On the contrary, Wright "began to write" because he saw a way out of despair; writing cleared a passage toward an objective he had at last begun to discern. Through writing, the internalized frustrations began to rush from Wright's psyche into a form as congenial to his needs (if not his talents) as the Prairie House. That he began his autobiography and his writings on cities simultaneously suggests his confidence that his new departure would permit him to do for himself what he had refused to allow time to do on his behalf: consign his early years to the past. He was willing to do so now because, with a subject to absorb him as completely as the family dwelling had thirty years before, he at last had a grip on the future. With the cathedral project and the beginning of *The Disappearing City*, the process of shifting his allegiance from cultural destiny to inner conviction, with which Wright was preoccupied during the middle years, now neared its end. It had been nothing less than the reformation of a gentleman of culture to a true Romantic, with an inspired vision and with the tools to project that vision beyond any obstacle that might now lie in his path.

Though of course never built, the cathedral was a recurring symbol of resurrection throughout his career, making a last appearance in the set of drawings for the Utopian Broadacre City that Wright completed a year before he died. New York does not appear in these drawings; even its ruins had apparently vanished from his memory. But Wright marked its site in his own geography with his greatest monument to the mother-art that, by the end of his life, had richly rewarded his faith.

■ SELF CITY

As its image on the Frank Lloyd Wright two-cent stamp suggests, the Guggenheim Museum takes a privileged place among Wright's buildings, a position of honor not in keeping with the lower rank to which its inadequacies as a musuem must inevitably consign it. But as a major cultural landmark in a world capital of culture, it has been seen firsthand by far more persons than any other Wright design. Inordinately photogenic, the Guggenheim is a mecca for weekend photographers, an essential illustration for art history textbooks, a reliable backdrop for fashion.

Indeed, nearing completion in the last year of Wright's life, the building made a splendid backdrop for a definitive portrait of the master himself: dark cloaked, confident, serenely gazing over concrete ramparts made to his specifications as though molded by his hands. Though Wright died before it was finished, the building's opening was perfectly timed to celebrate his life's work. The Guggenheim was not the greatest achievement of his career, but it looked like the crowning creation; looked, in fact, like a crown, a top-heavy four-tiered tiara fashioned to honor the prophet of architecture in his own land.

Wright had not built the skyscraper cathedral. New York was still there. The new museum both expressed and magnified the vitality of the city's culture; and New York hardly seemed the most appropriate site for the cenotaph of an American hero dedicated to the city's demise.

Yet it is appropriate that Wright's single most famous building should fall below the standard of his finest work. For the fame of Frank Lloyd Wright was itself a creation of his later years, a period in which his reputation rested more solidly on the architect himself than on his architecture. The Guggenheim is but one of scores of buildings that testify to the resurgence of Wright's career in the final twenty-five years of his life, among them Fallingwater, the Johnson wax company headquarters, Taliesin West, Beth Sholom Synagogue (a miniaturized suburban adaptation of the cathedral's tentlike glass pyramid), as well as a number of less dramatic buildings that recovered and extended the Oak Park tradition of innovative excellence in domestic design. But just as the Guggenheim tends to dominate even the greatest masterpieces of painting displayed upon its sloping walls, so Wright's figure overshadowed even the finest work of his later years.

Except as a means of prodding a commission for a recalcitrant client, Wright would have had little use for Flaubert's view that "l'homme c'est rien, l'oeuvre c'est tout." He emerged from the middle years an artist for whom the self and the work were of equal importance, and the self somewhat more equal. Where another architect might strive to create an enduring masterpiece, Wright sought immortality as much for who he was as what he made. "Not only do I intend to be the greatest architect who has yet lived, but the greatest who will ever live. Yes," he confessed to a friend, "I intend to be the greatest architect of all time."

While the quality of his oeuvre entitled him to make such a claim, Wright cared less for critical response to his work than for the projection of a public profile seen by those who had never entered a building by Frank Lloyd Wright, nor could ever afford to build one. This was not an objective appreciated by critics, but then alienating critics had long been a favorite pastime. What he sought in these years was public recognition; what he attained was a Rushmore-like position that soared above its foundation in buildings, an image ultimately as detached from architecture as Lincoln's was from politics.

Now the sensible view is that, whatever its interest to the biographer, the moralist, or the student of American publicity, this tendency toward self-aggrandizement has no significance that could be considered architectural; that Wright's egotism was a character flaw that occasionally marred his architecture and impedes our appreciation of it—a defect we may forgive in consideration of his hardships of middle age, but must forget if we are to arrive at an accurate assessment of his work.

And it is true that the inflation of ego was in part a legacy of the middle years, an addiction to attention born of the need to counteract notoriety and compensate for the lack of opportunities to practice his art. But although he published his autobiography precisely to stir up such opportunities, Wright's emphasis upon the self long preceded the decline of his practice.

In the autobiography, for example, Wright recounts, with much pride and some malice, how in the first year of his Chicago practice he drove a colleague into early retirement because, as the man confessed bitterly to Wright, "I've found out there's no joy in architecture for me except as I see you do it. . . . You *are* the thing you do. I'm not and I never will be." And in 1900 Wright set the tone for his future public relations in "The Architect," his first major speech. From the beginning, it was not just his work but his person that he wished to place before the public.

In Oak Park, however, Wright's personality was a local phenomenon; his buildings and drawings were what brought him international acclaim by the end of his first career. In later years it was the reverse: Wright was a personality known to a public many times the size of that familiar with his buildings, an architect whose architecture was almost an appendage to his personality, an architect who appeared to design houses much as a millionaire might build them—profligately, compulsively, but funded with capital from the full-time enterprise that was Frank Lloyd Wright.

The argument that Wright's egotism satisfied artistic as well as emotional needs might begin by recalling Alexander Woollcott's attribution of Wright's failure to his social incompatibility with those in a position to support his work. But, as Norris Kelly Smith has observed, the conflict between Wright's artistic aims and the medium in which he expressed them had been evident in the flourishing success of his Oak Park days.

He could design a harmonious room, but when his clients moved in with their possessions it was painfully apparent to him that they were not really in harmony with it—that simply by being their separate selves they were defacing a work of art which had ostensibly been made for them but which was in fact designed to set forth an ideal they did not fully understand or accept. He could design a subtly balanced and harmonious exterior, such as that of the Robie house, but there it stood on its narrow city lot, soon to be surrounded by houses that had nothing in common with it, so that instead of contributing to an image of urban harmony it seemed simply eccentric and incongruous—the interior situation turned inside out.

Before 1910 the problem of the exterior was perhaps the most vexing, though in an unbuilt design for a summer bungalow colony that year Wright made one attempt to solve it. But after 1910, with fewer opportunities to build harmonious rooms, much less to see them defaced, Wright found this problem far more soluble. By the end of the middle years, his determination to design the perfect house had been overtaken by a compulsion to engineer the perfect society, a harmonious world order, a government not of laws but of aesthetics, of architecture, and of Wright.

From the 1930s on, a client who commissioned a home from Wright got more than a perfect house. He obtained honorary citizenship in "Usonia," Wright's name for the "real" America that would arise one day west of the Hudson River. And Wright himself subordinated the ideal of the perfect house to the creation of a repertory of various forms appropriate to this society's diversity. If a house was set on a prairie, it became a prototype for the "cottage for level ground." If set on a hillside, it became a "typical home for sloping ground," a model for future Usonian architects to be created in Wright's image. Whether or not such a house was built, its true site was on a landscape of Wright's imagination. Each commission added another variation to the Usonian theme, another architectural adornment to this Utopian country's imaginary capital: the city that to Wright must be "everywhere and nowhere," the state of mind he called Broadacre City.

A Jolly-Jump-Up illustration to *The Disappearing City*, an attempt to give architectural form to the vision born of Wright's "worm's eye view" of New York in 1925 and 1926, Broadacre City was concisely described by Winthrop Sargeant in 1946 in the pages of *Life* magazine:

In 1935, Wright presented his answer to what he thought ailed the U.S. He called it "Broadacres." Physically it consisted of a large relief map on which models of farms, factories and railroads sprawled in a rather attractive mixture of urban and rural scenery. But this intricate model was only a jumping-off place for an elaborate structure of social, economic and moral ideas that has kept Wright smoldering like an Old Testament prophet ever since.

Of course Wright had been smoldering for years without, so to speak, catching fire, and the concept of Broadacre City addressed itself more directly to his problems than to what "ailed the U.S." To a psychologist it might appear that the years of unemployment had bred an unbounded fantasy of a world covered all over, Sherwin Williams–style, with Frank Lloyd Wright houses.

But if Broadacre City was the most extreme expression of an ego inflated to compensate for frustration, it is also the most compelling demonstration that the egotism of Wright's later years was not just braggadocio, nor the classic example of an artist exploiting his personality to fill the vacuum left by a waning talent. What it represented was the purpose to which Wright applied that talent during these years, a purpose for which the self was of critical importance. Indeed, the persona of Frank Lloyd Wright, the smoldering Old Testament prophet of modern architecture, was a creation as intricate as his imaginary city. Together, self and city defined the terms of his second career.

A decade after the unveiling, Henry-Russell Hitchcock wrote that Broadacres was of interest chiefly because it "brings into coherent relationship the many remarkable individual projects of the ten preceding years when so very little was actually built," and at the time it did seem logical to suppose that the need for such an outlet would evaporate with Wright's renewed capacity to build. But in 1958, with more commissions than at any time in his career, Wright prepared a second set of drawings for Broadacres, and his enduring interest suggests that the project had not been primarily a retrospective of the years of failure, but a vista of the "more universal destiny" that now loomed straight ahead.

Smith has commented that "the ultimate importance of Broadacres lay in the fact that it was sprung from the wholly personal center of Wright's own mind." But since the same can be said for perhaps the majority of Wright's designs, what distinguishes Broadacres is that it was not a product, like a building, a book, or a drawing, but rather a *process* for which the model itself, as Sargeant perceived, was no more than a "jumping-off place" for Wright's thoughts on matters quite alien to architecture. And if the intricacy of the Broadacres model owed more to Wright's complex imagination than to his commitment to practical planning, the project also offered him a means of extending that imagination toward his culture.

Indeed, the very appeal of The City as a metaphor was that it offered unlimited resources for proving the significance of Wright's self on the broadest possible cultural level. As a reaction to the real city, Broadacres provided Wright with infinite mirror images of precisely those resources with which the real city had been culturally endowed: resources of art, politics, economics, progress—a fund as bottomless as the city was tall. Ten years earlier Wright had proposed to blast this treasure from the earth to prepare his steel and glass cathedral. Now, sagely, he drew upon it to demonstrate that his self possessed a cultural value as broadly based as the most densely integrated, richly diversified metropolis. Just as Broadacres had no physical limits, so it provided Wright with a perpetual frontier to expand the meaning of the self beyond the compass of the individual project, however remarkable. By the end of his life, it was clearer that the purpose of Broadacres was not to collect unbuilt projects into a pleasing arrangement, but to bring Wright himself "into coherent relationship" with the culture he prepared to rejoin after twenty-five years' absence.

The boundaries of Broadacre City were not of space, but of time: a period extending over the last quarter-century of Wright's career, from the 1935 scale model to the last set of drawings completed the year before he died. Within this span of time, Wright achieved his more universal destiny on a scale almost as boundless as Broadacres. If in so doing he frequently "abandoned the great in order to reach the gigantic," he did so to illuminate his culture more brilliantly, if with less assured distinction, than in the great achievements of his art.

The self of Frank Lloyd Wright does not, of course, lend itself to formal evaluation. But the purpose of Wright's city was to advance a conception of architecture beyond conventional definitions, beyond even the most formally advanced ideas of the European Modern Movement, indeed beyond form altogether toward innovations in architectural content.

Just as it is inaccurate to regard Broadacre City as no more than an outlet for frustrated creativity, so to dismiss the persona of Wright is to ignore the content of his architecture from 1935 forward, a period in which he confronted directly problems that had afflicted his architecture since the earliest days of his practice, problems buildings alone could not solve but only reflect. If Wright's first career was, in Hitchcock's phrase, an exhaustive study of architectural expression "in the nature of materials," the second career was a no less thorough exploration into the nature of architecture itself: an examination of the American architect's relationship to his culture.

■ THE INCENTIVE ZONE

Vincent Scully has pointed out that by 1935 Wright's Utopian vision of a decentralized America was "entirely in accord with the way things were going in America anyway." For some Usonians, the problem was much the same as that of their real-life city-cousin counterparts: what if you didn't want to flee to the suburbs?

"So that those from the city wouldn't feel lost in that vision of the country," Wright offered to house unreconstructed city lovers in a series of apartment towers, dotted about the landscape of Broadacres rather like high-rise pillars of salt for those who dared look back at the disappearing city. In 1953 one of those towers was actually built, in the small town of Bartlesville, Oklahoma. "An idea that had to wait over thirty years for full realization," the tower's design actually preceded Broadacre City's by six years, and was, in fact, Wright's second major design for New York City.

Commissioned in 1928 by Willam Norman Guthrie, the same progressive Episcopalian rector under whose auspices Wright had proposed the Steel Cathedral, the St. Mark's Apartment Tower consisted of two 14-story and one 18-story residential towers, flanking three sides of St. Mark's-in-the-Bouwerie. After the stock market crash in 1929, plans to construct the towers were halted, then canceled.

By any standard the collapse of the St. Mark's Project must be counted a major loss to New York architecture—by any standard, that is, but Wright's own. Viewed in the context of his hardening stance against the city, the project exposed him at his most flagrantly opportunistic. Well into writing *The Disappearing City* by the time he designed the towers, Wright hardly merits sympathy for being deprived of the opportunity to contribute to the city's "pig-piling" in a part of town, the Lower East Side, already notorious for the density of its population. And one drawing, ominously labeled "First Group," suggests that the three towers were only the beginning of a scheme that would have anticipated the six-block stretch of nearby Stuyvesant Town by almost twenty years.

Unlike the cathedral, the St. Mark's Project was a practical, not to say worldly, venture designed to provide the parish with tax-free revenue in precisely the sort of steeple-topping enterprise that had appalled Henry

James and moved Wright himself to wrath. Apparently the one way the Church could escape censure for leading men into merchantdom and so becoming itself a merchant was to engage Wright to endow its real estate holdings with "the poetic principle."

Though on record as opposing tall buildings within the central city, Wright proposed the tower for two more urban locations before it finally came to rest on the Oklahoma plain. But here Wright surpassed himself in pitchman's fast talk, pawning off an old design like a con artist peddling the Brooklyn Bridge. "The tree that escaped the crowded forest . . . a finger pointing in the plain"—with a good deal more poetry than principle, Wright quick-changed disappointment into affirmation, exile into daring escape. "Now the skyscraper will come into its own on the rolling plains of Oklahoma," where indeed the Price Tower arguably became Wright's most "New York" building: not just because, though a mere sixteen stories, it was the closest he came to the skyline, but because it so brashly embodied the hustler's "Broadway Creed" for which he most reviled New York.

Certainly the flat, rolling plain was a more suitable location for Wright's high-rising individualism; nonetheless, the Price Tower is strikingly inconsistent with two qualities commonly associated with Wright's architecture. Most glaring, perhaps, is the tower's violation of his principle that a building derive organically from the nature of its site: he made no attempt to hide the fact that the design was originally intended for an urban environment. Equally odd is that so prolific a master of conspicuous creation should prefer to recycle an old design instead of taking the opportunity to create an entirely new one. No one would raise an eyebrow at Mies van der Rohe for building fifties skyscrapers based on twenties models, but Wright's tower—though he made no effort to conceal its vintage—soars aloft in a faintly unpleasant air of mothballs.

These two anomalies, one of space, the other of time, were therefore not accidental aberrations; they were features of the design, and so identified by Wright. The tower's passage over space and time was a calculated move, part of the process by which Wright brought himself "into coherent relationship" with his culture. Like an exclamation mark on the American horizon, the building punctuated Wright's remarks on the cultural meaning of the self and its antithesis, the city.

To depict Wright's later work as "an exploration of American culture" suggests a bloodless interest in academic issues; it was more a matter of survival. The St. Mark's Project emerged from the period in which Wright began to confront the architects of the European Modern Movement directly, to reject the honor of distinguished forerunner, and to promote himself as a visible alternative to Modern doctrine. If as late as 1926 he was capable of designing a work that, like the cathedral, strongly evoked European parallels, by the end of the decade he undertook to make his opposition to Modernism irrevocable and public.

In 1928, the year the towers were commissioned, Wright expressed his initial misgivings over Modernism in a review of an English translation of Le Corbusier's 1923 manifesto, *Vers une architecture*. Four years later he agreed to participate in the Museum of Modern Art's historic International Style exhibition, not as a member of the group, nor as an influence on their development, but, so he claimed, as an adversary to their teachings.

Lewis Mumford has decried the "America First" tendency that surfaced at this time as "a coarse, dark vein in the fine granite of [Wright's] mind"; but, if Usonianism did lapse into jingoism, it is hard to see in what other terms Wright could have confronted the equally indiscriminate endorsement of European Modernism among young American intellectuals.

"Isn't he dead?" Philip Johnson is said to have asked when Hitchcock suggested including Wright in the International Style exhibition; when informed otherwise, Johnson hailed him as "our greatest nineteenth-century architect." Even after his career's renewal, Wright continued to be over-shadowed by those Europeans toward whom the mainstream of western architecture was felt to have flowed. (Thus, in the final revised edition of his *Pioneers of Modern Design*, 1975, Pevsner lets stand this assessment: "To sum up, Frank Lloyd Wright's outstanding importance lies in the fact that nobody else had by 1904 come so near to the style of today in his actual buildings.")

Though it is reasonable to conclude that the rise of European Modernism contributed to Wright's decline after 1910 by seizing the leadership in modern architecture, one might also argue that in thus isolating Wright it made it possible for him to succeed ultimately as both architect and artist on his own terms to a degree that before 1910 had not been possible. And the city was instrumental to Wright as a means of defining his terms, clarifying the issues that he believed separated him from his European colleagues. Indeed, with the growing acceptance of Modernism among American (urban) intellectuals, the city sometimes functioned as a surrogate for Modernism in Wright's Usonian campaign.

Gertrude Stein preferred Chicago's skyscrapers to Manhattan's because, not confined to an island, Chicago's architects had no topographical reason to build vertically. "Choice" she explained, "is always more pleasing than anything necessary."

By the same token, in characterizing the Price Tower as "the tree that escaped the crowded forest," Wright clearly tried to create an impression that its transfer from New York to Oklahoma was his personal choice, as though he had withdrawn the design from the city for high-minded moral and aesthetic reasons and awarded it, after several decades of deliberation, to a worthier recipient of his gifts. Yet the opportunism gaily flaunted here, like the egotism from which it sprang, was neither a character flaw nor a lovably roguish foible, but the approach to a problem central to his art.

This problem was not uniquely Wright's; it was the condition Woollcott had appraised in Wright's failure: the architect's need for a social position in order to practice his art. Any architect, pariah or paragon, must cope with the capriciousness of a clientele, not only in taste, but in when, where, what, and, most frustrating in Wright's case, whether to build. While the architect's dependence on patronage has always been a problem in the conduct of his profession, in American culture it became, perhaps for the first time, a considerable factor in the architect's view of his art as well, as Henry Hobson Richardson realized in observing that the First Law of Architecture was "Get the Job."

Where artists in less expensive materials might work in comparative independence, confining themselves to respectably pragmatic gestures that preserved some semblance of detachment from their patrons, the architect's medium compelled him toward more overt forms of opportunism, away from choice, toward necessity. As the most expensive art, architecture was the art most likely to preserve traditional class ties, least likely to effect a smooth transition, or indeed any transition at all, from conservatively centralized sources of wealth to more broadly conceived democratic ideals. The more people read books, viewed paintings, attended concerts, the less architecture even seemed like an art at all.

For a commercial architect content to work in any style, on any project, Richardson's Law had no profound implications. For an architect of loftier ambitions the issue of patronage was crucial: the task of creating an art by such an undependable and conservative process was an aesthetic as well as a professional challenge.

Louis Sullivan had failed to meet this challenge. Classically inclined, briefly Beaux-Arts trained, he aimed to express democracy in architecture, but his conception of his own role in the process retained from aristocratic conventions the architect's traditional passivity. In theory equality replaced hierarchy, but for the practicing architect liberty did not replace servitude to his culture's ideals. The suspension bridge replaced the imperial arch, but the architect remained anonymous.

To Wright, Sullivan's exalted view of democracy was sentimental, a morbid humility doomed to defeat. If Sullivan was, in Mumford's phrase, "the first American architect to think consciously of his relations with civilization," Wright was the first who consciously determined to change them.

Where a classicist might pause to listen, a romantic speaks aloud; rather than wait around for democracy to call, Wright surmised that in a democracy an architect derived his authority not from "the people"—that sentimental euphemism for the coalition between "the mobocracy" and "them asses"— but from the self. The distinction between Sullivan and Wright was discernible even in their falling-out over Wright's "bootleg" house; where Sullivan sought to be dutifully responsive to his society, Wright's instinct was to take the initiative; indeed this response, in Wright's view, was the one his society most demanded. One either takes action or becomes a victim, and Sullivan had already become the latter.

Outspoken in his defense of democratic virtues against the aristocratic connotations of prevailing American taste, Sullivan shrank from initiative as though it were of the enemy camp. Like showmanship—"children of Barnum" was his epithet for practitioners of the American Renaissance style—initiative was unworthy of an architecture presumed subordinate to the high ideals served. Of course, these ideals were themselves at variance with the reality of his own commercial practice, compromised without redeeming irony by his office buildings, department stores, and banks. Where Sullivan's buildings begged the question of whether free enterprise deserved the spiritual emphasis he tried to give it, Wright responded to the client's worldliness with a pragmatism of his own.

To Wright, the architect might be a social surrogate because he had so deputized himself; he could not claim the authority of "the people" without first proclaiming his own. Behind Wright's famous choice of "honest arrogance" over "hypocritical humility" was the intuition that, far from being detrimental to the creation of a native democratic architecture, initiative was nothing less than the democratic equivalent to aristocratic patronage; initiative was both the means and the issue with which he broke from the European model and assumed the artistic, as well as the social position that democratic society demanded.

It was in this connection that Wright's ego became central to his confrontation with the Modern Movement. Long a cherished feature of the Romanticism he claimed as his tradition, egocentricity now became the proof of Wright's progress beyond the most advanced forms of modern architecture.

For all their gleaming appearance of modernity, in Wright's view modern buildings of the 1920s issued from an obsolete artistic premise beside which Monticello, for all its Palladian window dressing, looked more up to date. With revolutionary forms and radical rhetoric, the Modern proponents called upon the architect to assume an artistic position as traditional as Sullivan's, for like Sullivan they hoped to derive their artistic authority from their society—in their case retroactively, from the future society they intended to shape and "educate."

While the Romantic tradition from which Wright's egotism sprang was itself European in origin, the Modern Movement had no wish to align itself with or to perpetuate this tradition. Indeed its objective, as James Marston Fitch wrote of Gropius, was "to cross a new frontier in architecture into areas where design by the individual genius [was] no longer possible."

Such an aim, remarkably similar to Sullivan's search for an architectural system or rule "so broad as to admit of no exception," could only strengthen Wright's conviction that the Americanization of architecture was virtually synonymous with its transformation from a decorative branch of social service to an art. Americans, he believed, had crossed the frontier into areas where design by the individual genius, accountable to no sovereignty but his own, was possible for the first time in history.

In reality, of course, Wright was neither more nor less dependent upon the patron than were his European contemporaries; neither more nor less demanding of those who paid for the privilege of inhabiting his designs. If there was a distinction between the relationships that each sought with society, it was one that had to be dramatized. The American Architect was a role that had still to be played. And for Wright, the theater was the city.

There were as yet no "modern" buildings in New York when Wright motored east in 1929 to consult with the Reverend Guthrie on the St. Mark's Project; but, like the Regionalist painters who despised the city not for its native artists but for its intellectual receptivity to European modern art, Wright recognized the city as a port of entry for ideas that would not materialize into curtain walls for several decades. By 1929 New York had become for him roughly what the White City of 1893 had been for Sullivan: the symbolic beachhead for an imaginary invasion. Just as Sullivan had portrayed the World's Fair's classical forms as an unwarranted eastern intrusion on unspoiled American soil, so the definitive American architectural statement of Manhattan was, in Wright's eyes, the results of an aesthetic epidemic that should have been quarantined on Ellis Island.

But even before the 1932 International Style show granted architecture the visa that painting had obtained at the Armory Show two decades before, New York embodied the architectural paradigm that Wright held obsolete.

Just as he would later brand Mies "a reactionary" for trying to perfect the nineteenth-century box, so, on his 1929 visit, gazing up at the symbols of "the American Century," he was moved to remark that the "man-eating skyscrapers . . . riveted steel skeletons" were "nineteenth-century architecture. Not twentieth."

The city's willing capitulation to foreign invasion could be seen not just in the legacy of the City Beautiful Movement—steel forms embellished with classical orders, entablatures, cornices, academic statuary—but in the subordination of the architect to his expendable Old World role. Indeed, New York combined the worst of the old, the architect's passivity, with the worst of the new, no all-powerful patron to enable an architect to realize a vision unmarred by the competition of the mob.

Again like the Regionalist painters, Wright's attitude rested upon time-honored American prejudice against the city as a place of physical filth and moral corruption, a cattle yard where the sensitive soul is trampled underfoot by the hurrying crowd. But most of all, for Wright the city's squalor, its inhumane oppression of its citizens, were poorly disguised metaphors for the architect's subservience to a patron, indeed for all the indignities artists in other forms were to some extent spared.

The "forest" from which Wright's "tree" finally made its escape was composed not of "pig-piled" human beings but of other trees: other buildings. What was wrong with the city was not that it was overcrowded, immoral, and dirty, but that it denied an architect the opportunity to perform a solo without distraction from the competition. The city's worst corruption was visited not upon the morals of its citizens, but upon the morale of its designers. The New York architect's art was not only compromised but somewhat beside the point. Laid out on an engineer's grid, the city's form magnified not just Wright's insignificance, but every architect's, not least those whose projects had actually been erected. The Woolworth Building's Gothic pinnacles advertised not Cass Gilbert's art, but Woolworth's nickels and dimes. Rockefeller Center's "crime of crimes" was a comparable miscarriage of cultural justice. And to whom did the names Shreve, Lamb, & Harmon mean anything at all?

In his Oak Park days Wright had lived up to the letter of Richardson's Law. In his later years he sought to place himself above it by devising an architectural philosophy—more accurately a strategy—to accommodate the law's broader implications. The need to cultivate clients, to revise designs to conform to popular or individual taste: these were minor irritations. For Wright, "the Job" was to be truly self-employed, a job for which his middle years amply qualified him.

In the subordination of the building to the urban fabric, Wright found a dramatic metaphor for the Old World architect's subservience to society. And just as the frontier was the standard literary salvation from the city's dense, oppressive weight, so the Price Tower's escape to the Oklahoma plains dramatized Wright's passage across the American frontier toward an architecture of individual genius.

The year 1929 was not, of course, an auspicious one in which to take a stand for rugged individualism; but then that had not after all been the purpose of the original St. Mark's design. The tower was a work whose form preceded its most important function—the escape—by twenty-four years.

Fallingwater (1936) and the Johnson wax company headquarters (1936–1939) are the works that placed Wright back at the top of his profession. But, while neither building signified a detour like the Imperial Hotel and the Los Angeles houses, neither was so directly addressed to the central themes of Wright's later work as the St. Mark's Project and its subsequent manifestations.

An indication of the importance Wright himself gave the design in the development of his architecture is that, of his hundreds of buildings and unbuilt projects, the Price Tower is the only work to which he devoted an entire book: *The Story of the Tower: The Tree That Escaped the Crowded Forest*. The moral of the story is the subtitle: however well it graced its physical site, the tower's meaning reverberated back to the site that had refused it.

Among Wright's later buildings the Price Tower is not unique evidence that by 1953 he had progressed from an architecture noted for its harmonious wedding to site to an architecture so idiosyncratic it was equally out of place anywhere in the world, from Ellis Island to Beverly Hills, Venice to Baghdad, a style more Isolationist than International. Yet he continued to claim that each design was the logical expression of its site, and, in a sense, each was. For from Wright's point of view, the most distinctive feature a site could possess was a client willing to erect a Frank Lloyd Wright building on it. Until 1953 this was a feature conspicuously lacking in New York.

But while the book's title betrayed a long-held grudge, it contained a positive meaning also. For the tower's transformation from an urban design to the building that best embodied his opposition to the city was a reflection of Wright's own transformation in the decade that produced it. The polarity between tree and forest, between the city and self, was a key to the transformation.

Between 1925, when he began writing *The Disappearing City*, and 1935, when he unveiled Broadacres, Wright evolved from an embittered, embattled failure to an artist sufficiently motivated to again achieve success. The disappearing city was the self reconstituted; the simultaneous writing of that book and the autobiography constituted a process through which he conquered the emotional and artistic conflicts of the preceding fifteen years and laid constructive groundwork for the remaining twenty-five. Once he had discovered the city as a means of expressing the self, he ceased to be an architect consigned to the past and became one whose most productive years lay ahead. And in changing the title of the final (1958) version of *The Disappearing City* to *The Living City*, he summarized his own evolution from an architect fast disappearing into history books into a thriving twentieth-century institution.

If Wright's perambulating tower was an antimonument to the site for which it had been created, it was also a tribute to his discovery that the city was itself a movable famine on which his negativity could feast until finally satisfied. Though the original design sought accommodation with the city, by 1929 Wright could at last say without bravado that "something was coming clearer. . . . No, not rebellion. Conviction."

In 1929 that something was still several years on the horizon. But the horizon had always been Wright's natural habitat; six years before Broadacres brought the design into focus, the St. Mark's Project took the first step since the prairie houses that did not lead to a dead end: it breached an opening through the wall of concrete hollyhocks, textile-blocks, lava-stone lanterns, cubo-futurist caryatids, Mayan, Aztec, and Japanese forms, toward the fulfillment of his second career.

If the St. Mark's Project may thus be described as the first major work of Wright's later period, its realized form twenty-four years later dramatized the difference between this period and that in Oak Park; for Wright now aggressively claimed the prairie that he had once so compliantly accommodated. Where the Oak Park houses stretched out receptively toward the horizon, the Price Tower stood sharply perpendicular, tall above the plains, visible for miles around, as Wright himself now towered above a landscape on which his buildings stood as so many monuments to his successful return.

Of course the irony of the Price Tower is that, unlike the suburban shopping mall, the small-town commercial skyscraper is not a symbol of rebellion against the city, but of allegiance to it, like a regional stockbroker affiliated with a Wall Street firm. Just as the tower's meaning for Wright lay in its relationship to the forest from which it escaped, so the Price Tower was part of the Manhattanization of small-town America: a symbol of New York's hegemony over the nation's culture. As all roads led to Rome, so all skyscrapers point toward Gotham.

Perhaps this is why, after finally succeeding in building the Tower, Wright restored the design to its conceptual purity five years later, in the second set of drawings for Broadacre City. With its function as inviolate as its form, the skyscraper at last came into its own on the same fictitious landscape where the cathedral arose to mark the vanished city.

Speaking of Wright's method of constructing Broadacre City from a repertory of recycled forms, such as the St. Mark's Project, Norris Kelly Smith has written:

Wright's introduction of these various projects should not, I think, be attributed to expediency or to a thrifty desire on his part to make further use of existing material—though he was given to doing exactly this in putting together his frequently repetitious books. What he wanted to make clear, I believe, is that there is an underlying principle which establishes the unity of his life's work, and that that principle is best expressed in Broadacre City. To judge Broadacres is to judge everything he created— and vice versa. We must try to discover and to assess that general principle.

In a thoughtful analysis that would have greatly pleased one who claimed to be the first architect of stature in over four hundred years, Smith has located this general principle outside the traditions of western culture. In his view Broadacre City was essentially a vision of Zion, an eschatological preparation for a Judaic paradise ultimately derived "from the ancient patterns of Hebrew expression."

To an architect devoutly American, fiercely proud of his Welsh ancestry, a Unitarian who invoked ancient Hebrew expressions mainly to condemn "Mosaic . . . 'interest' " and defy Isaian taboo, this interpretation is not easily reconciled. Granted, however, that Broadacre City does make clear Wright's intent to express some kind of unifying theme, one may well search western culture in vain to discover a fundamental principle.

Given the general ambiguity of Organic Architecture, as well as the lengths to which Smith has gone to clarify it, it may be nearer the truth to say that the underlying theme expressed in Broadacre City was not a principle, but a dilemma; that the many contradictions in Wright's architectural philosophy, and indeed his own insistence upon the importance of "principles" he could neither fully articulate nor consistently uphold, can only be accounted for by a profound dilemma that no principle or set of principles could happily resolve.

If Broadacre City makes one thing clear, it is that the source of its theme was the city: a source wholly contained within the culture of Wright's second "time, his day, his age," that of mid-twentieth-century America.

To judge Broadacres outside that context is to adhere too faithfully to Wright's own practice of lifting himself above the culture that produced him. It is also to overlook the fact that the purpose of Broadacres was precisely to restore his place within that culture after a quarter-century's absence.

■ WRIGHT, INC.

It is tempting to interpret Broadacre City as Wright's elaborate revenge against New York for the collapse of the St. Mark's Project (and he was not alone in feeling that because the stock market had crashed on Wall Street, New York was largely to blame for the Great Depression). And it is tempting, also, to interpret the project's emphasis on decentralization as Wright's retaliation for being himself so cruelly "decentralized"—thrust by historians if not by history from the center of modern architectural innovation to the outskirts, demoted from a leader to a has-been. For Broadacres emerged from a period in which, as Robert Twombly notes, Wright "was considered even by many of his admirers as an eccentric, opinionated, flamboyant, arrogant, slightly screwy old man with strange ideas who talked too much."

For that matter, it is easy to dismiss Broadacre City altogether as "too much talk." Whether Yeats is correct to say that "we make out of the quarrel with others, rhetoric, but of the quarrel with ourself, poetry," undeniably Broadacre City launched the major campaign in Wright's lifelong war of truth against the world of others; and the bombastic rhetoric with which he promoted it does lack the poetic grace found among even his least distinguished buildings.

And yet, while Wright's jeremiads played every variation on the role of professional outsider, it would be wrong to infer that the "underlying principle" Broadacres expressed was primarily composed of hostility, misanthropy, alienation. Viewed apart from the overcharged rhetoric, Wright's Utopia does disclose an inner argument, a quarrel with the self. Its poetry is nearer the epic scale of Taliesin, Wright's cherished Druid bard, than that of the sonnet; its conception is heroic, with Wright of course the hero, but what it recounts is not simple reaction to the existing city, but Wright's inescapable attraction to it also.

In 1954 Wright informed the New York Times of his plans to move his practice to New York. Confirming what cynics had maintained for years, the Wisconsin State Supreme Court had recently charged that the Taliesin Fellowship, Wright's apprentice corps, was not a legitimate educational institution, but a private business venture. Rather than pay the back taxes demanded, Wright somewhat tastelessly threatened to burn Taliesin down yet again and move into the Plaza Hotel.

A fund-raising testimonial dinner enabled Wright to pay the taxes, and Taliesin remained intact. But his threat had not been idle—merely redundant, for Wright had already engaged a suite at the Plaza, a lease he retained for the rest of his life. Nicknamed "Taliesin the Third" by his apprentices, decorated in yearningly urbane style by Wright himself, the suite was in later years the most telling sign of Wright's ambivalence toward New York.

But Alexander Woollcott had years before observed the personality streak that characterized Wright's relationship to the city: "I know what perverse and tactless mockery of all who would serve him dances ever in his eyes. I know how near the surface, always, is the untamed imp in him that bids him upset the very apple cart he is hungrily approaching." If Woollcott knew better than most that Broadacre City was an emphatic kick in the apple cart, it was because he knew that New Yorkers figured prominently among those who would serve Wright. Woollcott knew that Charles MacArthur, the playwright, Joseph Urban, the Ziegfeld designer, and he himself had been instrumental in the creation of Frank Lloyd Wright, Inc., a corporation formed in 1927 for the purpose of paying off Wright's debts, enabling him to resume his practice after three years of legal setbacks. The St. Mark's Project was itself one of the first products of this corporation, for which Wright designed a letterhead that read:

Chicago   New York   Los Angeles   Tokio
Frank Lloyd Wright Incorporated

In fact, the "corporation" was headquartered at Taliesin, which the corporation's sponsors had redeemed from bank foreclosure and where Wright now resided as a salaried employee.

Woollcott knew that the architect who later boasted of his efforts to "help Japan to her feet" had himself been helped at this critical time in his career by citizens of the metropolis whose disappearance he now contrived to conjure. In 1931, while Wright was in New York lecturing at the New School on ideas published the following year in *The Disappearing City*, Woollcott chaired a meeting at New York's Town Hall to protest Wright's exclusion from the architectural committee of the 1933 Chicago World's Fair. During the same visit Lewis Mumford rallied the city's architectural community to give a birthday party for Wright, at which the guest of honor was moved to tears by the outpouring of affection at a time when he was still unable to secure commissions.

But moral and financial support was the very reverse of the city's greatest service to Frank Lloyd Wright. Edgar Tafel, the New York architect who worked as an apprentice on the construction of the great scale model of Broadacre City, observed that "every architectural episode in Mr. Wright's life had to have a villain," and Broadacre City was no exception. "No building moved ahead until the villain was established," Tafel continued; and if Wright's writings leave little doubt about the identity of Broadacre's villain, the site of the project's debut revealed the extent of Wright's dependence upon the villain for the project's realization.

In 1935 Wright took his proposal for the elimination of New York to Rockefeller Center, the city's new architectural symbolic heart. The site was appropriate, for the city itself had penetrated clear to "the wholly personal center" of the mind from which Broadacres had sprung. In so doing, it released the accumulated energy of the middle years and exposed a philosophical contradiction Wright himself had discovered at their outset.

In 1910 Wright's architectural practice came unstuck in a philosophical tug-of-war without a winner. In his introduction to the Wasmuth monograph published that year, he tried to demonstrate his descent from the tradition of the great Gothic builders, and to extoll the social consensus their buildings expressed as a prerequisite to all great architecture. And yet his scandalously antisocial actions that year, indeed the very theme of the essay itself— "The Sovereignty of the Individual"—pointed in quite a different direction. Far from supporting the social consensus of his own day, Wright raged against it, maintaining that the individual's right to reject social conventions took precedence to his duty to conform. His essay repudiated the influence of the Renaissance upon architecture, yet drew upon humanist assumptions to support his concept of individual freedom. "Renaissance" for self, "Gothic" for others—Wright's philosophy was as eclectic and impure as the revival architecture he despised.

In Europe between 1910 and 1925, when Wright began turning his attention to the city, a hypothetical architectural consensus—best symbolized by Gropius's Bauhaus buildings at Dessau—had been achieved, at least among progressive designers if not among Gropius's "million workers." But Wright's refusal to join them spoke for more than his age and individual temperament.

Speaking of the ancient Greeks, W. H. Auden proposed that "civilization be measured by the degree of diversity attained, the degree of unity retained." But how do you go about retaining something you never possessed? In America the progress toward an indigenous culture appeared to reverse the process: it was unity that served as the ideal to be achieved, while diversity and individuality came to be viewed as the traditional qualities most worthy of preservation.

If the aim of the Modern Movement was in part to enable individual artists to create forms that reflected a cultural unity among themselves, Wright's objective was roughly the reverse: to single-handedly create forms that reflected the diversity of his culture, of which he held his own individuality to be the emblem. The problem was not that so paradoxical an ideal could not be represented in architecture, but that the representation had already been achieved. For to Wright, as to many before him and since, this was the genius of New York City.

In New York, competition was the consensus; the city's form was competition crystallized, unified by a universal license to break rank, build taller, overtower, outshine. The skyscraper, as Wright himself sarcastically put it, was the "*ne plus ultra* of *e pluribus unum*"; and the skyline was a phenomenon so apparently organic it resembled nothing so much as a natural wonder.

Toward the end of the nineteenth century Montgomery Schuyler had written that, while few of New York's skyscrapers possessed great architectural merit individually, "it is in the aggregation that the immense impressiveness lies. It is not an architectural vision, but it does, most tremendously, 'look like business.'"

But by the 1920s the question of whether the skyline was or was not an "architectural vision" had become increasingly moot. Whatever one chose to call it—happenstance, greed, collective cultural projection, or a dream in the mind of Hugh Ferriss—the skyline possessed in the eyes of the world an authority greater than that any architect could command, a tremendously American impressiveness no architectural vision could equal without substantially revising prevailing conceptions of what might constitute "architecture."

In "Significant Insignificance," the chapter in *An Autobiography* describing his 1929 trip to New York, Wright tries hard to remain tremendously unimpressed by the urban aggregation, planting in the mouth of his four-year-old daughter the complaint later voiced by Le Corbusier: that the skyscrapers were not tall enough. But the sarcasm breaks down into "An Angry Prophecy and a Preachment" on the city's vices, and in a burst of anger Wright's "autobiography" turns into a soapbox from which he launches a rambling, contorted tirade, chapter after chapter of barely coherent philosophizing on Rent, Time, Traffic, Land, New Freedom, Youth, Poverty, Catastrophe, Conscience, Heresy, The Enemy, Great Power, Appeasement, More, Echo, on and on through a voyage of fulmination from which he recovers his composure, over a hundred pages later, when he arrives at the gates of Broadacre City.

If the city's "insignificance" was capable of provoking such an outburst, the reason was not because it violated Wright's philosophy, but because it realized it, resolved its contradictions in a glittering paradox of high and low, mighty and poor, unity and diversity, Renaissance assertion bound up by Gothic belief, in a vision—architectural or not—that in a few square miles feverishly reconciled the American cult of individualism with the ideal of unity.

A city could resolve the paradox, then, if at some cost in human and aesthetic values. But could an architect do the same, at any price? How could an individual be a consensus?

He might begin by claiming that the existing consensus was the wrong one, perhaps on moral grounds. The Steel Cathedral was such a beginning; and, as a holy city, Broadacres never overcame its roots in Wright's appeal to American religiosity. But to this ecclesiastical foundation it added appeals to patriotism ("the real America begins west of Buffalo"), to progress (the modern city is obsolete), with just the slightest hint of bigotry ("By way of the ancient Mosaic invention of 'interest,' money is now a commodity for sale"). Upon this platform of platitudes Wright erected his city to end all cities.

But the most significant difference between the cathedral and Broadacre City was that the latter was not "architecture"—no more strictly an "architectural vision" than Schuyler's aggregation, King's Dream of New York, or Hugh Ferriss's magic mountains. The cathedral after all was just another building, however inflated its scale and infeasible its construction. Even as fantasy it was pale compared to the eclectic thicket of spires rising in the 1920s. Unlike the cathedral, but like Ferriss's visions, Broadacres transcended Schuyler's conception of what an "architectural vision" might constitute.

"It is as desirable to build a chicken-coop as a cathedral," Wright instructed a group of students in 1939, for by 1935 he had already discovered that in a democratic culture it was even more desirable. For if no twentieth-century cathedral could convey the collective belief expressed in Chartres, Reims, or Amiens, a chicken coop—or, say, a modest house—might propagate, adding up incrementally to match the power of the Gothic achievement or, more pertinently (to mix Wright's barnyard metaphors), the awesome "pig-piling" of the modern metropolis.

Forty years earlier Daniel Burnham had surmised that the best way for architecture to compete with the city was to become one. A single building was at best a "little plan," very lovely, perhaps worth a gold medal, but with "no power to stir men's blood."

Broadacres was Wright's White City. To give architecture the "tremendous impressiveness" of the city, to make architecture itself "look like business," this was the business of Frank Lloyd Wright, Inc., this the incentive that led Wright to become, as Sybil Moholy-Nagy noted, the first architect in history to design an entire continent.

Not strictly true, actually, for Wright's comprehensive plan for America divided the continent into three parts. Two of these—Usonia North and Usonia South—were designated the areas most receptive to Wright's vision. The third part, roughly corresponding to the original thirteen colonies, would be termed New England and left alone more or less to pursue its misguided ideals of bastardized European culture.

By the end of his life Wright maintained headquarters in all three territories: the original Taliesin in Wisconsin, Taliesin West in Arizona, and Taliesin the Third in New York City. It was the last of these that held the greatest strategic importance in the approximate realization of his dream.

■ ASLEEP AT THE WHEEL

Was Broadacres prophetic? Or was it, as Vincent Scully has suggested, a shrewd tag-along with "the way things were going in America anyway"? Had Wright's proposals found wider acceptance, could chaotic urban sprawl have been avoided? Or did his emphasis upon individual sovereignty— self-interest—not preclude the very order his plan promised to insure?

Was it even a plan? Would Broadacre City be the creation of an "organic society"—the cathedral dismembered in exploded view? Or, like some vast continental behaviorist experiment, would Broadacres have modified American society toward a more organic way of life? Could it have been built bit by bit, or must it be the product of an overnight mass conversion?

To all of the above, yes and no. Like the term "Organic Architecture" of which it was the most complete expression, Broadacres was compounded of contradictions, paradoxes, and confusion; an idea to whose fundamental meaning only Wright remained privy; a process in which the only constant was the counterpoise of the imaginary city against the real one.

A model of the St. Mark's Project was a regular feature of Wright's traveling Broadacre City exhibition. Enormously out of scale with the Broadacres model, looming over it in installation like a feudal donjon over a lord's domain, the tower was a constant reminder of the underlying sense in which Broadacre City was a punitive paradise—a penitentiary, in the original, literal meaning of the term: a place to which innately good transgressors would be placed to "willingly" mend their shameful ways. Indeed, the "disappearing city" was so much the focus of Wright's plans that he was as indifferent as any real estate developer to the extent to which their implementation would have obliterated the countryside also, sowing the inevitable harvest of suburban sprawl. The dispossessed city dweller could at least move into a St. Mark's tower and ride the elevator in fond remembrance of the skylines past, but where could country folk turn to escape the spread of decentralized civilization? In the city that was everywhere and nowhere, every Usonian would be a cosmopolite, every hitchhiker a boulevardier, and "man in possession of his earth" a captive, universal Man About Town.

If the Price Tower violated Wright's principle of reciprocity between building and site, Broadacre City suspended it entirely. Here, in stark relief on a twelve-by-twelve-foot scale model, a wholly imaginary landscape supplanted the American soil from which Organic Architecture had supposedly sprung, a topography as artificial as the most tortured European topiary. Here was the landscape of Wright's own mind fully liberated from compromise, from the demoralizing effects of patronage, from the undependability of an art made irregularly on commission.

In this freedom, however, lay a problem: the transgression of a principle far more important than that of landscaping, indeed, the most elemental principle that Broadacres was ostensibly designed to uphold. Having imaginatively dispensed with the conditions that curtailed his own individual sovereignty, Wright proceeded to set forth concepts of social engineering that would effectively have checked the autonomy of others. For when all the Whitmanesque windbag rhetoric extolling the pioneer spirit is swept away, what remains is a society constructed upon the strict hierarchical model of Wright's own Taliesin Fellowship: a government of architecture, a society in which the architect is granted ultimate executive power.

"The agent of state in all matters of land allotment or improvement, or in matters affecting the harmony of the whole, is the architect," Wright proposed, to which Smith has commented that "in other words, the entire life of Broadacres would have come under his jurisdiction, for what is there that does not affect the harmony of the whole?" Just as Wright's cathedral had perverted its Gothic model by taking its form from a single architect, so Broadacres turned an about-face from Wright's customary Romanticism by laying down laws for social organization as severe as the most harmonious neoclassical diagram.

By prohibiting the intrusion of designs not authored, or at least authorized, by Wright himself, Broadacres solved the problem of the defacement of his individual buildings with a vengeance. But it was one thing to allow an individual building to express its architect's autonomy at the expense of a private patron's occasional discomfort. It was quite another to expect an entire society to make a similar sacrifice, particularly when the whole point of the enterprise was to accommodate the individuality of its members.

While his concern for the integrity of the work of art was understandable, Wright's effort to translate his aesthetic aims into political policies veered uncomfortably close to Walter Benjamin's hypothesis regarding Hitler, that the logical result of fascism is the introduction of aesthetics into political life. With the architect installed as chief of state, one envisions a Usonian secret police specially trained in the permissible colors for lampshades and the organic placement of ashtrays; underground networks of renegade antique dealers; brisk black-market trade in Breuer cane chairs.

It is easy, therefore, to view Broadacres as proof that within every self-styled individualist is a dictator longing to break free, just as it is difficult not to interpret Wright's insistence upon controlling every detail of a private house's furnishings as at least inherently repressive. Since the executive architect had the final word, Wright's crusade for individual sovereignty cannot escape comparison with Huey Long's exactly contemporary platform, "Every man a king, but no man wears a crown." Long wore the crown in Louisiana, and in Broadacres Wright was king.

Yet perhaps what is most disturbing about Broadacres is not that Wright's political system was designed to be self-serving, but that one so committed to the *art* of architecture should have ventured into politics at all. There is some irony in this, for in 1935, when the plan first appeared, it was severely criticized not for being political to a degree unbecoming to an artist, but for not being political enough. What offended the then-Marxist art critic Meyer Schapiro, for example, was not that Wright had compromised his art but that he had neglected his Marx; turned his back on the social, political, and economic issues with which many intellectuals, equally dedicated to creating a more equitable social environment, were primarily concerned.

Thus Lewis Mumford, though well aware of the intricacies of Wright's proposals and the many years he had devoted to formulating them, was correct to write in 1953 that he "has never faced the paramount problem of modern architecture—to translate its great individual accomplishments into an appropriate common form. . . . If the contemporary architect has not yet found an adequate answer to this problem, Wright characteristically has not even asked the question." And thus it is rare to find any mention of Wright or Broadacres in intellectual histories of the political activities of artists and writers during the Depression, for he engaged in no such activities. Though the author of one of the most comprehensively planned Utopias of that or any other time, as Smith observes, Wright

had nothing whatever to say about the political strategies that would be relied upon to bring all this about. . . . Instead of engaging in political action that might have affected public policy at some level, he and his apprentices spent long hours in the mid-thirties constructing a large model of Broadacres that was later exhibited at various places, presumably in the quite vain expectation that its example would be contagious.

But was this Wright's sincere expectation? Did he truly wish to be a dictator, even of design? Did he want the world to conform strictly to his own image? While one might be justified in interpreting Broadacres as the uncovering of Wright's latent fascism, it may be nearer the truth to say that Broadacres itself was the disguise. Perhaps all the long hours spent in constructing the model, all the drawings, plans, lecture-demonstrations, pamphlets, position papers on Rent, Money, and traffic control constituted an elaborate attempt to conceal—not least from Wright himself—that fundamentally, as the Marxist critics recognized, *there was no plan at all.*

In *The Living City* Wright breaks away for a moment from his inventory of New York's ugliness and evil to wax poetic on the "myriad beauties" of the city seen by night:

In human terms yet undefined, the nocturnal monster yields rhythmical perspectives, glowing spotted walls of light, dotted lines, a world of fascinating reflections hung upon other reflections ranging along vistas of the street or pendent as the wisteria hangs its violet racemes on a trellis or the trees. Then the skyscraper is, in the dusk, a shimmering, prismatic verticality; gossamer veil of a festive scene, hanging there against the backdrop of a black night sky to dazzle, entertain, and amaze, in great masses. Lighted interiors come through the veil with a sense of life and well-being. The City then seems alive. It does live as illusion lives.

Of course, the nighttime illusion of beauty was to be resisted, like a whore's. Many writers have described the city as though it had no more substance than a mirage, but Wright's metaphors had an ulterior motive: to vaporize the existing city into a condition no more palpable than Broadacres. Through the magical thinking of mock politics and sham practicalities, Wright met the real city on a common plane, bathed in the Romantic half-light of the city's apparently delirious disorder.

"Night is but a shadow cast by the sun," Wright cried, contrasting New York to his city as darkness fleeing before the dawn. But if New York was a vision of night, Broadacres was born in the dappled light of a daydream. To call it a city at all was the act of a dreamer, for Wright's city was to the city what Orwell's memory hole was to memory. And despite the intricacy of its plans, its very name continued to recall its origins in reverie: Broad Acre was the name of a field on Wright's newly purchased Arizona ranch. Like a vision of classical civilization prompted by Attic ruins, the vista of timeless America rose from Wright's own backyard.

Yet it is hardly exceptional for a Utopia to be a dream. Indeed, what is unique about Wright's is that it *was* so "entirely in accord with the way things were going in America anyway." What is ultimately most disturbing about Broadacre City is not that it was more unrealistic than other Utopias, but so much less so; that its features so closely resembled those of the real America—yet transformed, the way a dream can distort household objects into threatening nightmare specters. Wright's vision reverses the process, for here the repertory eyesores of the modern American landscape (tract housing, highways, shopping centers, parking lots, industrial parks, the occasional high-rise headquarters of a "relocated" corporation) are transformed back into the makings of the American dream. In this sense Broadacre City (particularly in its 1958 version) must be regarded as an overripe, somewhat degenerate contribution to the Utopian tradition: more Madison Avenue than Fourier, a vision in which existing forms of middle-class life are depicted in the guise of an unattainable paradise.

Broadacre City's emulation of American reality paralleled its counterfeit politics. Just as it was both distastefully political and disdainfully detached from politics, so it was too real to be Utopian and too dreamlike to be of practical importance. The paradoxes of Broadacres—more elaborately worked out than in any Utopia in history, yet more privately obsessive; so near the reality of urban America, yet as distant as night from day— should not be interpreted as confusion on Wright's part, nor as ignorance of what was going on. They were intentional, the heart of the design.

When asked whether Broadacres was technically feasible, Wright would sometimes say yes, sometimes no, then habitually describe it as "the city that was everywhere and nowhere." Given the scheme's self-evident megalomania, it is easy to overlook the fact that the city's second essential quality—that of being "nowhere"—was as important as the first. For Wright's refusal to state unequivocally whether Broadacres was a vision or a plan—so in keeping with his culture's dilemma over whether to be shaped by idealistic dreamers or can-do materialist technicians—derived from the plan's basic purpose. Equivocation was its very nature, its function, and its form.

To say that Broadacres had no real plan is not to say that it was not practical, and in fact Wright did offer some practical advice on how it might be achieved:

There is only one solution, one principle, one proceeding which can rid the city of its congestion—decentralization. Go out, un-divide the division, un-subdivide the division, and then subdivide the un-subdivision.... Clients have asked me: "How far should we go out, Mr. Wright?" I say: "Just ten times as far as you think you ought to go." So my suggestion would be to go just as far as you can go—and go soon and go fast....

And of course the second suggestion, here implied, is to become a client of Mr. Wright. Go out. Buy Wright. The principles and politics of Broadacres were essentially those of the real estate speculator.

The profit he sought was not financial, however, but cultural. As Mumford has observed, the implicit goal of Wright's policy of personal manifest destiny was to impute "to his own 'Usonian' architecture a monopoly of the democratic virtues and of organic design." The word "monopoly" is particularly apt, for Wright's scheme had much in common with a more famous scale model also designed to promote the building of houses. Parker Brothers first published the game Monopoly in 1935, the year that Wright unveiled Broadacres. Both were creatures of the Depression, offering a means to build in fantasy what could not be constructed in fact. Both were initially derived from the Single-Tax land-reform theories of Henry George; and both severed all connection with the political thought that had inspired them, transmogrifying a socialist doctrine into respective schemes of rampant self-interest.

But while a major motive behind Wright's model was to raise income by building houses, and perhaps a hotel or two, the primary function of Broadacres was artistic. As with the Price Tower, self-interest was a point of departure from which Wright proceeded toward an elucidation of his art and its relationship to his culture.

The idea that architecture is a social art conveys the meaning that buildings occupy a more prominent place in daily life than do other works of art. It suggests that a building be as responsive to social criteria (from the comfort, safety, and taste of its inhabitants to the civic obligations that may attend its function and its occupation of a given site) as to such formal criteria as volume, rhythm, proportion, and scale. It suggests that in the social criteria of architecture rests the essential distinction between a building and a sculpture; that a successful building is one in which these two sets of standards are most effectively integrated. It suggests ultimately that a building may offer the fullest expression of unity between the art and the life of a culture.

Whether the suggestion can be taken and acted upon would seem to depend upon the particular culture in question. While such examples as the Japanese house and the Gothic cathedral affirm that such a synthesis might be possible, the identification of such examples as ideals (and both were so identified by Gropius as well as by Wright) may signify a culture in which the synthesis is not actually possible. It can be achieved, at best, only symbolically, through the means of art and, paradoxically, by designating the building as a work of art distinct from its environment, isolated from the daily life around it.

This is to say that a culture that exhibits a Japanese house in a museum (as the Museum of Modern Art did in 1954) is unlikely to produce its own equivalent. It is to say that a culture that must make the fundamental distinction explicit in Pevsner's famous remark that "a bicycle shed is a building; Lincoln Cathedral is a piece of architecture" is a culture unlikely to produce a Lincoln Cathedral.

The solution proposed by the Bauhaus was to model architecture of all types and sizes upon the bicycle shed. It was a solution that depended upon the architect's willingness to relinquish the role of individual genius, and it failed to hold, in part, because only artists were capable of upholding such an ideal, and the greatest of them were ultimately reluctant to make such a sacrifice.

The solution proposed by Wright was to endow the smallest building—bicycle shed or chicken coop—with the significance of Lincoln Cathedral. This was the meaning of La Miniatura, the two-bedroom house that "represented about as much studious labor over a drawing board and attention to getting construction started as the Cathedral of St. John the Divine in New York City."

But Wright's position of individual genius had its own problems—for one thing, only an unsuccessful architect had the time for such studious labor over a bungalow; for another, not everyone would want to inhabit such a work, even if he could afford one—as well as a deeper artistic dilemma to which Broadacre City was primarily addressed.

If poets are, as Shelley asserted, "the unacknowledged legislators of the world," then architects have historically been the artists most determined to win the world's acknowledgment of their legislative talents. Or perhaps, as the artists with the least amount of independence from society's actual legislators, architects are more inclined than other artists to overcompensate for their lack of autonomy in the projection of Utopias where architecture rules supreme.

To the extent Chekhov is correct to say that the only true subject of art is the difference between life as it is and life as it should be, the architect is in an artistic bind. His objective differs from Chekhov's in that he ordinarily aims to make life as it is more nearly approximate life as it should be. His practice is to create the immediate environment of everyday life, not works of art surrounded by frames or mounted on pedestals, bound between covers or set on stages. If this provides a challenge to his imagination as well as to his power, it may also, by Chekhov's criterion, set limits upon his artistic vision. For the more nearly the world approximates his vision—the more nearly life as it is resembles his view of life as it should be—the closer he may move toward neutralizing the discrepancy between the real and the ideal that constitutes his artistic subject.

For an architect like Louis Sullivan, determined to aim for high ideals within the framework of the commercial status quo—banks like temples, office buildings like cathedrals—there was no great conflict between architecture's social and aesthetic criteria; not until the conflict broke him. But for an architect like Wright, determined, in part by Sullivan's sad example, to accomplish for architecture and architects what Beethoven had achieved for music and musicians, this conflict could not be avoided.

This helps to explain Wright's obsession with the myth that his early work had gone unappreciated, and why, in the second period of his success, he clung even more tenaciously to the role of the outsider. It may also explain why, the farther America traveled down the road toward the decentralization he had advocated, the louder Wright complained that no one was heeding his advice.

True, he had reason to protest that decentralization was proceeding chaotically, that the hour was growing late for comprehensive planning. But since he never took the slightest political action toward having his proposals enacted—since Broadacres must be "everywhere and nowhere"—it is more likely that the real America was vexing not because it differed from his vision, but because it corresponded all too closely. "Here I am at it again," he shouted along the lecture circuit, "but what is the use?" And indeed there was no use, no need, for him to be at it again, as billions poured into the Highway Trust.

In a statement similar to Chekhov's, Gertrude Stein professed that

After all everybody, that is everybody who writes is interested in living inside themselves in order to tell what is inside themselves. That is why writers have to have two countries, the one where they belong and the one in which they live really. The second one is romantic, it is separate from themselves, it is not real but it is really there.

Even more literally than Stein, Wright, though not a writer, needed these two countries. Unlike Stein, he did not have to travel to Europe to locate his other country, for modern architecture was his country and from the 1930s on he was an expatriate simply by remaining at home.

But despite the critical success of the International Style, "the way things were going in America anyway" conformed more nearly to his vision than to Gropius's or Le Corbusier's, and Wright stood in constant danger of losing his outsider's advantage by becoming a prophet honored in his own land. At the end of the highway his two counties merged into one, his inner life externalized and despoiled.

In the Landlord's Game, the original board game from which Charles Darrow fashioned Monopoly in 1935, the player who "won" the game was in effect the loser—the villain the game was designed to expose. It was much the same with Broadacre City. The more nearly America came toward realizing Wright's vision of decentralization, the more he lost the artistic authority of this position, exposing to deeper scrutiny the gross authoritarianism of his system.

The solution to this dilemma lay in a sharp distinction between the vision of Broadacres itself—the model, the drawings, the exhortations to decentralization and organic design—and Wright's ongoing process of promoting this vision before the public. In theory and in practice Broadacres disclosed entirely different meanings.

Smith has aptly compared Wright and the Taliesin Fellowship to Arthur and the Round Table; and if, to extend the comparison, the great Broadacre City model was their round table, its realization was their grail: an emblem of purity that to bind them together in common purpose must be both possible and unattainable. While the model envisioned an America recast in Wright's image, promoting it served an opposite function in which the model acted as a wedge to keep the vision and the reality as far apart as heaven and earth in any hell-fire preacher's sermon.

To be everywhere and nowhere: this was not Wright's uncertainty about how Broadacres would be created; it was the project's true form. To be either one alone would have neutralized its function. It could not be so "everywhere" as to liquidate Wright's Romantic ideal, nor so "nowhere" as to deprive him of the oportunity to pretend that it was feasible—perhaps inevitable, at some future date, after he had stopped practicing his art and stilled the urge to "range to purely imaginary regions."

If Broadacre City originated quite primitively as a dream of America covered coast-to-coast with Frank Lloyd Wright houses, in practice the project developed into Wright's method of mediating between that private world of his imagination and the real America in which his works of art must physically reside. It was a medium between the aesthetic criteria of his forms and the social procedures through which these forms were brought into being. In this sense it was a symbolic treatment of architecture itself: the road map of an artistic intuition guided by the politics of architectural practice.

As Wright wrote in the preamble to the "Broadacre City" chapter of his autobiography, "I am not fond of thinking: preferring to dream—until circumstances force me to think, which the circumstances in which I live are perpetually doing." Doesn't this sum up the divided condition of the artist as architect? And doesn't Broadacre City represent Wright's attempt to mediate between those two states—the dreamlike vision of the Romantic artist, repeatedly shocked awake by the practical and social demands of his worldly profession? The artist must dream; the businessman must think; the head of Frank Lloyd Wright, Inc.—like any practicing architect—must do both.

As a Romantic artist, Wright had to reject the claims and impurities of civilization in the strongest possible terms. As an architect, he often had to accept them as the terms of his license to practice. What began when Wright "began to write" about the big city, and what continued throughout the process of designing and promoting his own vision of Broadacre City, was the extended dialogue of a Romantic with civilization, an attempt to negotiate a working relationship with the civilization that he was obliged as a Romantic artist to reject, but with which he was also obliged as an architect to cooperate.

While undertaken initially to alleviate Wright's personal problems, the design of Broadacre City was also the means by which Wright brought "into coherent relationship" with his culture the dilemma that had stalled his practice years before. Between the aim to make the architect a self-sufficient artist in the Romantic sense, and the aim to render forms appropriate to an entire society in a neoclassical sense, there was a clear contradiction, a conflict equivalent to, indeed arising from, the opposed positions espoused in his 1910 essay "The Sovereignty of the Individual." Broadacres enabled Wright to strike a conceptual balance between these two objectives.

From the 1930s on, with Broadacre City as his fulcrum, Wright pursued the two directions that in 1910 had proved the contradictory stumbling block in his philosophy. One path led approximately toward "art"—toward the Guggenheim Museum and other similarly flamboyant buildings in which he flaunted his unique and individual sovereignty, his mastery in the field of design. The other path led, similarly, toward "life"—toward a series of houses in which he sought to extend the field, to determine how far his mastery could go toward achieving an American version of the Japanese ideal. Both paths converged eventually on New York, the source of the visionary city in which Wright sought to reconcile these two conflicting aims.

To an art lover with less than moderately elastic knees, the Guggenheim's spiral ramp might seem more appropriate in a parking garage than in a museum; and Wright's only other existing work in Manhattan, the Mercedes–Benz showroom at Fifty-sixth Street and Park Avenue, is an often overlooked clue to the fact that the Guggenheim's basic form did indeed derive from Wright's passionate preoccupation with the car.

His first spiral, the unbuilt Gordon Strong Automobile Objective Project of 1925, is perhaps the first architectural monument, other than a bridge, conceived expressly for the car. As its title suggests, the sole function of this roadway spiraling up a mountainside to a planetarium at the summit was simply to provide an excuse for pleasure driving. Rather than run a highway past a scenic wonder to provide automobile access, Wright's project was designed not to be seen from the car, but to be an extension *of* the car, to express all that Wright felt the car would come to represent in his culture. And the planetarium showed precisely of what cosmic significance Wright knew the car to be: decades before nations had seriously undertaken to explore, much less colonize, outer space, Wright grasped intuitively that the culture of the highway, barely born, would one day come to maturity among the stars.

If the ramp of the Mercedes–Benz showroom provides a visual clue to the Guggenheim's descent from the automobile, three other New York designs, none of them containing spirals, further illustrate the aesthetic impact of the car upon Wright's work. Two of them are New York designs in the sense that, like the scale model of Broadacre City, they were designed to exploit the city's matchless potential for public relations.

The Usonian House (1953) was the first Wright building actually erected in New York City, and, ironically, it was the last private residence to be built on Fifth Avenue. It was also the shortest lived. As the centerpiece of a traveling exhibition of Wright's work, "Sixty Years of Living Architecture," the Usonian House stood for less than a year on the future site of the Guggenheim Museum.

In 1957 Wright created the Air House, a two-room inflatable structure commissioned by the United States Rubber Company as a showpiece for the International Home Show at the New York Coliseum.

Though the Cass House, built on Staten Island in 1959, is the only Wright-designed residence standing in New York City, it of the three is the one *not* intended for a New York location, but was the first in a line of prefabricated housing Wright designed in the 1950s for the benefit of those who could not afford to commission an original Wright design. It is ironic that this Pre-Fab, designed as it was to facilitate the city's disappearance by providing low-cost Usonian housing, should be the only Wright house in New York: while the unwilling urban refugees made it as far as Oklahoma, the eager emigrés couldn't even get past the city limits.

But in their betrayal of Wright's artistic principles, all three houses left the Price Tower miles behind. Here at last all pretense of a building's appropriateness to its site and its client is completely abandoned, as the Air House somewhat rudely confirms that the Usonian vision was rooted in air, while the Usonian House flaunts the degree to which a Wright-designed house was a house designed for Wright, in which residents were often made to feel like guests at a private viewing of his art.

Wright liked to insist that his buildings did not belong on art historical pedestals, that they could be experienced only as living environments, not as museums. But he unveiled the Usonian House as though it were a *chef-d'oeuvre sans pareil* ("the first truly democratic expression of our democracy in Architecture" was the phrase he coined for the opening) and he peddled the Pre-Fabs somewhat like signature scarves. Even worse, the Cass House, wryly described by the *AIA Guide to New York City* as a "cream colored masonite building with tacky metal roof, totally lacking dignity or style," showed how shamelessly Wright closed the gap between himself and those who abused his earlier innovations in the little houses made of ticky-tacky on the hillside. Nor was it seemly that this housing, designed to accommodate those eager to follow Wright out of the city, was architecturally negligible compared to the stylish high-rise barracks in which he proposed to detain those who refused to leave voluntarily.

None of these designs could be considered major works. They were, however, variations on what Wright himself considered the most challenging theme of his later career. "I would rather solve [the small house-problem] than build anything I can think of," he declared; and if these three houses prove that he never really solved it, they also show that it was not in any conventional sense an architectural problem.

In concept if not in result, these experiments in low-cost housing came within spitting distance of the Modern Movement's search for a "living machine," and indeed quite surpassed the flimsy "cardboard architecture" for which Wright loudly reproached the International Style. Eventually, to the basic line of Pre-Fabs, Usonians, and Usonian Automatics, Wright added mass-produced fixtures and furnishings, carpets, wallpapers, end tables, a range of industrially influenced designs, some of which actually went into production, while others—designs for helicopters, cars—never left the drawing board.

Commerically, these ventures were no more successful than were Bauhaus experiments in merchandising well-designed cutlery, teapots, or lighting fixtures, and, aesthetically, considerably less so. But, like the Bauhaus, Wright was inspired more by the idea of the thing than by the thing itself. In place of the European dream of a modern environment organized by pure technology, his aspirations more nearly resembled those of the American dream's folk hero, Horatio Alger. If his ventures were not profitable, it was doubtless because he did not sincerely want to be an industrial magnate but felt that his broad vision of America could not be complete without a Usonian version of the native cultural strain that had produced the car, the assembly line, and the art of selling them to the public.

Without the car, of course, there could have been no Broadacre City; indeed the dilemma was that as decentralization progressed from the 1940s on, there would be a Broadacre City anyhow, of sorts—without Wright. Henry Ford had not only announced that "we shall solve the City Problem by leaving the city," he had also provided the means to actually do so.

In the process the American car began to look more like home than the American house. An Englishman's home might be his castle; an American's would be his Ford. The small-house problem for most Americans was how to make the average house look like something other than an adjunct to the two-car garage, and in this regard Wright was no different from most Americans. For him, the small-house problem was how to make architecture seem less inconsequential compared to the car and its demonstrated power to transform the American environment on the continental scale Wright had hoped would be architecture's manifest destiny. At most, Wright could hope to equal Ford's achievement by housing the urban exodus, at least symbolically, within the artistic means at his command.

The extent and nature of these means were in fact the issues raised by the small-house problem. For if Broadacre City was Wright's attempt to achieve imaginatively in art what Henry Ford and the car had achieved in reality, the three houses presented Wright's attempt to push beyond the realm of art into Ford's domain. The small-house problem posed the question: how far into this territory could he go? It was perhaps a sadly misguided yearning, almost a renunciation of his own artistic values. At the same time it was perhaps one of the most challenging aesthetic problems he ever faced.

Wright was not merely paying lip service to social conscience when he stated that "the house of moderate cost is not only America's major architectural problem but the most difficult for her major architects." For these houses, three of the most trivial designs he ever produced, were at the heart of his investigation into the nature of his art and the relationship of that art to the American culture of his time. These shamefully conventional buildings illustrate why, in the course of that investigation, Wright was compelled to push architecture beyond conventional definitions.

In his 1948 analysis of American culture, *Made in America*, John Kouwenhoven discerned a profound conflict between the "cultivated" tradition of American art derived from European models, and the "vernacular" style epitomized on the American continent by the practical ventures of the mechanical engineer. Kouwenhoven's basic implication—that any building recognizable as a "work of art" was, as such, less vitally American a cultural artifact than the balloon frame or the grain elevator—was itself perhaps the view of a somewhat overcultivated sensibility. Yet it was a precise assessment of the artistic dilemma that Wright faced in undertaking to solve the small-house problem. Unless he could find a way to make his masterpieces appear to emanate from an authentic American vernacular, he risked having his greatest achievements regarded as fraudulent: as un-American as New York.

One the one hand, Wright wished to create an architecture that could capture the serene, organic authority he had admired in Italy and Japan; on the other, he angrily rebutted Mumford's prescription for "pooling resources" with other designers, contending that "you can never get [Organic Architecture] through any form of collectivism. A true work of art must be induced as inspiration and cannot be induced or inspired through 'teamwork.' " In large part, the solution to the small-house problem appeared to rest on the question whether these two aims were compatible: the organic vernacular and the "true work of art."

The Japanese example suggested that they were, but this was itself incompatible with Wright's chauvinism, and in any case the modular Japanese house was entirely too organic to accommodate the individual inspiration behind Wright's description of the true work of art. The anonymous Japanese architect was a worthy model for others, perhaps, but not for Frank Lloyd Wright.

A closer paradigm was Henry Ford, for in his own line of work he had solved a problem similar to Wright's. Ford had no more invented the car than Wright had invented the house. But what Ford had achieved was a true cultural vernacular, a category generally held to be "anonymous," and in the process of so doing achieved the worldwide eminence of "Henry Ford." Ford's individuality was not dissolved by his success at marketing a product people soon came to take for granted; on the contrary, it was magnified. To command the power of anonymous native genius, yet be renowned as the individual who had unleashed that power: this was the incentive behind solving the small-house problem.

True, Henry Ford was not an artist. But Wright was willing to overlook this because, as he announced in a lecture four years before unveiling Broadacre City, "today we have a scientist or an inventor in place of a Shakespeare or a Dante. Captains of industry are modern substitutes, not only for kings and potentates, but, I am afraid, for great artists as well."

Wright did not want to be a captain of industry, even if he enjoyed living like one; what he sought was not Ford's economic but his cultural status, and this no American artist had ever achieved. It was not just a craving for personal fame, it was a bid on behalf of his art. Approvingly, he (mis)quoted Ford's most famous dictum: "No wonder sensible Henry says 'art is the bunk.' He is right; all that he has known by that name is no more than what he says it is. And pretty much all that all America knows, too, is likewise."

But architecture was bigger than art; there it stood, big as life. If we took a house even more for granted than a car, why couldn't Wright's drawing board produce an impact on culture as great as Ford's? The answer is that a house is not a car, and, unlike Buckminster Fuller, for example, Wright couldn't fool himself into thinking that it could be. He was ultimately neither willing to give up "the bunk," nor able to pass from his own sphere of culture to Henry Ford's. While he might scoff at the cultivated tradition and its patrons Mrs. Plasterbilt, Mrs. Gablemore, and Miss Flat-top, his sarcasm could not conceal his own contribution to this tradition.

"To put it bluntly," Norris Kelly Smith observed, "architecture has always been the art of the establishment," and in this sense it hardly mattered how that architecture came trimmed: plaster fronts, looming gables, modern tops, or Wright's own deeply overhanging eaves. The most strenuous exercise of the imagination could not dissolve the fact that in Wright's chosen field of private residential architecture, the distinction between cultivated and vernacular was virtually synonymous with the economic distinction between rich and poor. The poor, if they were lucky, got housing; the rich got architecture—if they were lucky, by Frank Lloyd Wright.

While he claimed to be "embarrassed" when someone wanted him to design a house for $250,000, because "very wealthy people usually go to some fashionable architect, not to a known radical who is never fashionable if he can help it," he was neither so radical, so embarrassed, or such a fool, as to return the fee. And he conceded that his clients came from "the upper middle third of the democratic strata in our country."

There is no irony in the fact that the Cass House, designed to penetrate beneath that economic floor into the reservoir of huddled masses yearning to become un-"pig-piled," is situated not amid the vast tracts of speculative housing that have covered Staten Island since the opening of the Verrazano–Narrows Bridge, but in the island's most exclusive residential district. For the Cass House only confirms that the small-house problem was insoluble because it was not even a problem.

Wright was quick to recognize that the traffic problem of great cities was not really a problem, but a euphemism for some of the most dangerous and distressing conditions of modern urban life; what he did not recognize was that the small-house problem was not so much a problem as a condition of his art. It could no more be solved by prefabrication than the traffic problem could be solved by building new highways. So long as cars and fuels remained attractively priced, there would be a traffic problem. So long as architecture remained a rich man's art, Wright was himself part of the small-house problem and could hardly be expected to come up with a solution.

Even if cost were not the issue, Wright's fierce individualism stood implacably between himself and a solution. For as much as he wanted to transcend the category of art, he would not abandon the freedom of the Romantic artist, nor his pride in his unique creations. He had, after all, terminated his first career partly to dissociate himself from those he felt had robbed his ideas to create the idea of a "Prairie School"; and now, by the 1950s, there was nowhere he could go to escape the effect of his innovations upon the proliferating open-plan ranch house. What was most dispiriting about the Pre-Fabs was that they were redundant.

"What would you say is the greatest disappointment in your career?" asked Hugh Downs in a nationally televised interview to mark the opening of the Usonian House exhibition.

"Well, I think I touched on it a moment ago when I said that instead of emulation I have seen chiefly imitation. Imitation by the imitators of imitation."

And it was true that by 1953 Wright had more reason to be alarmed than flattered by his imitators, as urban decentralization threatened to liquidate his own Romantic dream in a vista of carports, split-levels, lawn sprinklers washing away the Usonian dream to make way for the weekend barbecue. Wright's influence by then had already been felt more widely than any architect could hope for—but that influence had bred not affordable Taliesins for sovereign individualists, but rather the standard living modules for a decade saturated with blind faith in bland conformity. And Wright's reply inadvertently suggests something worse: in the quest of his ideal, or rather as the result of that quest, Wright had himself become an imitation.

What the three houses reveal is that the closer Wright came to achieving a vernacular architecture, the closer he came to an architecture that in the worst sense was indistinguishable from the millions of Wright-derived buildings that provoked him to rage against the perversion of his ideas. In trying to make architecture seem more consequential than the car—more consequential than art—Wright produced the most inconsequential designs of his entire career. The search for a synthesis between the cultivated and vernacular modes brought him to the frontier of his philosophy, brought him straight to the border, in fact, of Gropius's territory: the land where architecture did not depend on genius; brought him there without distinction, and brought him back, inevitably, to New York.

The Natural House is Wright's most charming book, indeed the only book among his published seventeen to which one could ascribe a quality like charm. Though much of the text consists of excerpts from earlier books, skillful editing has created a fresh context for the familiar stories, and a good-natured grandfatherly tone replaces the voice of vituperation we have learned to expect. Once again Wright recounts the triumphs and trials of his career; but a mellow, autumnal light dispels the Sturm und Drang that drenched earlier accounts of the Imperial Hotel, perfidious colleagues, and the citizen against the city.

An endearing old codger, the author of this book tells jokes on himself: how "all my life my legs have been banged up somewhere by the chairs I have designed"; how "the boards in the ceiling over my bedroom at Taliesin West, overheated during the day, began to pull and crack and miniature explosions occur at about three o'clock in the cool of the morning"; and how "it has been said that were I three inches taller than 5′ 8 1/2″ all my houses would have been quite different in proportion. Probably."

The Natural House is Wright's record of his attempt to solve the small-house problem, or, as the dust jacket would have it, "the world's greatest architect here meets the urgent problem of suitable shelter for The Family in a democracy, in a magnificent and—as was to be expected—challenging book. Here, presented at last in full detail, is the *natural* house."

It is primarily a book of photographs, depicting houses "of infinite variety for people of limited means—in which living has become for their owners a purposeful new adventure in freedom and dignity." Though in black and white, and not luxuriously reproduced, these pictures comprise perhaps the most faithful illustration of his achievement that Wright ever produced, almost fulfilling the book's promise to convey graphically "the principles which have given a new birth to architecture in this country."

"Principles" perhaps overstates the case, for while Wright gives generous handyman hints on how to build your own house out of textile-blocks, he comes no closer in this book than elsewhere to defining Organic Architecture per se. And yet, lulled by the mellow tone of his prose, confronted with photographs of his life's work, one at last begins to see, as though through the architect's eyes, the vision that his sermons and melodramas only clouded: an organic America, an America of warm-toned wood, crisp brick walls, blazing hearths, democratic vistas, and unlimited free parking; an America in which cars do not pollute, vegetables are fresh, and progress enters the house through the back door like a cheerful delivery boy.

A heady vision, and one most Americans were eager to work for in the years of postwar prosperity. Yet isn't the charm after all a bit thick, even for the times? Could this role of the affable, self-deprecating gaffer be somewhat calculated? Grateful though we are for a glimpse of the charismatic side of Wright's personality with which he must have concluded many a sale, we might want to call in a contractor of our choice to check for flaws in the real estate Wright is offering.

Here on page 204: should a book devoted to low-cost housing in good conscience depict a floor plan on which, all too clearly, we see a "maid's room"? Or here on page 208, a plan for another house that includes not only a "servant's room" but downstairs living quarters conspicuously labeled "chauffeur"? Again, the sylvan settings shown in the photographs suggest that some of these dwellings may be second houses, weekend or summer retreats built for clients for whom the servant problem is apt to be more pressing than that of the small house.

Most of the houses have no servants' quarters, but to read the small print is to realize that the natural house does not grow on trees. Nine pages are devoted to the Willey house: cost, $10,000. But the only complete exterior view of this house is an artist's rendering of a preliminary version that cost $6,000 more. And why, in describing, on page 118, a house built in 1953, should the caption read: "Fifteen years ago, this was about a 15,000 dollar house"? Why not the price in 1953? or the price in 1852?

And, finally, upon closer inspection the photographs themselves disclose that the small-house problem was best left in the hands of the interior decorator than assigned to the architect. Take away the plants, put out the blazing fire, remove the priceless Oriental screens and pre-Columbian terracottas, discard the Calder by the front door, fold up the vicuña blanket thrown casually across the bed, and the difference between Broadacre City and Levittown vanishes down the highway along with Ezra Stoller's wide-angle lens.

Of course, the book's prevarications in construction costs, furnishings, and the staff required to maintain the houses only underscore the fact that the small-house problem was economic, not architectural. Lacking the means, perhaps ultimately even the will, to find a solution through economic restructuring, the substitute for the solution was cosmetic, an image, dream-housing, or, in a word: salesmanship. And the means to achieve this solution came not from Henry Ford but from another friend of Wright's, Bruce Barton, the tycoon of American dreams. The model was not the car but the advertisement used to sell it; the method came not from Detroit but from Madison Avenue. Like the kickoff to a saturation ad campaign, the Usonian House marked the final conversion of Wright's sacred "Cause of Architecture" into a purified, Usonian version of his detested Broadway Creed.

Yet if it was misleading of Wright to present his vision as universally accessible, it would be wrong to accuse him of cynicism or fraud. From the outset the product of Wright, Inc., had been imagery: not cars, not helicopters, nor even houses. They were not deceptions, these pictures; they were entirely faithful depictions of his dreams, more accurate ren-derings than either his landmark buildings or the scale model of Broadacre City itself, of the dream and the extent to which his culture had allowed him to realize it. Although he professed to deplore that "the universal modern art is really salesmanship," *The Natural House* showed he under-stood completely that advertising is the American art form nearest our dreams, if not our ideals. And thus, in that it came closest to presenting the vision of Broadacres whole, Wright's book more than any of the buildings depicted in its pages, was itself his most successful solution to the small-house problem. And it was yours for under ten dollars.

In the center of the book, a special section is devoted to the Usonian House exhibition in New York, complete with a dedication speech by Wright, photographs by Stoller, even a glowing press notice, reprinted from *Architectural Forum*, attesting that

thousands of New Yorkers who walked through it experienced for the first time the design qualities Wright has talked about since the turn of the century: spaciousness and sunlight, human scale, warmth and solidity, a feeling of shelter, and a sense of the outdoors.

But not even Stoller's camera can disguise the fact that the house was, and looked like, a temporary rental office, a model suite set up to sell not houses but the Usonian vision of its designer. And Wright's remarks make quite clear that the most important element of that vision was not "spaciousness," nor sunlight, nor any of the building's "design qualities."

To say the house planted by myself on the good earth of the Chicago prairie as early as 1900, or earlier, was the first truly democratic expression of our democracy in Architecture would start a controversy with professional addicts who believe Architecture has no political (therefore no social) significance. So, let's say that the spirit of democracy—freedom of the individual as an individual—took hold of the house as it then was. . . .

Thus a basic change came about in this affair of a culture for the civilization of these United States. What then took place has since floundered, flourished and faded under different names by different architects in an endless procession of expedients.

Here the original comes back to say hello to you afresh and to see if you recognize it for what it was and still is—a home for our people in the spirit in which our Democracy was conceived: the individual integrate and free in an environment of his own.

That so notoriously procrustean an architect could claim to have created "the first truly democratic expression of our democracy in Architecture" suggests a master of the Big Lie that by its very audacity can hardly be denied. Yet in his own mind Wright was convinced that he had, indeed, shown that it was possible for an architect single-handedly to create houses "of infinite variety," houses for the individual "free in an environment of his own."

And Wright seemed equally convinced that his architecture had established these free individuals in coherent relationship with each other. In 1930 he had seen with perfect clarity that the car, radio, and television would overhaul both the physical environment and the psychological conception of community. But he would not see or acknowledge the extent to which the very instruments that were bringing Broadacre City into an approximation of reality had superseded architecture's capacity to endow society with symbolic cohesion. Indeed, Wright's attacks upon the city, his insistence upon the city's obsolescence, may have been partly motivated by the need to externalize his fear of architecture's "obsolescence," its diminished capacity to provide symbols of social cohesion comparable in influence to those supplied by the car manufacturer, the highway builder, the television broadcaster. And if Wright was correct in stating that the centralized city could no longer provide society with symbolic stable unity, he was naïve to suppose that simply by advocating cars, gas stations, and radio networks he could keep the art of architecture two steps ahead of decentralization, or preserve architecture's traditional cultural eminence as a language of social symbols.

Yet to create an architecture "in the spirit in which our Democracy was conceived," to create a "unity in diversity"—these intentions were the very content of his art, the very rationale behind his conception of architecture as "the scientific art of making structure express ideas." And it would be as foolish to dispute them as to dispute the objective truth of any artist's ideals. Wright's failure to accomplish his stated social goals subtracts nothing from the supreme success of his artistic achievements, and if the results of his effort to reach beyond his talent and indeed beyond architecture itself may invite ridicule, they also clearly affirm that it is the nature of Romantic art to challenge the limitations of the artistic medium.

As its privileged place in *The Natural House* indicates, the Usonian House was in part a kind of homecoming, a tribute to the city that had sparked the vision of Broadacre City and helped Wright find the most effective means with which to project that vision. It was a tribute made in triumph, for Wright had by now indeed created a vision that, however imperfectly realized, could easily match the tremendous impressiveness of the city—and perhaps one day even surpass it. But for now the Usonian House represented the farthest extremity of his vision.

"So go far from the city, much farther than you think you can afford. You will soon find you never can go quite far enough." Then what was the point of going at all? No more than metaphor, perhaps: that infinitely receding horizon was an emblem of Wright's own Romantic quest for an ideal that could not, must not, materialize at the risk of losing the dream itself. And the three houses were Wright's attempt to test the outer limits of how far he could go before the dream liquidated itself in a torrent of humdrum reality.

In the dream of Broadacre City, Wright had implicitly accepted responsibility for the social welfare of the culture that had created him and nourished his vision. Yet his fundamental responsibility was to his art, and in any conflict between the two his gifts would determine the outcome. "Go way out into the country—what you regard as 'too far'—and when others follow . . . move on." With the Pre-Fabs, Wright had gone far enough. In less than a year the Usonian House would be torn down to make room for the Guggenheim Museum. The exchange was symbolic, for while Frank Lloyd Wright came to New York as quality in pursuit of quantity, New York came to Wright as quantity in pursuit of quality. If neither one precisely achieved its objective, the image would suffice.

■ TWO HOUSES AND A HOTEL

By 1953 Wright's trips to New York were becoming so frequent that he decided to rent Suite 223 at the Plaza Hotel on a permanent basis—permanent, that is, for the five years that remained him. He redecorated the suite's two rooms in a style that, at least to his eyes, struck the correct note of urban sophistication, recapturing, so he felt, the original elegance of the rooms before they had been ruined by the period furniture styles preferred by the management's "inferior desecrators."

In Wright's scheme, circular mirrors, set into the top of the room's arched windows, concealed indirect lighting. Deep red velvet curtains swept from ceiling to floor, their pull cords weighted at the ends by balls of clear crystal. On the walls, panels of gold Japanese paper were framed by light-rose-colored borders. Black lacquered tables and chairs, edged with red lacquer, completed the scheme. While the suite's small bedroom afforded the Wrights some privacy, "a bedlam of activity" reigned in the combination workroom, office, and sitting room where Wright entertained clients, gave interviews to the press, and worked on projects with the volunteer assistance of former apprentices who had "established themselves as architects and editors in the self-centered city," as Mrs. Wright noted with somewhat sour irony. "They take turns taking days off from their office work to help in various ways."

"The Taliesin atmosphere of work permeated the apartment for five years until January 7, 1959—the last time we were there," Olgivanna Wright later recalled. And her reminiscence of Suite 223 is a telling evocation of the place New York had made in the pattern of their lives. After Wright's death in April of 1959,

William Short, the superintendent of the Guggenheim Museum, and a few others carefully packed the furniture and a truck brought it to Taliesin. This furniture now graces our Forest House in Wisconsin a mile from Taliesin, giving it a touch of elegance. Looking out of the Forest House windows, I can see a smooth lawn, maple trees and pines. I also see Central Park, Fifth Avenue and 59th Street. I hear our Wisconsin meadow larks and cardinals, robins and mourning doves. I also hear the pigeons outside on the sill of the Plaza windows—forever cooing and fighting each other. I hear Mr. Wright saying, "Look at that speckled pigeon—he is the boss— the rest are afraid of him." And we watched him first strut on the thin iron rail, then take off for flight over the traffic signals among the blackened skyscrapers. Many lives within us for a time run parallel to one another, later to be fused until there is no separation.

This fond recollection of the park and the pigeons may seem somewhat out of character for a woman who was if anything even more outspoken than her husband in her distaste for urban life. Yet her memory's double exposure of Taliesin and New York was an accurate picture, for in later years Wright's town and country life became increasingly fused. As Mrs. Wright had written the year before his death,

For the last twenty years we have always stayed at the Hotel Plaza in New York City. I remember on one of those trips our good friend, the late Howard Myers, editor of the *Architectural Forum*, sent us a bouquet of flowers, and on the card was written, "Welcome to Taliesin the Third."

We all laughed then, thinking it a big joke. But the kindly jest proved to be prophecy. Now it truly is becoming Taliesin the third.

Wright retained the New York base primarily to supervise a number of projects under commission or construction in the East during these years: houses in Rye and Pleasantville, the Manhattan Sports Pavilion project, the Lenkurt Electric Company project on Long Island, the Mercedes–Benz (originally Hoffman Jaguar) showroom on Park Avenue, and, most notably of course, the museum whose patron, Solomon R. Guggenheim, also had a suite at the hotel.

But Wright's suite at the Plaza was more than a grand-luxe foreman's hut. It was a handsomely appointed symbol of Wright's hugely successful rejuvenation. His passage from the "worm's eye view" of New York in the twenties to a treetop-view suite at the Plaza in the fifties was just the kind of success story for which Manhattan has always provided a thrillingly dramatic backdrop. More than this, however, Taliesin the Third was both a logical culmination and a vital complement to Wright's life at the two "Usonian" Taliesins. This last Wright outpost *east* of Buffalo was instrumental in resolving the creative conflicts that had brought his career to a halt more than forty years before.

The precise value of the Taliesin Fellowship to Wright's work is not easily placed, in part because, like Broadacre City, the Fellowship was created under circumstances that do not discourage cynical interpretation. Just as Broadacres may be discounted or dismissed as a mere outlet for Wright's creative frustration, so the Taliesin Fellows, whose first project was to construct the large scale model, invite ridicule as heartily as do the lads lined up to paint Tom Sawyer's fence.

Whether or not the State of Wisconsin was justified in charging that the Fellowship was not a legitimate institution, Wright himself admitted that he was not cut out to be a teacher, indeed that architecture could not be taught. It may be true that the rigorous, sometimes capricious discipline imposed upon the Fellowship did reflect aggressions Wright might otherwise have released in buildings. Certainly the Fellowship was no more a fellowship than Broadacre City was a city.

Nor were the cynical mistaken in suspecting a financial motive. The Fellowship never made money, but it provided a small income, as well as a volunteer labor force, that enabled Taliesin to be economically self-sufficient throughout the worst years of the Depression, when Wright was not the only unemployed American architect, merely the best prepared.

But Wright had embarked on the course of the middle years in large part because commissions alone had not satisfied him; and now, at the period's close, perhaps his plan to reorganize the nation signified that it was his own life that needed a structure. This the Fellowship provided, better than a deluge of commissions; and, in the event, it proved one of the means by which Wright once again obtained them.

In admitting that he was not cut out to be a teacher, perhaps Wright recognized that Organic Architecture was not something that could be explained, only experienced. But education had always been part of the experience of his architecture, and often his buildings were explicitly pedagogical.

The Oak Park houses, for example, appeared less to express the virtues of marriage and family life than to instruct their inhabitants in these areas; and during the middle years this tutorial impulse advanced from the family unit to the wider social community. Thus Midway Gardens was designed to elevate the taste of the American public, and the Imperial Hotel was offered as a means to "help Japan to her feet" by instructing her how best to make a dignified entrance into the modern western world.

It was during the lean middle years, of course, that Wright's outpourings of pedantic prose confirmed that those who can't, teach; and by the end of this period he had found the most congenial form in which to express this impulse. In establishing the Fellowship in 1932, he put into practice a concept he had outlined in his Princeton lectures two years earlier, calling for the creation of "style centers"—schools to prepare "sensitive, unspoiled students" for the day when "art must take the lead in education." If the "little gas station" was the heart of Broadacre City, the style center was evidently its brain, a training ground not only for future artists, but for legislators once the County Architect had assumed the executive chair of Usonion government.

Because the Fellowship was obviously conceived as a prototype for future such franchised style centers, one might say that the Fellowship was the closest Wright came to actually realizing Broadacre City in any way. It may be nearer the truth, however, to say that the school was designed to make up for Broadacres's worst defects. For Taliesin was not, like, say, Le Corbusier's Chandigarh, a miniature version of an architect's Utopian forms. It was rather an admission of how little Wright's vision actually depended on such forms—on architecture as conventionally defined.

"Architecture," wrote Adrian Stokes, "is limited to forms without events"; and it may be that most architectural Utopias, with their yearning for the reins of social planning, spring overblown from just this deficiency. But even before Broadacre City, the lack of events was a defect of which Wright was often made cruelly aware. In the Oak Park houses, to reiterate Smith's observation, "when his clients moved in with their possessions it was painfully apparent . . . that simply by being their separate selves they were defacing a work of art which had ostensibly been made for them but which was in fact designed to set forth an ideal they did not fully understand or accept."

In Wright's public buildings, the frustration was intensified. With the sad air of an open house celebration to which nobody came, Midway Gardens collapsed because of Wright's inability to control the one event—public response—upon which its success depended; and it took an act of God to make the Imperial Hotel an event worthy of wide public attention. Like other Utopias, Broadacre City, in all its immaculate, white, transcontinental ghost-town splendor, made the absence of events only that much more glaring.

The Fellowship cut the glare. Useful as a labor force to build the Broadacres model, Wright's apprentices made a far more important contribution by structuring his vision with concrete events. For practical purposes, these events took the convenient form of "education." But the Taliesin syllabus was not a method for training "sensitive, unspoiled students" but a means of populating these events with persons other than the insensitive clients who so often spoiled the harmony of his designs. "The Fellowship . . . is not on trial," read Wright's prospectus; "the apprentice is."

If Wright lacked patrons to provide him with the means and materials to articulate space, the Fellowship was primarily a means of structuring his time, of which he obviously had much to spare. This was not an achievement easily translated into rational architectural forms; but then the very severe rationality of Broadacre City's forms was another typically Usonian defect the Fellowship helped to neutralize. Deficient in events, Broadacres was equally bereft in spirit, as though in evicting the "separate selves" that marred his real buildings, Wright had inadvertently extinguished his own.

Norma Evenson's pronouncement that "for any city perfection is death" sits heavily upon this vision by the modern architect most sensitive to the example of living forms; how could Wright reconcile this boundless, precisely compartmentalized necropolis with the organic ideas his buildings so vitally expressed? Again, the answer lay in education.

"I'll think as I act as I am!" went the refrain to Wright's "Taliesin Work Song" (1933); no model of intellectual clarity, perhaps, but it accurately set the tempo for the Fellowship's antirational spirit (Olgivanna Wright composed the tune). Unlike the Bauhaus, which sought an educational method of objective social and aesthetic criteria, Wright's method, such as it was, flowed from "the inspirational leadership and the fellowship of genuinely creative architects." The assumption of benefits accruing from personal contact with a genius was the principal content of the Fellowship's academic form. Thus, Robert Twombly has observed that Wright's school had less in common with the Bauhaus than with Gurdjieff's Institute for the Harmonious Development of Man, at which Wright's wife, the acting "dean" of Taliesin, had once been a student.

And yet one need only look to the nearest Collegiate Gothic campus, or to Princeton, for example, where Wright first proposed the school, to perceive that the Fellowship's mixture of education, faith, and architecture was a wholly American proposition; that Wright's educational philosophy, while unconventional in form, shared with the most conventional American institutions of higher learning a mystical belief in the power of education to improve the individual and his society. In a sense the Fellowship recast the 1926 Steel Cathedral in a more truly indigenous form, drawing upon education rather than religion as the traditional American medium between the real and the ideal. "Improvement," more than knowledge, was education's major objective, and the Fellowship was itself a metaphor for the architect's need to "educate the public" as spiritual preparation necessary to enter the holy Usonian city.

Nor were Wright's charismatic methods particularly iconoclastic for the 1930s, a time when the belief was widespread among American intellectuals that, in Frederick Schuman's words, "the masses of men are moved not by reason, nor even by economic self-interest, but by emotions, mysticism, and mythology. . . . Societies are held together never by cold intellect but by nonlogical symbols of warmly felt collective experience." The attempt to express this collective experience into appropriate forms of art was another phenomenon common to the time. Ted Shawn's Jacob's Pillow, Katherine Frazier's Playhouse-in-the-Hills, Katrina Trask's Yaddo represented a range of comparable ventures in which dance, poetry, music, and painting were brought together in a spirit similar to Taliesin's reverential aesthetics. And it was in this spirit that the Fellowship preserved the glow of Broadacre City's extinguished creative spark.

Like other art colonies, the Fellowship was at once a retreat from the world and a breeding ground for a culture to be carried back to the world not only as works of art but in the minds of those transformed by the collective experience. Behind the construction of the Broadacres model was the assumption "that the example," in Edmund Wilson's phrase, "would prove contagious."

But whether or not Wright actually expected, or even wholeheartedly wished for, the example to prove contagious, in practice the Fellowship's function was not centrifugal, but centripetal. The educational format did not lay down the basis for broadcasting the strange ideas of this cranky old man, but served as a magnet enabling the erstwhile outcast to bring the world to his door on his terms. If the objective of Broadacre City remained an elusive grail, the Fellowship capably netted more worldly prizes.

Wright's ability to attract students gave him not only renewed personal confidence, as well as eleven hundred dollars a student a year, but a valuable pretext to actively enlist the support of others, thus helping him conquer the image of a bitter, embattled eccentric. Particularly in the climate of 1930s collectivism, those reluctant to support Wright personally were willing to assist a venture no longer purely personal, for the prospectus suggested that Wright had at least partly surrendered his ego to a social cause.

It was by thus appearing to submerge his individuality in the format of an institution that Wright attained, for the very first time, the comparative autonomy of the modern artist, free from the architect's traditional subservience to the tastes of a wealthy clientele. And when one of Wright's students persuaded his father to commission a building from Wright in 1935, the result—Fallingwater—not only signaled the start of Wright's "second career" but dramatized the Fellowship's role in subordinating cultivated taste to Wright's authority.

Students and commissions were not the most auspicious catches that fell into the Taliesin net in the 1930s, however. The Taliesin prospectus advertised that "leaders in thought, artists and philosophers from many countries may come to occasionally share for a time in our activities." Honorariums were not offered, and not everyone accepted with pleasure; Olgivanna Wright reported one antiphonal refusal in 1934:

[Alice B. Toklas]: "No, thank you. Thank you, no. We are flying to Minneapolis tonight. We love to fly to Minneapolis. . . . Oh, but we love to fly."
[Gertrude Stein]: "We do really. Really we do like to fly. We always fly everywhere because we like to fly."

But others accepted, and if the practice did little to convert leaders of American arts and letters to the philosophy of Organic Architecture, it was instrumental in reconciling Wright to the wider cultural sphere from which he had ceremoniously withdrawn two decades before. Even in Oak Park he had put his social life to professional use, and now, twenty years after abandoning the suburban gentleman's life, he prepared its equivalent on the vast Usonian scale through which he achieved at last the "more universal destiny" of which he had long been conscious.

It had taken him over two decades to reach this point. In his decision not to return to Chicago in 1924, Wright had assumed intuitively that he was his own best client, that his fortune could not be left to the capricious taste of a cosmopolitan public, that his architecture could not prosper until he himself had achieved a cultural significance wider than his buildings.

The Fellowship was the instrument by which these objectives were achieved. If New York had been a catalyst to propel Wright's lapsed architectural practice into a constructive theory, the Fellowship provided the means by which he converted theory back into practice. Having done so, he returned in due course to the source of his development, to Taliesin the Third. The Fellowship granted no diplomas, indeed produced but one graduate: Wright himself.

In the rambling prospectus for the Taliesin Fellowship that appears in the 1943 edition of his autobiography, Wright announced that "The Big City is no longer a place for more than the exterior application of some cliche or sterile formula, where life is concerned. Therefore the TALIESIN FELLOWSHIP chooses to live and work in the country." But Wright knew well that the city was useful for far more than he allowed. While publicly concurring with Sullivan's belief that "nature is the source of power; and the city, the arena in which that power is dissipated," Wright understood that the city is also a theater in which ideas are disseminated to the widest possible audience. While the founders of other art colonies shared his belief that the country was a more appropriate setting in which to devise an authentically indigenous American culture, few of them took so strong a stand against the city; and none of them showed so shrewd an understanding of the city as a stage for social drama. And as if to deny, at least to disguise, his dependence, Wright's abuse of the city escalated with his increasing use of its resources.

In 1930 Wright's initial proposal to establish the Fellowship coincided with the first New York exhibition of his work, at the Architectural League. Two years later the Fellowship's opening session coincided with Wright's participation in the Museum of Modern Art's International Style show as a less than loyal opponent. That same year a meeting organized to protest Wright's exclusion from the planning committee of the 1933 Chicago World's Fair was staged not in Chicago, but at Town Hall in New York. Two years later Wright was back in town with the Fellowship's custom-built Trojan horse, the model of Broadacre City. And the climax came in 1940 when the Museum of Modern Art's retrospective of his work, including models and drawings of such recent commissions as Fallingwater, the Johnson administration building, and the first Jacobs House, restored him firmly in the public eye as an architect of renewed vitality. The acclaim with which the show was greeted more than justified the confidence his apprentices had placed in him well before the triumph of his "second career." Indeed, their confidence played no small part in restoring Wright's own.

From the outset, then, there had been a polarity between the Fellowship and the city: between the place where Wright found truth in art, and the place where he went to pit that truth against the world. But as the 1954 "threat" to move to New York indicated, by the 1950s the balance had begun to shift from the studio to the showroom.

At his two country estates, Wright continued to design buildings—forms without events. In New York, he exhibited the main event, the top-of-the-line product of Wright, Inc.: Wright himself. By the end of his "second career," he had exploited the territory of fame as successfully as the Oak Park houses had articulated the prairie, as though posterity had replaced the midwestern horizon, and Wright's celebrity was the vehicle designed to carry him there.

At Taliesin the Third, Wright had turned 180 degrees away from the days, thirty years before, when he had come to New York to escape "the newspapers' pursuit of news." Now he came to obtain the maximum coverage. "At times Mr. Wright is interviewed by newspapermen in one room," noted his wife, "while several clients wait in another." The protocol is suggestive. In New York, Wright's more conventional "professional" obligations were subordinated to the business of calling up such writers and editors as Douglas Haskell, Edgar Kaufmann, Jr., Cranston Jones, and "young Brendan Gill," who by then had replaced Woollcott as Wright's most widely read self-appointed New York publicist.

Yet Wright's purpose in coming to the city was not just to bask in a flattering shade of limelight, but on the contrary to preserve the posture of an iconoclast, as though without the world against him there could be no truth. Taliesin the Third crystallized his relationship with the city; to maintain a permanent apartment at an address used primarily for transients dramatized the role of Professional Outsider, one of Wright's most highly prized creations.

It was in this role that Wright appeared in one of his major urban dramas, a recurring public debate with Robert Moses on the future of the city in a series of published exchanges in the *New York Times*. While Moses insisted that his parkway system insured that future by making the city more livable, Wright, of course, claimed the opposite, maintaining that "Robert Moses is struggling to release New York to the country. He thinks he is doing the opposite. But he isn't. New York's Moses is another kind of Moses leading his people *out* from congestion rather than *into* it—leading the people from the city." Public "enemies," privately the two were cordial friends, in fact distantly related by marriage, and, as Olgivanna Wright admitted, "he simply cannot contain himself in the pleasure of being the cousin of Robert Moses!"

After years of red-tape delays, it was no doubt a pleasure to expedite the Guggenheim's construction by placing a call to a friendly cousin; but perhaps the chief pleasure of his relationship to Moses was the opportunity to re-enact, for fun, the kind of sparring match he had conducted years before, in another city, with Daniel Burnham.

In contrast to the withering contempt Wright brought to disputes within his own field, his "feud" with "cousin Bob," as with "Uncle Dan" long ago, was suffused with affection and respect. He relished the connection, perhaps because Moses—unlike such architects as Le Corbusier, Sullivan, and Wright himself, artists whose power was limited to the scope of art— was an individual, like Burnham and Henry Ford, with literal, not just symbolic clout; someone with the power to realize a vision on the scale of Wright's imagination. Perhaps the relationship sustained his hope to break beyond art into the wider sphere of life he felt was architecture's true field of action.

Indeed, in Wright's cherished view, Moses, Ford, and Wright himself constituted a great triumvirate, a giant environmental cartel: one to open the gates of the city, one to provide the fleeing residents with chariots, one to house the exodus in the promised land across the River Hudson. But as a backdrop against which to mount this tableau, Wright needed the City Ugly as much as Burnham did the City Beautiful; and upon a stage setting no more substantial than Burnham's plaster facades Wright made his most successful bid to join the league of big-time builders.

In his only government building, the posthumously completed Marin County Civic Center in California, Wright contrasts the design's low, hill-hugging horizontality with a single vertical element: the tall, sharply tapering pinnacle of a broadcasting tower. It was a symbolic treatment, Wright's acknowledgment of the power of the mass media in mid-twentieth-century America, including media that threatened to make the printed word as obsolete as the cathedral. And in view of Wright's designation of the County Architect as his government's chief executive, the tower expresses the importance of the media in his own work at the time of the building's design, symbolizing his emphasis upon the dissemination of ideas above and beyond the design and construction of buildings.

But Wright had long before recognized the media's value as a cultural tool, and in 1930 he had explicitly mated it and the car as twin instruments of decentralization:

To many such traffic stations, destined to become neighborhood centers, will be added, perhaps, features for special entertainment not yet available by a man's own fireside. But soon there will be little not reaching him at his own fireside by broadcasting, television, and publication. In cultural means, the machine is improving rapidly and constantly.

The financial dependence today of public television upon the oil industry makes Wright's image of the gas/TV station seem much less outlandish now than it did fifty years ago. But, in any case, no small part of "improvement" was that the "cultural means" afforded by technology enabled Wright to pass from his sphere into Ford's. All Wright could do with a car was custom paint it his personal shade of Cherokee Red and drive it; with television, he could get much more mileage.

Half a century after the Chicago World's Fair, Wright's Plaza suite overlooked the best view in New York: Central Park, the masterpiece of one of Louis Sullivan's most detested East Coast enemies, Frederick Law Olmsted, who had also laid out the landscape for the Fair. Contrasted with the seedy hotel in which Sullivan had died, Wright's splendid accommodations (he claimed they had once been Diamond Jim Brady's) might be taken as proof that American architecture had indeed recovered fifty years after the Fair, just when Sullivan said it would. But if the spirit of Sullivan prevailed at Taliesins East and West, where Wright worked to achieve his mentor's "rule that would admit no exceptions," Taliesin the Third was pure Burnham, a midway booth in which Wright unveiled big plans "to stir men's blood": the Guggenheim Museum, the Mile-High Illinois, as well as smaller plans that enhanced the figure of Wright himself.

In *The Natural House* Wright confessed that the one kind of building he would rather design more than the small house was "the modern theater," and in a sense at Taliesin the Third he did both. If the Plaza suite was the sound stage, the small house was the show: it was Frank Lloyd Wright starring in "Air House," Frank Lloyd Wright now appearing in "Pre-Fab." Trifles though the designs may have been, they were suitable star vehicles for a personality people wanted to see.

"The Broadway Creed has covered the country pretty much until it has Hollywood on its other end," Wright observed knowingly. And though unable to cover the country with buildings, he was adept at borrowing techniques from the "other end." In the earliest days of the Fellowship, he had used the picture show as a means of extending hospitality and allaying suspicion in the Spring Green community; now he used a publicist's flair to extend his reputation around the world. Like a seasoned contract player, he knew precisely what was expected and had no wish to disappoint his fans. His walking stick and cape were theatrical props, like Dietrich's cigarette; his irascibility was polished to the point of caricature. If he was too old for front-page love-nest exposés, his quips were far more dependable copy.

There are those for whom such theatrics were troubling in an artist of such integrity, the resemblance to Burnham disturbing to a view of American architectural history that has placed them poles apart. Yet it was not a sudden, late intrusion, nor, unless one takes the political implications of Broadacres seriously, was it especially corrupt. Though Taliesin the Third was to some degree a hypocritical betrayal of the Fellowship's uncompromising stance, it was also a clear epiphany of Wright's true intentions, a fulfillment of the Fellowship's charter to take Wright's message to the world.

And in a sense it was all fulfilled according to Wright's earliest conception of the architect's task; only the means had changed. Wright was still "an individual working out his problems . . . knowing well his tools, his opportunity, and—most important—himself," and the 1950s were crowded with opportunities for him to use new tools to express that self with a freedom he had not before known. If the central problem he faced in Broadacre City was to extend the radius of the individual concealed within the mystical dogma of Organic Architecture, by the 1950s he had grasped the fact that there were more sophisticated means to that end than the mass production of houses. He understood that mass media stood ready to project the image of Frank Lloyd Wright into the heart of America without the artistic compromise his three houses had extracted.

For if the three houses had shown that Wright's genius was ultimately incompatible with the ideal of a vernacular architecture that he pursued, his genius was in itself an ideal commodity in the sphere of popular culture. If Wright's art was denied full admittance to this sphere, his self was not. And it was as a professional genius, launched by the Broadway Creed on waves of air, that Wright himself, his image and name, entered triumphantly into the vernacular culture of his time.

Yet there was another, deeper side to Wright's New York life, apart from the triumph, the quotes, the lights and cameras, the spurious solutions to America's social problems. If the city helped Wright attain his cultural objectives by providing him with a public stage, it also served a private need, resolved an inner chord whose reverberations echoed back to New York in 1925, the time of darkness before the dawn.

Vincent Scully has lamented Wright's lack of irony, but clearly with ambivalence he was amply endowed, or cursed. His relationship to the city was one illustration, and it was in writing of the city that Wright came closest to defining the inner conflicts behind the many dualities that surfaced in his work again and again: the city that was everywhere and nowhere, the "known radical" dedicated to "the cause conservative," the arch-Romantic seeking to organize society along lines of classical harmony.

In the opening pages of The Disappearing City, Wright tried to describe the history of human settlements by means of an allegory:

Go back far enough in time. Mankind was divided into cave-dwelling agrarians and wandering tribes of hunter-warriors; and we might find the wanderer swinging from branch to branch in the leafy bower of the tree, insured by the curl at the end of his tail, while the more stolid lover of the wall lurked, for safety, hidden in some hole in the ground or in a cave: the ape? . . .

The cave-dweller became cliff-dweller. He began to build cities. Establishment was his idea. His God was a malicious murderer. His own statue, made by himself, more terrible than himself, was really his God; a God also hiding away. . . .

But his swifter, more mobile brother devised a more adaptable and elusive dwelling-place—the folding tent.

He, nomad, went in changing seasons from place to place, over the whole earth following the laws of change: natural to him.

He was the Adventurer.

His God was a Spirit: like a wind, devastating or beneficent as he was himself.

It may seem odd that an architect should ally himself with the tree-swinger against the lover of solid walls, and in view of Wright's celebrated marriage of building to site (culminating in the literally cavelike "berm" houses of the 1940s,) it is puzzling that he saw himself as an Adventurer battling the Cave Dwellers. As he composed the parable not long after he had been dubbed an adventurer in the worst sense, however, and lived literally a nomad's life (not "following the laws of change" but fleeing those of the criminal code), one need not go back to prehistory to find the source of his inspiration.

Yet Wright retained the parable in the final edition of the book, prepared a year before he died, and it is a telling assessment of his ambivalence and why he was drawn to the city to resolve it. Perhaps the truth, as Robert Fishman has observed, is that the Cave Dweller and the Adventurer "were in fact personifications of two conflicting impulses present in all of Wright's work."

If the two archetypes were the closest Wright came to defining the conflict, they show, as well, how incapable he was of recognizing it as something inside himself: "Both human divergencies set up enmity. Enmity each toward the other." It was a fulltime struggle, one that precluded irony, and one that he never finally resolved in his art. In his life, however, he resolved the conflict with irony to spare.

For by the last decade of his life, Taliesin, with its retinue of admirers, its fortress mentality, its hostility to change and to ideas not conceived by Wright himself, had become nothing more than a cave dweller's abode. "Turn that off!" Wright shouted at an apprentice with a radio tuned to jazz. "It sounds vile in this atmosphere." Once Taliesin had fulfilled the task of bringing the world to Wright, it became increasingly moribund, hidebound to his innate conservatism. And once again, as before in 1910, Wright was compelled to go off in search of adventure, and it was to Taliesin the Third that he journeyed to meet challenge in the Adventurer's role, to renew the qualities within himself that he prized most highly.

To have carried out the threat to move to New York would have been catastrophic, in its way, as his departure from Oak Park had been forty years before. And he did not cut his ties this time, perhaps intuitively aware of the dangers of antagonizing the troglodyte dwelling deep within him. Instead he created an environment of balanced polarities, one that enabled him to house the two sides of his nature in equilibrium.

But Broadacre City had been designed as the Adventurer's capital; and perhaps it is more fitting than ironic that of Wright's own three residences, it was the one within the city that housed the spirit to which he had dedicated his plan for the city's destruction.

■ **ART BUILDING**

On December 21, 1956, twenty-one New York painters delivered to the trustees of the Guggenheim Museum a petition protesting Frank Lloyd Wright's design for the new museum. Construction on the building had already begun, after more than a decade's delay; nonetheless, the authors of the petition (including Franz Kline, Willem de Kooning, Milton Avery, Philip Guston, Adolph Gottlieb, and Robert Motherwell) strongly urged the trustees to reject the design as "not suitable for a sympathetic display of painting and sculpture."

Whether it is fair to say with Robert Twombly that the protesting artists "condemned in architecture the very spirit of adventure they claimed for themselves" in painting, it is likely that their censure was provoked by more than the Guggenheim's flawed facilities for the display of art. It is for the same reason that picture postcards of the building have always outsold those depicting its collection that the Guggenheim has always been most disturbing: the museum is too much a work of art itself to adequately serve the work of other artists. Neither technical improvements in lighting and installation nor the passage of twenty years has done much to erode Lewis Mumford's 1959 assessment that "you may go into this building to see Kandinsky or Jackson Pollock; you remain to see Frank Lloyd Wright."

Contending that artists would paint better pictures under the influence of his revolutionary gallery, Wright replied to the protesting painters, "I am sufficiently familiar with the incubus of habit that besets your minds to understand that you know all too little of the nature of the mother art—architecture." And perhaps Wright was more familiar with the activity of their minds than he, they, or many art historians have ever recognized: for if time has not improved the Guggenheim's suitability for the display of modern painting, it has brought into sharper focus the remarkable affinities between Wright and the painters of the New York School, affinities as obscured by antipathy as those between the architect and the city itself.

In a sense Wright's relations with the painters replayed his treatment of the Modern Movement in architecture years before, as an un-American aberration, objectionable on patriotic as well as aesthetic grounds. While provincial, his attitude was not unreasonable, for in the 1950s it was commonplace to emphasize the descent of Abstract Expressionist painting from School of Paris precedent. As Robert Rosenblum has commented, "the grandeur of the American achievement seemed to demand a search for equally grand roots, especially to justify the sense that the spearhead of European modernism had now crossed the Atlantic."

Commissioned as it was to display a collection composed principally of European paintings, the Guggenheim was thus at once a link in this dubious transatlantic pedigree and a convenient pretext for Wright to inveigh against the New York artists as yet another alien invasion of Modern taste. The paradox is that, to the public eye, Wright's museum seemed so perfectly to herald the triumph of American abstract painting and to honor the city that had nurtured it. Though the Guggenheim collection was neither American nor, by 1959, strictly modern, the museum itself was extravagantly both; and the debate provoked by its design merged promiscuously with the controversy surrounding American abstract painting in the 1940s and 50s, and appeared, at least to the uninformed, to express it: to symbolize architecturally the exuberant effrontery of "abstract art." Indeed, the year of Wright's first design for the building (1943) and the year of the museum's opening (1959) so conveniently bracketed the period of Abstract Expressionism's rise to international acclaim that to watch the spiral rise on Fifth Avenue in the late 1950s was to observe the transfiguration of the New York painters' notoriety into fame, of their downtown action-gestures into uptown museum icons of spiraling value. Newspaper coverage of the painters' protest against the museum was itself evidence of their prestige.

In mere months the 1960s would begin the task of sweeping Abstract Expressionism not only into museums but into history books, rendering the Guggenheim something of a memorial edifice to more than its recently deceased designer. Built despite the disapproval of New York's painters, for whom in any case it was·not designed, the Guggenheim nonetheless stands in retrospect as a monument to New York in the era of "modern art."

Yet one would not of course expect Wright to submit graciously to the task of erecting a triumphal monument to others; and it is not surprising that he attempted to dismiss the painters, as he had the Modern Movement, by pointing to precedents in his own work, claiming, for example, that he had been making "what they now call 'non-objective' art" to adorn his buildings since before the turn of the century. But the New York painters could not be dismissed, for the reason that, unlike the artists of the Bauhaus, they did not "pervert" Wright's original intentions but fulfilled them faithfully, although in another medium and in ignorance of his earlier work. It was gratuitous for Wright to claim that painters would paint better under the influence of his museum, for the Guggenheim is nothing if not an epiphany of interest and influences common to them both.

Vincent Scully's comparison of the Guggenheim to a Pollock canvas is not idle, for Pollock's description of his mode of painting echoes Wright's comparison of the Guggenheim to an unbroken ocean wave. "My concern is with the rhythms of nature," Pollock said, "the way the ocean moves. . . . The ocean is what the expanse of the west was for me." Again, Pollock's statement "I work from the inside out, like nature" could not have worded more precisely "the latest sense of organic architecture" Wright claimed to have embodied in the Guggenheim's fluid design.

The words of another New York painter, Arshile Gorky, could be mistaken for Wright's statement comparing the Guggenheim to traditional museums. "I am breaching the static barrier, penetrating rigidity," Gorky wrote. "I am destroying the confinement of the inert wall to achieve fluidity, motion, warmth in expressing feelingness, the pulsation of nature as it throbs." And however poorly their paintings might show there, a group exhibition at the Guggenheim of the protesting painters would disclose similar parallels with Wright's work at every turn of the spiral: mutual emphasis upon subjective self-expression, preoccupation with publicizing the heroic joys and despairs of artistic creation, and a like impulse to reach back to primitive art and organic forms to locate intuitive links between the mind of the individual artist and his collective culture.

As for the European legacy ascribed to the New York School: though many of the artists had been born abroad, and all of them admired Picasso, Barnett Newman was neither unique nor insincere in professing he would "rather walk on the Tundra than go to Paris." And perhaps it was here, in their mutually "nineteenth-century" preoccupation with exploring uncharted, uncultivated space, that Wright and the New York School stood closest on common American ground, a proximity that provoked Wright's deepest resentment.

"I take SPACE to be the central fact to man born in America, from Folsom cave to now," wrote the poet Charles Olson in 1947. "I spell it large because it comes large here. Large, and without mercy." To Wright, the practice of architecture could be as merciless as the raw material it was designed to modify.

The indignation behind Wright's huffy invocation of "the mother-art" was provoked not simply by the painters' failure to acknowledge his "T-square" ornament as a source of abstract painting, but by their presuming to dictate terms to a superior form of art. Clearly, as an artist working in the medium directly concerned with "the central fact to man born in America," Wright deserved to be seated at the fountainhead of his culture, not criticized or patronized by artists in an inferior medium.

How galling, after laboring for decades to establish architecture as the central American art, to be upstaged in old age by painters, on the international as well as the American scene; and implicitly asked, moreover, to serve them in their glory. That art itself had become virtually synonymous with painting, that the history of Modern Art was traced not on blueprints but on canvas, were obvious grounds for resentment. How natural that the mother-art, like any self-respecting American mother, should not suffer quietly her offspring's neglect; the Guggenheim was a clear opportunity to redress her grievance.

The word "painter" had long been one of Wright's most withering epithets for architects he didn't like, from the Renaissance to the modern age: "Michelangelo was no architect; he was a painter—not a very good one." "Corbusier should have been a painter. He was a bad one but he should have kept on. No painter can understand architecture." In the cultural hierarchy governed by the mother-art, the ideal painter was a muralist eagerly subordinate to the architect's design, the next best kind of painter was a house painter, and after that painting more or less descended to the level of graffiti. Better to hang a Japanese print than corrupt the house with an easel painter's "mere artistic activity."

Wright began airing such philistine sentiments during the design of Midway Gardens, a time when his opinion was almost justified by America's lack of confidence in its own achievement in painting. Coincident with the Armory Show in 1913, he could reasonably argue that American painters and sculptors "were unable to rise at that time" to the Gardens' continental-style "synthesis of the arts," and so, like the Little Red Hen, he himself "made designs for all to harmonize with the architecture."

He tried to repeat the pattern in the Guggenheim: in his renderings of the museum's interior, fragments of his Midway Gardens decorations fill up rectangles where Kandinskys and Klees were meant to be installed. But this time his condescending criticism missed the mark. Over forty years after the Armory Show, American painters not only were sufficiently confident of their power to rise to the level of Wright's achievement, but with the WPA a thing of the past were less than eager to enlist as decorative muralists to any architect's conception.

If "no painter can understand architecture," Wright himself could not understand, or would not accept, that what the New York painters sought in their work was not what he had achieved in ornament, but what he had sought in the whole of his architecture. The fundamental question raised by the conflict between Wright and the painters was not whether his abstract designs had been wrongfully neglected, as his renderings implicitly charged, but whether the painters' medium was not more suitable to the central aims of his own work. Wright asked,

What is it to be an artist? Simply to make objective in form what was subjective in idea. It is to make things within and yet beyond the power of the ordinary man. The artist may feel no deeper, may see no further but has the gift that enables him to put that insight into form in whatever medium he uses.

Yet the problem was that some media might be better suited than others to express such a conception of art. Painting was an ideal medium for making "objective in form what was subjective in idea" with the greatest possible economy. Architecture, as Wright well knew, was perhaps the most problematic of all; the work of art must be inhabitable, and pleasing to those who inhabit it.

Like Wright, the painters tended to view their task as heroic, "beyond the power of the ordinary man." (Gorky: "Abstract art . . . is an exploration into unknown areas." Gottlieb and Rothko, in a joint statement: "To us art is an adventure into an unknown world, which can be explored only by those willing to take the risks.") Unlike Wright, however, the painters were not required to equip the results of their quests with front doors and modern conveniences, nor were they required to apologize or compensate for the deliberate self-interestedness of the adventure.

Where Wright had to cope with clients who complained of being treated like guests in their own houses, that is to say in Wright's works of art, the painters had no cause to disguise the subjectivity of their visions in order to sell a painting, no need to quote Emerson in order to justify their self-expression. Contrasted with Wright's compulsion to maintain that the Prairie House, for example, derived organically from the prairie, came Clyfford

Still's contention that "the fact that I grew up on the prairies has nothing to do with my paintings, with what people think they find in them. I paint only myself, not nature.' Or Gorky's claim: "I do not paint in front of, but from within nature." Or Pollock's: "I am Nature."

How could Wright not resent their liberation from the need to hide behind Mother Nature, without whose authority his forms might be condemned as the arbitrary impositions of his ego? Pollock's conception of painting paralleled not only his intentions in the Guggenheim, but also the "dream of open space and endless movement," in Vincent Scully's phrase, that lay at the heart of Broadacre City. "There was a reviewer a while back who wrote that my pictures didn't have any beginning or any end," Pollock said. "He didn't mean it as a compliment, but it was. It was a fine compliment." And one that Wright would have welcomed for the city that was everywhere and nowhere.

Like Wright, the painters pursued a vision subjective in origin, continental in scope. "Maybe the world is a dream and everything in it is your self," proposed Arthur Dove. "My imagination, it would seem, has its own geography," echoed Mark Tobey. But unlike Broadacre City, the geography of Abstract Expressionism required no literal identification with America itself, as had been true among the Hudson River painters; nor did it depend upon a transformation of the landscape by civilization; their geography, rather, was that landscape, rendered subjectively, projected in a form of "action on canvas" that required no further construction to be fully realized.

In a scrap of twisted metal no bigger than a breadbox, Federick Kiesler's Endless House made a complete poetic statement that three decades of rhetoric, plans, models, and drawings for Broadacre City brought no closer to fruition. On portable rectangles of canvas, Gottlieb, Kline, and O'Keeffe accomplished what Wright could never produce—not a prospectus but a work complete in itself, a transformed continent, a fully realized dream whose inaccessibility to others was not only acceptable, but expected.

Wright's Romanticism was arrested at boundaries unknown to artists whose medium possessed the facility if not actually to capture the grail, at least to bring back from the search facsimiles faithful to a degree Wright had never known. His medium kept the subjective idea trapped within his mind, never to emerge fully into objective form with the defiant authority of Pollock's drip, Newman's zip, or Rothko's shimmering rectangle.

Or almost never; for of course that is what Wright's spiral was: a contour traced in a dream, brought back intact from his own geography. What else but a building brought back from a dream would be windowless, have walls and floors and tilt and twist, begin on the top floor, spiral in toward the center like an enigma? Where else but in a dream would a patron be convinced that so grotesque a conception was both feasible and a great work of art?

"The cult of space can become as dull as that of the object," said Tobey. "The dimension that counts for the creative person is the Space he creates within himself." And this is the space Wright uniquely created in the Guggenheim. Even farther removed than the Price Tower from the Prairie House's horizontal gesture, the museum's centripetal coil acknowledged finally what Wright's medium had previously forced him to conceal, that America's true frontier was not the prairie but the human mind. "Go out. . . . go out . . . " was for Wright's clients; the artist himself turned in toward the intuition that "the central fact to man born in America" could not be located on the horizon by a pointing eave, but in the emotional impact of that distance upon the mind.

If in architecture the American scale of space had been successfully captured only by the skyscraper and the highway, the Guggenheim's interior held its own with both by turning the scale upside down and inward. The defensively introspective impulse that in the Los Angeles houses had produced fortresses of gloom here was transfigured as it broke through recklessly into the Guggenheim's sun-splashed rotunda: cascading light, a wishing-well fountain, the pleasure garden of a mind liberated at last from the compulsion to make Organic Architecture intelligible in any language save its own sensuous form.

True, as Lewis Mumford suggested, Wright had "claimed the privileges of the painter and sculptor without fully accepting the responsibilities of [his] own profession." Yet even Mumford conceded that the Guggenheim's very "absurdities as a museum thus become its ultimate glory as a work of art." What is rarely appreciated, however, either by the building's admirers or by its critics, is that the Guggenheim *had* to be absurd, for reasons that recapitulate the entire history of Wright's relationship with New York.

"When a Samson Agonistes has made sport for the Philistines, he can, if he be a sculptor, say, or a poet, or painter, retreat to the wilderness and fulfill his destiny. Your architect, on the other hand, must work in and with a community." What Alexander Woollcott meant is that no architect could be a truly Romantic artist, nor could a truly Romantic artist accept the responsibilities of the architect's profession. The Guggenheim Museum was the culmination of Wright's campaign to prove otherwise, a campaign he had been waging for half a century. In 1910 he abandoned his successful Oak Park practice because, as he stated in his autobiography, "this absorbing, consuming phase of my experience as an architect ended about 1909. . . . I was losing grip on my work and even interest in it. . . . Because I did not know what I wanted, I wanted to go away." What caused Wright to lose interest in his work was, more than anything else, his success. Wright's success, and the ease with which he had achieved it, had deprived him of the opportunity to enact the role of the Romantic outsider, a role essential to his conception of art. He was losing his grip because Romantic art withers in the atmosphere that architecture requires to survive.

Wright may not have known what he wanted, but what he needed was adversity; this, in any case, is what he found; this is what he devoted his life to for two decades after quitting Oak Park. "I know how flagrantly he himself had invited some of the thunderbolts that have struck him," Woollcott wrote in 1930; by then, of course, whether by accident or by design, Wright had spent enough time in the wilderness to enact the authentic Romantic role.

To Wright, Romanticism and modernity were inseparable. The "retreat to the wilderness" was not just an alternative route along which an artist could fulfill his destiny; it was an essential part of the destiny he must fulfill. It was for this belief that he propagated the ironic falsehood that his career had always been a courageous stuggle of "Truth Against the World"; for this that he plunged into the middle years that enabled him to convert that falsehood into truth; for this that he came to depend on New York City as a means of perpetually renewing his license to play the Professional Outsider. The debt Wright owed New York was the debt any Romantic artist owes the society he must reject, the society without which his rejection has no meaning, the world without which he is helpless to define his truth.

To the New York School of painters Wright owed a special debt, for by December 1956 it had been some time since he had faced any major adversity. Indeed, New York had never been an adversary at all outside Wright's own mind. The controversy stirred up by the Abstract Expressionists was like a farewell public performance of the clash that, until then, had taken place solely in his imagination. The painters' solemn committee of outrage played straight into Wright's waiting hands, their somewhat philistine commonsense objections sounding an ironic welcoming chorus to his most uninhibitedly Romantic building. To show that an architect could hold his own with the most advanced representatives of the Romantic tradition, and on their ground, was the primary function of Wright's art museum, a function the Guggenheim's absurd and glorious form followed to precise perfection. To those of us who cherish the building's bumptious presence in our midst, Wright had settled his debt to New York in lavish style.

ILLUSTRATIONS

Frank Lloyd Wright in New York City. Photo-
graphed with model of the Price Tower at
the exhibition "Sixty Years of Living Architecture" in an exhibition pavilion built on
the future site of the Guggenheim Museum,
Fifth Avenue and Eighty-ninth Street, 1953.
(Photograph © P. E. Guerrero)

Project: Steel Cathedral including Minor Cathedrals for a Million People, 1926. Elevation.
(© 1955 The Frank Lloyd Wright Foundation)
"It consisted of the major faiths grouped around a central courtyard. Wright hoped that the focus of religious activity would shift from the tabernacles to the courtyard. There the universal religion of Broadacre City would be celebrated with magnificent pageantry drawn from the four elements: earth, air, fire, and water. The service would be a union of all the arts, a great communal dance in harmony with the 'Organic Whole.' "—Robert Fishman, *Urban Utopias of the Twentieth Century*

Project: Steel Cathedral, 1926. Plan.
(© 1955 The Frank Lloyd Wright Foundation)

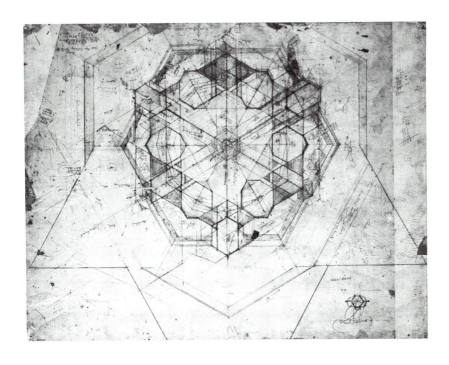

123

Embossed letterhead, "Chicago New York
Los Angeles Tokio, Frank Lloyd Wright
Incorporated." 1927.
(Collection of Edgar Tafel; photograph
Suzanne O'Keefe)

Project: St. Mark's Apartment Tower, 1929.
Perspective.
(© 1962 The Frank Lloyd Wright
Foundation)

Project: St. Mark's Apartment Tower, 1929.
Aerial perspective.
(© 1962 The Frank Lloyd Wright
Foundation)

FIRST GROVP

IN THE BOUWERIE. NEW YORK CITY FRANK LLOYD WRIGHT. ARCHITECT

Broadacre City: "Typical street view at civic center with new type vertical body car and helicopter taxi in flight. . . . In distance, universal (nonsectarian) cathedral. Tower at right, combination apartments and offices."—Frank Lloyd Wright, *The Living City*
(© 1958 The Frank Lloyd Wright Foundation)

Mercedes-Benz (originally, Hoffman Jaguar)
showroom, as executed by Wright (1955),
Park Avenue and Fifty-sixth Street.
(Photograph Muriel Muschamp)

Mercedes-Benz showroom, renovated
according to original Wright designs by
Taliesin Associated Architects, 1982.
(Photograph courtesy Mercedes-Benz of
North America)

Usonian House and Exhibition Pavilion,
Fifth Avenue and Eighty-ninth Street, 1953.
Night view of pavilion.
(Photograph © P. E. Guerrero)

Entrance to Usonian House, 1953.
(Photograph © P. E. Guerrero)

Usonian House, opening reception, 1953.
(Photograph © P. E. Guerrero)

Air House, International Home Show, New
York Coliseum, 1957.
(© Domus)

Air House, 1957. Interior, with gracious
living.
(© Domus)

Crimson Beech, Wright's first Pre-Fab,
Staten Island, 1959.
(Photograph © P. E. Guerrero)

"Taliesin the Third," Suite 223 at the Plaza
Hotel, New York City, 1958.
(Photograph © P. E. Guerrero)

"Taliesin the Third." Living room, 1958.
(Photograph © P. E. Guerrero)

Two views of Wright's desk, "Taliesin the
Third."
(Photograph © P. E. Guerrero)

Solomon R. Guggenheim Museum, "Scheme
B," 1943. Elevation.
(© 1962 The Frank Lloyd Wright
Foundation)

Solomon R. Guggenheim Museum, "Scheme
C," 1943. Elevation.
(© 1962 The Frank Lloyd Wright
Foundation)

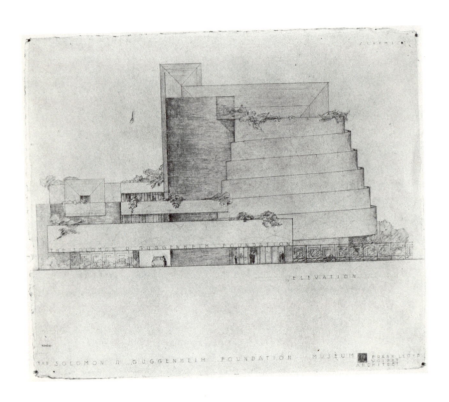

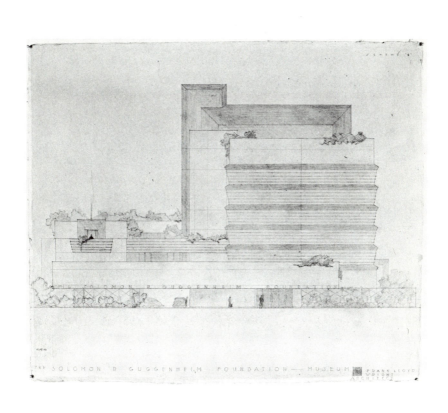

Solomon R. Guggenheim Museum, ten-story
version, 1943–1959. Elevation and section.
(© 1962 The Frank Lloyd Wright
Foundation)

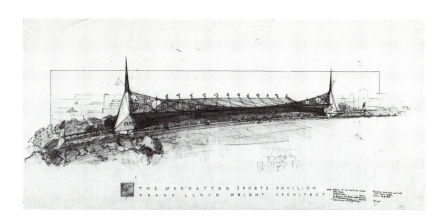

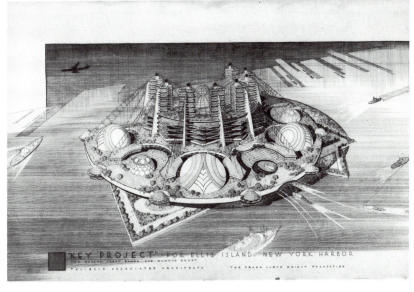

Project: Manhattan Sports Pavilion, 1956.
Aerial perspective.
(© 1962 The Frank Lloyd Wright
Foundation)

"Key Project," Apartment and Hotel Towers
and Gardens, Ellis Island, 1959–61. Taliesin
Associated Architects. "The last project
developed by Frank Lloyd Wright: a self-
contained city unit to be built on the site of
Ellis Island in New York Harbor."—Arthur
Drexler, *The Drawings of Frank Lloyd
Wright*
(© 1962 The Frank Lloyd Wright
Foundation)

1 9 6 0 – 1 9 8 0

ABOUT TOWN AND THE BUILDING

Whether the Guggenheim is or is not a good museum was long ago resolved as a matter of personal taste. You like it or you don't; you admit to mixed feelings; you compare it to the Whitney; you move on to books and plays. Despite the obvious flaws in the building's overall conception and functional detail, it was also clear from the outset that in the Guggenheim the city had acquired a new addition to its roster of front-rank landmark attractions—the Statue of Liberty, the Empire State Building, Times Square, and the Stock Exchange—monuments whose precise significance in architectural history is as uncertain as their place in the tourist's viewfinder is secure.

But the Guggenheim raised questions posed by none of its picture-postcard-rack peers. Perhaps because the museum enjoys none of the physical advantages of site and scale that ordinarily set architectural monuments off from their surroundings, its very distinction always provoked accusations of aesthetic impropriety. The Guggenheim did not sit alone on an island, like the Statue of Liberty; did not straddle a river or join two cities, like the Brooklyn Bridge; was not a self-contained district, like Central Park or Radio City; did not hold its head in the clouds like the Empire State Building, aloof to the murmur of public opinion.

The small, seven-story museum had only presence of mind to keep its less than dignified distance from its well-heeled, high-rising Fifth Avenue neighbors—the presence of a mind not notably neighborly. While the building's interior soothed with splashing light and water, hanging plants, the powdered curves of a skilled seductress, its brazen exterior undulated like a fat *fille de joie* importuning passersby on the city's most solemnly decorous street. The spectacle was wondrous, but, like Mae West, begged reproof. Well within the decade following its completion, whatever controversy remained attached to the Guggenheim had passed from the inside out, so to speak: from the museum's functional inadequacies for the display of art to its public display of such showy sensuousness on the city's blandest stretch of buildings. No one has seriously suggested masking the Guggenheim's plastic exuberance with a tasteful limestone facade, much less tearing it down; but no New York building is an island, and as the 1960s unfolded the bell tolled ever louder for any architect brash enough to think so.

In the strictest sense the questions raised by the Guggenheim were aesthetic ones: should a building be architecturally consistent with its immediate surroundings? What should be the latitude of permissible variations? But as the most famous work of urban architecture by America's most famous architect, the building became emblematic of conflicts ranging far beyond aesthetic etiquette into areas where architecture merges almost imperceptibly with ethics, economics, and social philosophy. Is the concept of legislating architectural consistence itself consistent with the values of free enterprise that presumably underwrite a city's very existence? The American city is not, after all, an extended palace household, subject to the control of a ruler's taste. Who is to say what variations in building form will be tolerated, and who is to say that the objective of consistency is desirable, even on aesthetic grounds?

If such an objective is claimed to represent a social consensus, are the claims of society inimical to the creation of masterpieces, as Wright charged in his tirades against the Mobocracy? Or, conversely, is the freedom to create monuments claimed by an architect like Wright demonstrably anti-social? Certainly to some observers the Guggenheim Museum came to typify an arrogance allegedly prevalent among architects in general, perhaps inherent in the medium itself, perhaps a perversion perpetrated by Modernism: an extravagant pursuit of artistic or theoretical goals conducted at an intolerable social cost. Ironically, Wright's openly confessed "honest arrogance" came to be perceived as symptomatic not just in works of individual virtuosity, like the Guggenheim, but in the characteristically "sterile" postwar architecture, cast in the International Style, that to many appeared to blight the city with forms of unredeemed bleakness.

To an observer like Jane Jacobs, for example, there was no appreciable philosophic difference between Wright's egocentric flamboyance and the virtual anonymity of public housing projects based upon Le Corbusier's pre-World War II prototypes for urban renewal. While to many people such projects indicated that the architect had abdicated entirely in favor of the building contractor and the cost accountant, others agreed with Jacobs that "an imitation of Le Corbusier shouts 'Look what I made!' Like a great, visible ego it tells of someone's achievement."

As imitations, of course, such projects succeeded only in discrediting the ideas of Le Corbusier; even Jacobs would be hard pressed to recall the names of these great visible egos. But Wright's unmistakably authentic shout continues to reverberate down to the present through a series of unresolved issues raised by many contemporary projects, questions ranging from whether an architect has a responsibility for the social consequences of the projects he undertakes, to whether genius justifies all; questions that, in the past twenty-five years, have helped crystallize new approaches to architecture around the term "urbanism."

The *Random House Dictionary* defines urbanism as "1. the way of life of persons who live in large cities; urbanization. 2. see city planning." Neither definition is precise, indeed it could be said that these meanings have been historically mutually exclusive: on the whole, city planning has failed to connect constructively with the vast majority of those who live in large cities, because urbanization has outpaced the development of techniques to plan it. In this sense, one might say that the concept of urbanism has arisen to bridge the gap between the planner's reach and his grasp.

Some people use the term as though it were synonymous with urbanology, the study of cities; others recognize that it has an unmistakably ideological slant: a kind of architectural consciousness-raising devised to get architects more involved with social issues. A major difficulty in obtaining a precise definition of urbanism may be our failure to ask whether urbanism is not a phenomenon unique to our time. To speak, for example, of the "urbanism" of ancient Rome, medieval Paris, or colonial Philadelphia obscures the possibility that urbanism may be a concept with no application to periods before the term itself was coined—before we began to be aware, at the time of the 1910 census, that ours was a predominantly urban culture. Since there have always been large cities, there has always been an urban way of life, there has always been urbanization; and city planning itself is not a modern innovation. But Urbanism, like Modernism, is a modern phenomenon, a lively part in the intellectual life of the contemporary city. It is an umbrella term covering a variety of attempts to orient ourselves to the reality of living in an urban culture, to adjust our environmental expectations accordingly, and to adjust our environment to meet these expectations.

In the specific context of architecture, the word "Urbanism" is often used adjectivally, to connote characteristics of design considered desirable in an urban building by particular observers. Thus, as a restaurant might be given separate ratings for "atmosphere" and "service," a building might be described as "good architecture and bad urbanism" or vice versa, as any building proposed for an urban site has become subject to assessment according to criteria different from those that might apply to works designed for a more isolated setting.

Is the building sensitive to the adjacent environment, to community needs, to long-range planning objectives? Have provisions been made for access to public transportation, for energy conservation, for such amenities as neighborhood parks, community meeting rooms, shops and restaurants to preserve or enhance the liveliness of the street? Is the projected use of a proposed building—residential, industrial, commercial—compatible with the long-range interests of the immediate community and the city as a whole? Like a businessman running for political office, the contemporary urban building is expected to demonstrate the virtues of good citizenship in ways that often influence its design as decisively as do the client's needs and the architect's talents.

144

In other words, Urbanism is more than an approach to the design of individual buildings: it is the approach to a renewed conception of architecture as a whole, an approach that subordinates the individual building to its environment, its visual effects to the measure of its social, economic, even its biological impact upon that environment. Just as the city itself has spread outward from the traditional center to the physical outskirts of civilization itself, so one of the major preoccupations of Urbanism has been to discern patterns of influence between the architect's work on the individual building and the wider concerns of society as a whole. Indeed, in the broadest possible sense within the architectural context, one might define Urbanism as the process of determining what architecture ought to be in the present age of urbanization.

In certain respects, the impact of urbanization on architectural design resembles that made by industrial mechanization at the advent of Modernism. The Greeks, the Romans, even Stone Age men had "machines," at least as Lewis Mumford defines them; but mechanization was not a central fact of culture until the Modern age. Similarly, there were apparently cities before there was written history to record them; but urbanization did not become the central cultural fact until around the time Lewis Mumford started writing about it—until the time America ceased to be an agrarian culture.

Both mechanization and urbanization have been recognized by architects as major factors in the transformation of culture; yet each phenomenon has succeeded in transforming the physical environment generally without the advice and consent of architects. It was not an architect who invented the elevator that made the skyscraper possible; not architects who invented the train and the automobile that made urbanization possible. But both mechanization and urbanization challenged architects in ways that revolutionized not only the forms of their buildings but their conception of architecture itself.

Fifty years ago technology forced architects to reappraise their art, their profession, their social function, their cultural position. Like Modernism, Urbanism is also a term an impatient historian might begin to associate with a particular period—the 1960s and 70s—when architects began to be challenged by the "urban crisis" in part as a means of resolving the aesthetic crisis brought about in their own profession by the waning of Modernism as a dominant architectural mode. Yet Wright's work in the field of urban design—precipitated four decades earlier by Modernism's rise—anticipated many of the themes of which urbanism would be composed.

This book has depicted the relationship between Frank Lloyd Wright and New York City as a lopsided, if not one-sided, affair; the emphasis has been placed entirely on the city's influence on Wright, and with good reason. It would be pointless to claim that Wright's philosophy of Organic Architecture produced the slightest effect on the architecture of New York. Walking-tour guides might point out to the curious the Mercedes–Benz showroom, its truncated ramp an easily overlooked Guggenheim footnote tucked away in the corner of one of those "skinny glass boxes" despised by Wright. Serious students of the city's architecture may detect the influence of Wright in the work of Edgar Tafel, an earnest Wright disciple whose sensitively designed additions to older buildings offer an exact antithesis to the master's best-known building. For the rest, the Guggenheim will remain known as Wright's only New York work: an exotic shell cast up on a public beach, mounted like a treasured curio on the broad, bleak mantle of upper Fifth Avenue.

And if Wright's positive impact upon the city was minimal, his destructive influence was probably less than that. Though the case could be made that his long and loud espousal of urban decentralization helped to accelerate the city's decline, the case would be a weak one. Wright himself, of course, would be the first to plead a cheerful "Guilty!" Yet the evidence is circumstantial, and the final judgment must be that any connection between his assaults and the city's bruises is purely coincidental; it is as likely that his insults served to stiffen the morale of loyal New Yorkers as to convert them to Usonian ways.

Yet in this sense one could with some license interpret Urbanism as New York's "reply" to Wright, at least to the extent that Urbanism represented a response, formulated and voiced primarily by New Yorkers, to the artistic waywardness of architecture in which Wright played so definitive a part. Just as the jagged skyline represents Manhattan's most distinctive architectural export to other cities of the world, so the motley group of cultural convictions huddled beneath the umbrella of Urbanism are recited in the native vernacular, sharing the legacy of liberalism, of the melting pot, of New York's continuing role as the center of American intellectual life.

Yet if it is fair to say that Urbanism represented a repudiation of the "look what I made!" egotism manifested in such structures as the Guggenheim, it is also true that Urbanism has perpetuated many of the values Wright himself sought to manifest throughout his work in the field of theoretical urban design. He wrote, "Any city of *futurism* to be valid will be only more individual than in ages ago. Not less so." And much of the impetus behind the emergence of urbanism derived from the belief that there was more individualism and diversity in one New York City block than in a continent of conglomerate-owned suburban subdivisions; that the central city, even in decline, promised a range of possibilities far broader than that of a decentralized megalopolis constructed and serviced by the unprecedented concentration of wealth and homogenization of taste, attained under the auspices of multinational corporations, broadcasting networks, and fast-food chains. In the 1960s and 70s it was not the central city but the megalopolis that seemed most to warrant the epithets Wright had hurled at New York thirty years before: "triumph of the herd instinct . . . confusing personality by frustration of individuality . . . fibrous tumor . . . outgrown as overgrown . . . the Moloch that knows no God but more."

If the central city had dimmer prospects for a viable "futurity" in the twenty years after Wright's death, it was not because it had ignored the virtues of Usonian individuality but because it cherished them somewhat more dearly than American culture as a whole was willing to allow; too dearly, at least, for the comfort of those who retreated to the suburbs in search of a less heroically individualistic way of life.

Indeed, the Urbanist during this period assumed a cultural position analogous to the niche Wright had proposed for the County Architect—to discern a "unity in diversity," to oversee "a harmony of the whole"—and, like the County Architect, the urbanist sought involvement as much with social and political as with purely architectural issues. Just as Organic Architecture extended Wright's sphere of interest beyond formal matters to a consideration of American society, so Urbanism became a procedure for examining the social values of contemporary urban culture through the prism of the individual building.

It is as such a prism that the Guggenheim continued to stir occasional controversy long after debate on its merits as an art museum had ceased to be useful for anything but pick-up conversation along Museum Mile; and it was through the medium of such controversies that Urbanism began to make its impact felt, not only in the design of the city's individual buildings, but in the direction of contemporary architecture as a whole.

That the Guggenheim was in this sense more central to the emergence of Urbanism than it ever was to the evolution of Modernism is not in any direct way the consequence of Wright's urban theories. One needs no knowledge of Broadacre City, of Usonianism, of the private correspondence between the spiral and the car, even of Wright's public animosity to New York City, to reach one's own conclusions about the urban design issues raised by the Guggenheim. But the issues are themselves indicative of the increasing significance Urbanism attained in the decades after the Guggenheim was built. The conclusion of this book will attempt to clarify Wright's contribution to this development, and to assess the value and meaning of that contribution in the context of architecture and urbanism at the present time.

The idea that architecture is a social art suggests a number of interpretations in addition to the unique intimacy with which buildings, compared to other art forms, are bound up with daily life. It suggests, for example, that architecture is a collective art, most often the creation of a team rather than a single author. Then, too, architecture is the "social" art, long the only socially acceptable art, the traditional gentleman's pastime for those gentlemen of creative bent whose ambitions transcend the auction rooms of Sotheby's but stop short of the untidy Parnassus of paints, pens, and ideas. There are, in addition, two interpretations of the social art of more than passing semantic interest, two views of architecture's relation to society that are of central concern to the issues raised by Urbanism. Like the term "Urbanism" itself, one interpretation is objective, one ideological in implication.

The first interpretation is that architecture functions as a *social mirror*, reflecting in durable images a wide spectrum of the economic and political processes, customs, beliefs, temperaments, and tastes that combine to create a building in a particular form or style at a given place and time. Thus the pyramids may be "read" as diagrams of the theocratic social structure of ancient Egypt; Chartres as a system of interlocking variations on the theme of thirteenth-century unity; Versailles as an index of decorative formalities radiating from the person of Louis XIV. Nor is this reading simply the illusion of historical perspective; in their own time, these monuments were designed to reflect and to stabilize existing patterns of social order.

The second interpretation, a more recent view, would define architecture more or less as a "socialist" art, an art whose purpose is to change the existing patterns of social order as reflected in the built environment. From the assumption that society as a whole benefits from progressive, measurable improvements in the built environment derives the idea that architecture should be employed as a *social tool*, an instrument for attaining the enlightened goals of social reform. Attendant on this view is the belief that architects should conspicuously uphold an ethical responsibility to the society for which they build.

In Hammurabi's day, an architect might be executed if his building collapsed and crushed its inhabitants to death. More recently, social reformers have periodically sought to establish more sophisticated corollaries between the design of the entire built environment and the well-being of society as a whole, and to question whether, or to what extent, an architect, either individually or as a member of an organized profession, should be held morally responsible for the material condition of his culture. Should there be an architectural equivalent to the Hippocratic Oath? By what standards are we to judge whether or not such a responsibility has been met?

The idea that architects should actively seek to change rather than passively reflect the status quo has had a special significance in the culture of American democracy, in part because reform has long been considered an integral part of the American status quo. As the historian Robert H. Walker has written, "Americans have steadily assumed that their society should adjust itself toward a system wherein all citizens share more fully in the good things in life. The reformer begins by discovering this sentiment." And the course of American architecture has been significantly influenced by this sentiment also, perhaps because few things are so symbolic as architecture of "the good things in life."

"For Sullivan," Norris Kelly Smith writes, "architecture seemed to afford a means whereby the 'feudalism' of the existing social order could be transformed, by little more than environmental conditioning, into an ideal 'democracy.' " Yet Daniel Burnham, Sullivan's arch-antagonist, viewed architecture in similar terms: the mission of the White City, and of the City Beautiful Movement in general, was to reform the urban environment for the benefit of a population who could not afford to build private palaces. The same impulse informed Olmsted's design for Central Park, spurred the nationwide movement to create urban parks, animated both Wright's plans for Broadacre City and Robert Moses's system of parks and parkways in New York. It is the idea of reform that has guided the theoretical development of modern city planning, if more rarely its practice, and that found expression more recently in Buckminster Fuller's proposals for planning on a global scale. "Reform the environment, not man," Fuller has written; and implicit in all these projects is the assumption that "environmental conditioning" is at the very least a first step from which profound social change must inevitably follow.

The conception of architecture as a tool for social reform is not, however, an American phenomenon. The philosophical point of view from which it derives originated in Europe; was articulated by Rousseau more clearly than by the Founding Fathers; was embroidered by the philosophes; was rendered into Utopian architecture and town planning by Fourier and Owen well before Wright publicized the Prairie House as "the first truly democratic expression of our democracy in Architecture." While it was clearly to Wright's personal advantage to maintain that only an American enjoyed the cultural support to fully realize this point of view, his impulse was far surpassed by the more frankly socialist objectives of the early Modern Movement. Scheerbart preached the replacement of masonry by glass as a means of abolishing distinctions of social class and nationality; Gropius extolled the "new building" as a catalyst for the socialist solidarity of at least "one million workers"; and the notion that environmental reform would lead to social reform, rather than vice versa, underlay Le Corbusier's insistence that modern society faced an ultimate choice of "architecture or revolution."

The repudiation of Modern Utopianism formed a major plank in Urbanism's ideological platform. Yet, like Modernism, Urbanism drew heavily on the democratic sentiment of social reform to fuel its own cultural momentum. In this ideological sense, then, one could interpret Modernism and Urbanism as successive stages in a continuous cultural evolution, derived from a common idea: the idea that architecture must be progressively transformed from a "rich man's art" into an art more comfortably reconciled with democracy's social ideals. Occurring at the approximate juncture between these two stages, Wright's New York designs are a useful point of departure in examining this evolution and its influence upon the architect's role in contemporary culture.

All art is a rich man's art. You can buy a house designed by Frank Lloyd Wright for somewhat less than it will cost you to purchase an O'Keeffe canvas worthy of its living-room wall. It will not bankrupt you to buy a book, providing you do not make a habit of it, but a writer aiming to produce "literature" is often aiming in the direction of the "intelligent reader" whose intelligence was cultivated at a cost beyond the reach of the average American budget. The poor, devoted art lover is an invaluable institution, especially at grant-writing time; but he does not endow chairs in the humanities, underwrite the cost of producing new ballets, supply a sculptor with steel or a conductor with an orchestra. Museums are open to the public free of charge or at nominal cost; they would not be open at all were they unable to offer the art collector a reliable means of protecting investments and easing tax burdens. The idea that art is for everybody is not a cynical myth. But Pop Art was a way of turning a twenty-nine-cent soup can into a ten-thousand-dollar icon, in the process offering an ironic commentary on the glaring difference American culture continues to make between popular art and art. Popular art costs twenty-nine cents; real art aspires to the condition of six figures.

The point of these remarks is not to impute hypocrisy to artists, patrons, or cultural administrators, nor to suggest that works of art should be viewed in an economic, much less a Marxist, context. It is rather to suggest the influence of the marketplace on architecture's relationship to other forms of art. Woollcott's remarks of fifty years ago comparing architecture to other arts remain substantially true today; they are pertinent not only to comprehending Wright's professional difficulties during his middle years, but to understanding the evolution of architecture as an art form throughout the history of democratic culture.

One unfortunate corollary to the architect's dependence upon the patron is that, unlike other artists, he often comes to be identified with the patron's economic status. A fine painting testifies to a wealthy man's good taste; a fine house testifies to the condition of a life made possible by wealth. The identification of the architect with the privileged class that can afford to hire him is certainly unjust, for after all "good design costs no more," and therefore great architecture is a relative bargain. Nonetheless, the identification has a legitimate cultural basis. It is predicated not simply on the economic advantages of those who can afford to build private houses, but on the historical identification of architecture with social and political power. It is based on a history of architecture that, until fairly recently, was mainly a record of major monuments built by the dominant individuals and institutions of world civilization.

To say that architecture is a conservative art is to speak not so much of the alleged artistic timidity of architects or their patrons as of the ungainliness with which the medium lends itself to the liberal tendencies of democratic culture. A painting, a book, a poem, a symphony can be detached with relative ease from its association with the patron who supported the artist who created it. To strip these associations from a building would take more than a wrecker's ball or an angry mob; it would require the suppression of historical memory. An aroused society can depose the Bourbons and turn Versailles into a museum; even so, such a museum displays the work of the Bourbons far more prominently than that of the artists— Le Vau, Hardouin-Mansart, Le Nôtre—who actually created it. On the other hand, a Boucher portrait of Madame de Pompadour will be more greatly prized as the work of Boucher than as an image of his patroness. There can be no New Criticism of architecture, because a building is rooted as firmly in its social context as on its real estate. Even those buildings whose exact social context has been lost to historical memory—Stonehenge, for example—can rarely be appreciated as formal compositions until the imagination has made an effort to supply one: Druids, Stone Age astronomers, ancient astronauts.

Architecture can be "democratized" in several ways. One way is to clothe the institutions of democracy in the monumental *symbolic forms* of classical civilization; Washington D. C., owes its appearance to the idea that only the forms of classical antiquity could do justice to the noble concept of government by the people. Another way is to construct *social programs* to make "environmental conditioning" available to a greater percentage of the population. This is the approach taken by the United States Congress in the 1940s in adopting the goal of "decent housing for every United States citizen" as official government policy; building construction ranks second to agriculture in the nation's economy as a consequence of this policy. A third way is to revise or expand the *cultural interpretation* of architecture itself to include works of various types that have previously fallen outside the traditional scope of architectural history. This approach has been of critical importance to the evolution of architecture as a contemporary art form: for example, while the poor have always required shelter just as much as the rich, before William Morris it was rare to think that a poor man's shelter could be perceived as architecture just as legitimately as could a palace.

To the Modern architect, the historicist approach to democratization taken by architects of official government buildings was at best misguided, at worst a cynical perpetuation of the aristocratic impulses that democracy had ostensibly been designed to eliminate. The second and third approaches constituted the two fronts—one social, the other artistic—on which the architect fought to liberate his art from its traditional aristocratic associations.

The social approach led the Bauhaus designers to experiment with mass-produced household accessories, Le Corbusier with the Dom-ino concrete construction system, Wright with Pre-Fabs—all products conceived with the expectation that technology could be called upon to deliver to the many a range of architectural goods and services that until then had been the province of a few. The artistic approach led these designers to redefine architecture in words and projects that conveyed the message that only architecture that could be made available to the many deserved the cultural significance of building once commissioned by the few. A chicken coop became as desirable as a cathedral, if not more so. A block of workers' flats assumed the cultural significance of an imperial court, even though few workers showed enthusiasm for homes modeled after factories. Patrons who could afford otherwise preferred chicken coops and foreman's huts to retardataire mansions whose architectural status was now suspect. Small houses, exhibition pavilions, unbuilt visions, pamphlets, crafts: on the basis of "democracy" the architect filed his claim that these works were to the Modern age what palaces and cathedrals had been to ages past.

Each of these approaches was predicated on the impulse of reform, and in theory they were complementary. The machine would make it possible to produce architecture for the multitudes, and at the same time force a revolutionary reappraisal of what architecture ought to be. In 1910 Wright had been no less adamant than the Bauhaus in professing the belief that "the Machine can only murder the traditional forms of other peoples and earlier times. All of them"—and equally convinced that the architect was uniquely suited to preside over the birth of new ones. Under the architect's guidance, social and artistic reform would unite to bring about the harmonious world of the Modern future—Broadacre City, La Ville Radieuse: by any name, a world reformed and reconsecrated to democratic values.

As a social art, architecture has always been a mixture of social and artistic values; to paraphrase Emerson, a mixed art whose end is sometimes beauty and sometimes use. But the pressure to democratize architecture had an unsettling effect upon the mixture. In theory the Modern architect's programs for social and artistic reform were designed to restore to the built environment the authority and coherence that prevailed when architecture was expected to reflect, rather than to reform, society's most powerful institutions; in effect, to create an international District of Columbia stripped of cornices and columns. In practice, however, these two approaches to architecture's democratization headed off for the future in opposite directions.

Because Modern architects failed so dismally to arrive anywhere near the goal of revolutionizing the built environment in accordance with the democratic and socialist values expressed in their Utopian projects, it became commonplace to assume that the Modern revolution was confined entirely to matters of form: the elimination of applied ornament, the exterior expression of interior structure, the visual symbols of social and mechnical function.

But if the Modern architect's rhetoric did not succeed in changing society, it did announce a profound change in the architect's relation to society, a change at least as revolutionary as that of his formal vocabulary. Radical as these forms once appeared, even more radical was the change in the architect's *responsibility* for their creation. Indeed, without impugning the sincerity of the Modern architect's idealism, it could be said that while the avowed aim of Modernism was to reform architecture in conformity with democratic ideals, the achieved objective of the Modern era was to establish architecture as an autonomous art form, to place the architect on the same creative footing as the painter, the composer, the poet. Thus it was that Wright, having credited himself with creating "the first truly democratic expression of our democracy in Architecture," came to describe the Guggenheim Museum as though it were the masterpiece of the collection of paintings and sculptures it was designed to display; while Le Corbusier— having long since conquered his fear of "revolution"—came to think of architecture as an event in itself: "the knowing, accurate and magnificent interplay of shapes assembled in the light." While the overt objective of the Modern vision was to appropriate the social functions of architecture on behalf of those who had never had access to an architect's services, the real revolution of Modernism was the appropriation of the building's artistic functions on behalf of architects themselves.

To oversimplify the matter: before the Modern era, an important work of architecture expressed an explicit social program, one of church, of state, of a patron's power. After Modern architecture, the program expressed by our most significant buildings expressed the power of genius liberated by the architect's successful application of Richardson's Law: "Get the Job." One went to the cathedral to experience the splendor of Christianity, to the palace to be awed by the power of a prince. One entered the Modern building to witness the convictions of its designer translated into such expressive power as his budget and his talents allowed.

The success of this revolution is shown in the degree to which we have come to take it for granted: in the fact that we seldom pause to reflect that the history of architecture as an art form is a fairly recent chapter in the history of architecture, and that the two histories are neither synonymous nor entirely congruent. Nikolaus Pevsner's well-known definition—"the term architecture applies only to buildings designed with a view to aesthetic appeal"—is a good illustration of the triumph of the Modern revolution. What is significant about Pevsner's 1949 distinction is not whether or not it is true, but that it attempted to revise history in accordance with the one criterion by which Modern architects could claim cultural parity with the builders of Lincoln Cathedral, the Parthenon, and other monuments of established institutions. Modernism set a course in which the term "architecture" would apply to buildings designed with a view only to aesthetic appeal. Only by this standard could a chicken coop be considered as desirable as a cathedral.

In reviewing Wright's Usonian House exhibition, Lewis Mumford observed that many visitors to the show were apparently baffled by what they saw there—puzzled by what exactly they were meant to see in it. What, apart from the fame of its designer, was the point of erecting a rather ordinary-looking ranch house on New York's Fifth Avenue and opening it to public view?

The Usonian House did not seem to possess any of the extraordinary attributes for which a house is put on display. It was not, for example, ultramodern, full of technical marvels and timesaving devices, like the Homes of the Future typical of world's fairs and appliance-manufacturers' conventions. Indeed, as Mumford wrote, the house "had an almost old-fashioned, homey air." Yet it did not have any obvious antiquarian value, like the reconstructed houses of Williamsburg. Nor was it grand, like the short-lived chateaus that had lined Fifth Avenue in an earlier era, nor exotic, like the Japanese house displayed at the Museum of Modern Art the following season. It was not a novelty item, like the Air House; and though a Calder sculpture graced its entrance and a huge Wright-designed kettle softened the rectangular hearth, it contained no great works of art, like the Morgan or the Frick.

It was Mumford who pointed out that the reason that "Wright's exhibition has puzzled visitors . . . is that many of Wright's most audacious innovations have been generally absorbed during the last half-century; we have taken them in, just as we have taken in glass doors for offices, indirect lighting, steel office furniture—all inventions that stem from Wright or that he helped pioneer."

In a similar way we have taken in, have come to take for granted, Wright's celebrity, his fame as a great architect. We assume that, of course, an architect of his gifts should quite naturally be well known. And because we take his fame for granted, we ask, in a rhetorical tone that implies reproach, why he sought repeatedly to make such a public spectacle of himself; why he made such an issue of his ego; why so many of his buildings seemed to take self-advertisement as their principal function. Yet such questions betray an ignorance of Wright's legacy equal to that of those visitors who wandered through the Usonian House unaware that the open floor plan and indirect lighting were Wright innovations.

For the legacy of Wright's formal innovations was closely paralleled by the legacy of his fame. And just as we have come to take the open plan for granted, so we tend to overlook the significance of Wright's celebrity in the transfiguration of the architect from a talented social servant to an artist whose creative autonomy rivals that of artists in other fields. We fail to recognize the correlation between Wright's fame and his autonomy, or we tend to think that his fame was the result of his autonomy, whereas the Usonian House suggested that the reverse was more nearly true: no one would have thought to erect this ordinary house in that place had its author not been Frank Lloyd Wright.

If a student now dreams of becoming a "famous architect"; if he wishes to use his materials as freely as any other artist uses the materials of his art; if he wants his buildings to be acknowledged works of art, emanations of his own talent rather than his patron's taste, he owes these possibilities to Frank Lloyd Wright more than to any single predecessor.

There is perhaps no better illustration of the student's debt to Wright in this regard than that afforded by what, with a bit of license, one might call Wright's "thirteenth New York design": the living room from a house designed by him in 1913, installed in 1982 in the Metropolitan Museum of Art's new American Wing.

The Metropolitan numbers among its galleries dozens of "period rooms"; the museum-goer may walk through space and time in French Gothic, Italian Renaissance, Colonial New England, Elizabethan England. On the walls of these rooms he may view paintings by Boucher, Velázquez, Copley. On bookshelves he may inspect the spines of leather-bound volumes by Gibbon, Hardy, Montaigne, while on a music stand he might observe a sheet of music composed by Bach. Among the furnishings he must not touch are chairs by Chippendale, porcelain by Meissen, pewterware by Paul Revere. But the rooms themselves are anonymously titled; or else they bear the names of the patrons who inhabited them, like a natural history museum's recreated tableaus of Neanderthal, Cro-Magnon and Pre-Columbian Man. Frank Lloyd Wright's "Northome" is the exception to this rule.

Mr. and Mrs. Francis W. Little were the original owners of Northome; but museum literature announcing the installation referred to it as "the Frank Lloyd Wright period room," as though Wright himself constituted a period. And, in more than a purely formal sense, he did: he constituted, or at least presided over, a period in which the architect succeeded in appropriating from the patron his traditional privilege to dictate the aesthetic criteria of his work.

W. H. Auden wrote:

The two characteristics of art which make it possible for an art historian to divide the history of art into periods, are, firstly, a common style of expression over a certain period and, secondly, a common notion, explicit or implicit, of the hero, the kind of human being who most deserves to be celebrated, remembered and, if possible, imitated.

In the Wright room, we can observe that Wright gave the first of these characteristics to the Prairie School of the late nineteenth century, and the second to the world at large of the twentieth. "We have been at this three or four years and have got nowhere," complained Mr. Little in an angry letter to his architect, threatening to withdraw his commission.

What is the use of continuing it? Why not recognize frankly that the difference between us is fundamental and that it isn't in you to get the kind of house *we* want? You have made a very strong but unsuccessful effort to persuade us to like and accept something we don't like and don't want.

In the end, of course, Wright was successful. He would build the kind of house he wanted. And if the Wright room's leaded-glass windows and Stickley-style furnishings look backward to the Prairie Houses of his "first career," the fundamental difference that divided Wright and his patron looks forward to the major achievement of his later years: the architect-hero who most deserves to be celebrated, remembered, and, if possible, imitated.

This is not, of course, to claim that Wright was the first celebrity architect, the first architect in history whose name has outlasted those of his patrons. Palladio and Stanford White, to cite but two examples, are both far more celebrated than most of the patrons who employed their services, and were so even in their own time. As Kenneth Clark has pointed out, the Renaissance in particular reserved special esteem for the architect of genius. "Everyone knew that Brunelleschi had built the Pazzi Chapel, and that Bramante had been chief architect of St. Peter's, and so on down the scale to relatively inconspicuous buildings."

Yet it is unlikely that an architect of the Renaissance, or of any period before the Modern age, could have based his reputation almost entirely on "relatively inconspicuous buildings," as Wright did, for example. As Smith comments, "the buildings that have traditionally been regarded as works of architectural art have invariably been bound up with an organized social group, an established institution"; and before the Modern age it is doubtful that a private house, of fewer than a dozen rooms and well removed from public view, could have been so regarded.

The impulse to outshine the patron had recurred throughout architectural history; but what architect before Wright had made such an effort to justify this impulse as an artistic principle—as a symbol of the individual's superiority to any "organized social group" or "established institution"? Louis Sullivan, of course, had anticipated the streak of Romantic heroism that Wright was to exploit so fully. But Sullivan had failed; his example could serve only as a cautionary fable against the arrogance of proposing oneself as superior to the patron who paid the bills. Wright's career set quite a different example. The "honest arrogance" of the artist was now not only a viable option for the architect, but perhaps a necessary demonstration of his integrity as well. The inspired autonomous architect, "working out his problems" to the best of his individual talent, was the most appropriate instrument through which democratic society could articulate the highest forms of its art. The model was irresistible, even to the European Modernists who sought most strenuously to resist it.

In the opening pages of this book, I suggested that the significance of Wright's New York designs lay in their anticipation of the increasing influence of urbanism on architecture in the past twenty years. Yet the development just described contradicts this: never before in history has the art of architecture been so liberated as at present from the criterion of social accountability it is urbanism's apparent function to identify and uphold. Never before has the architect so naturally claimed, nor to such an extent been granted, the freedom to behave like an artist, to be endowed with the temperament of an artist, to be reviewed in the pages of art magazines like an artist, to write the rules of his medium and, more important, to break them at will, like an artist.

The architect's contemporary position in this regard is perhaps best summed up by Philip Johnson's blithe insistence that "all history disproves the idea that architecture is anything but an art." Whether or not this is history's lesson, it is a valuable part of Frank Lloyd Wright's legacy to American architecture. It is a legacy we value more today, perhaps, or at least enjoy with less misgiving, than we did in the years when Gropius was trying to persuade us to lay down our geniuses and march forward toward an architecture "where design by the individual genius is no longer possible." To reject this legacy is not only to reject Wright's contribution to our architectural heritage, but to ignore the Modern Movement's amply demonstrated lesson that architecture can indeed be an art, a form of creative activity handled more capably by some than by others, handled best of all by geniuses (such a Gropius himself) whose original works not even the most rabid urbanist would wish to outlaw or glibly dismiss as atavism. Wright consciously perceived himself as accomplishing for architecture what Beethoven achieved in the field of music, and one does not lightly dismiss his achievement without repudiating the efforts of artists since the late eighteenth century to secure the right to set their own terms for art.

Yet it is exactly this legacy that urbanism did challenge. Urbanism challenged the idea that architecture can or should be thought of as an event in itself. It challenged the idea that the formal and conceptual standards of Romantic art were adequate criteria for measuring architecture's past achievements or guiding its future development. It challenged the idea that architecture can or should aspire to become an autonomous art form without severely diminishing its own cultural power.

This challenge became more audible as the pronouncements of Modernism became less so. As the stylistic and ideological pressures of the Modern Movement began to weaken, it often appeared that the socio-aesthetic mixture of the "mixed art" had begun to separate somewhat like a vinaigrette, breaking down into its base ingredients of social and artistic values. In the 1960s and 70s some architects puritanically took upon themselves the burden of "use"; others devoted themselves ostentatiously to "beauty." And many devoted less time to making buildings either useful or beautiful than to polishing the "eloquence" with which they defended the merits of their respective points of view.

As Kenneth Frampton remarked of the profession's ambivalence during this period, "many of its more intelligent members have abandoned traditional practice, either to resort to direct social action or to indulge in the projection of architecture as a form of art." Thus, in the late 1960s, "advocacy architecture" arose on the one hand as a kind of architectural equivalent to the antiwar movement, while, on the other, the term "Post-Modernism" arose to identify a trend toward an artistic autonomy so complete that it often eschewed the form of the building, evidently preferring to retain, as drawing or model, the shape the architect had given it in the white splendor of his studio.

Yet in a sense the architects who took to these polemical poles did not so much abandon traditional practice as perpetuate practices well established during the Modern period. Thus, for example, the architect Ulrich Franzen argued that "the great drawback to functionalist theory [was that] modern architecture came to be seen as an ideology, a tool of technological progress," while actually, at least in Franzen's view, the great Modern architects, like great artists in any field, "simply did what they have always done, following the dictates of their own eyes and hearts." In the post-Modern era, "Post-Modern architecture" tended to follow the late Modern subordination of social to aesthetic ideals, focusing on formal solutions to the social and technical problems the architect is called upon to solve, often invoking Modernism as a precedent for avoiding unseemly social commitment. As Philip Johnson stated flatly, "Mies didn't give a damn who was running the government, but Hitler liked pitched roofs."

Mies van der Rohe's first Berlin building was the 1926 monument to the Communist leaders Rosa Luxemburg and Karl Liebknecht, complete with hammer and sickle. Was it really no more than a monument to Richardson's Law? In the post-Modern period, urbanism offered a means of restoring the social motivations that had informed the early Modern program, of reestablishing the social priorities that had helped to shape their forms.

In the opinion of James Marston Fitch, "the most disturbing aspect of life in the United States today is the widening discrepancy between privatized luxury and public amenity," and while "architects themselves are only partially responsible [for this problem], even so, their work shows certain characteristic deficiencies which they presumably could correct." Guided by the belief that architecture should continue to reflect with increasing accuracy democracy's social ideals, the urbanist numbered among his tasks the identification and correction of these deficiencies.

As the statements by Franzen and Johnson suggest, the dichotomy between "direct social action" and "the projection of architecture as a form of art" had its roots in the Modern tradition. It is to this tradition that one must turn to understand how the dichotomy came to exercise so strong an influence on many of the profession's "more intelligent members" in the period of Modernism's decline.

Speaking of Louis Sullivan, Mumford contended that perhaps an architect should not even attempt to transform the skyscraper into the "proud, soaring thing" Sullivan wanted to make it, because the commercial interests responsible for putting up such a building had no spiritual substance to speak of, hence no business competing with cathedrals. Nonetheless Sullivan's office buildings and banks raised the issue: can an architect actually reform the environment, or does he practice a language of metaphor, performing a cultural function that may help in some more elusive, spiritual way to reform those responsive to enlightened values? Can a building help move society measurably closer to its ideal, or must it remain no more than a symbolic beacon? Can it do both?

And how can it do either if a patron's mundane intentions are so clearly at odds with the architect's enlightened ideals? An architect might make his building's exterior honestly express its interior structure, but could his own high ideals amount to more than a decorative facade? Objectively appraised, how could this most cumbersomely material, publicly visible of all the arts hope to be more than sugar coating, a cynical exercise in public relations?

For Sullivan, for Wright, as for many European Modernists, the solution lay in polemical maneuvers that established the architect's right to create a poetic statement independent of the building's patron, or indeed of the very functions that a particular building might be commissioned to perform.

Yet to the degree that social reform was held a legitimate objective for architecture, such a solution was ultimately self-defeating: pushing architecture into the relatively rarefied realm of fine art only distanced the building farther from the social arena where the need for genuine reform was most evident. The consequences were sometimes more than faintly ridiculous, when not destructive: Le Corbusier erects a model industrial city in the strife-torn center of an Indian dust bowl; Wright turns an automobile ramp into an art museum, then sideswipes the viewer who comes to look at paintings; Gropius's pleas for artists to engage in humane, collective enterprise end up as a chilly, expensively catered Bauhaus reunion in the lobby of the Pan Am Building, New York's most insensitively sited skyscraper. Like speculative real estate, the Modern Future was auctioned off to the highest bidders to support the careers of those who had painted that future in radically different colors.

The paradox was that the more it became possible to conceive of architecture as an autonomous art, the more glaring became the discrepancies between the ideals to which this art was consecrated and the economic realities that brought forth the art objects—the buildings—themselves. It was one thing when a private house represented the unabashed patrician taste of a Vanderbilt, an Astor, or a Hearst, Americans whose architects professed no commitment to egalitarian ideals. It was quite another matter when a rich man's residence was designed by an artist who claimed to uphold the values expressed in the poetry of Walt Whitman or the paintings of Winslow Homer. And, as James Marston Fitch observed, "even Frank Lloyd Wright, for all his splendid display of nonconformism, did not really escape [being] the creature and prisoner of the wealthy. . . . He merely found patrons who were themselves rich nonconformists."

The more skillful Wright and other Modern architects became as poets of democracy, the more one was forced to take notice that they had offered themselves not as democracy's roving troubadours, at the service of twentieth-century lords, but as guardians of democratic decentralization of the traditional patron's authoritarian power. And while the resonance of their poetry had indeed earned them the right to appropriate the patron's artistic authority, they had shown themselves neither capable nor especially interested in carrying through their commitment to uphold the patron's social responsibility for the built environment as a whole.

The question was not, then, whether their beliefs were sincere, but whether their pursuit of artistic autonomy was not fundamentally antagonistic to the realization of their beliefs. In 1825 Robert Owen had gone to Indiana to build the Utopian community of New Harmony; when the town failed to materialize as the Holy City depicted in the renderings of his architect, Stedman Whitwell, Owen returned to England to work for social reform through direct political action. When the Utopian cities envisioned by Modern architects showed equally little promise, however, these men chose to invest their energies and talents not in social change but in the creation of Art Buildings for those wealthy enough to buy them.

To an Urbanist, a scheme like Broadacre City was offensive not simply because it was anti-city, but because it proposed the harmoniously constructed work of art as a paradigm for the built environment. The Urbanist challenged the cultural value of such a paradigm when examined outside the comparatively narrow scope of art history; and he insisted that architecture can and should be examined outside that scope.

On the surface the Modern urban Utopia appeared to indicate a strong social commitment on the part of its designer. But beneath its rosy rendering of the future, it suggested contempt for society in its determination to demolish rather than improve human settlements, and to replace them with art objects blown up to planetary proportions. The Utopia implied the architect's acceptance of a social contract in which he was granted permission to appropriate the traditional patron's artistic control in exchange for improving the environment of society as a whole. The Art Building abrogated this contract in settling for the opportunity to style the private environments of those who could afford them.

"*A city cannot be a work of art,*" wrote Jane Jacobs in 1961, a statement which, correct or not, focused on the precise point of Urbanism's divergence from Modernism. But in effect Urbanism began in an attempt to practice what Modernism had preached: to dislodge the authority of centralized power and wealth over the built environment and to distribute this authority on a more nearly equitable basis. Where Modern architecture succeeded in appropriating the patron's artistic authority, Urbanism evolved to assume social responsibility for the vast majority of the population who could not afford to build.

The Urbanist began by discovering that the city is not only the place where the sentiment of reform has traditionally been applied, but also the place where the social objective translated by Modern architects into artistic symbols should be rendered into actions more appropriate to the actual attainment of those aims. To the Urbanist, the central city was more essential to the course of architecture after than before urban decentralization, as the social inequities revealed by the suburban exodus made it all the more urgent that the spirit of reform should continue to guide architecture's evolution toward an environment more democratically constituted.

Within the decade after Wright's death, the decline of the central city did not, as he had predicted, fertilize the flowering of American democracy in the natural setting for which it had presumably always been destined. On the contrary, it unveiled publicly like a gaping wound how imperfectly America's social ideals were realized in the most highly visible of its cultural manifestations, the built environment.

The "we" who Henry Ford said "shall solve the City Problem by leaving the city" solved nothing at all, not even urban congestion, but rather dramatized the fundamental social problem by exposing all too vividly a "they" who could not afford to leave. Each highway built to pave the way for middle-class exodus made more inescapably glaring the defects and inequities of "the system" by whose authority the roads were paved. Decentralization made a reluctant Jacob Riis of every suburban commuter, of every urban architect and planner a potential "soft cop," in Robert Goodman's phrase, unwitting partner to policies geared "to prevent radical change and to perpetuate repression in the cities." And decentralization promised furthermore to spread these defects nationwide.

As the Art Building came to signify both disproportionate wealth and the subordination of social to aesthetic values, so the city became a symbol of the need to reexamine these priorities, of the need to translate Modern architecture's "great individual accomplishments into an appropriate common form," in Mumford's phrase, or at least into forms that appeared less eager to ignore the ideals our culture holds in common. As to Wright the city was "the crowded forest" from which the architect must escape to seek his artistic autonomy, so to the urbanist the city was an emblem of the social matrix from which the architect had irresponsibly strayed, to which he must be returned, dragged back kicking and screaming, if need be, from the impulse to make architecture "an event in itself."

Wright had created his "first truly democratic expression of our democracy in Architecture" at a moment when statistics were available to show that after a century and a half America had in fact made surprisingly little progress since colonial times toward economic equality. In his writings he sought to justify this imbalance by invoking Jefferson's concept of an American "aristoi" of the naturally gifted, conveniently overlooking the absence of the economic equality that Jefferson considered essential to the eventual attainment of this ideal.

If Wright's own genius was easily defensible on the grounds of "natural gifts," the economic privilege of his patrons—particularly when rendered by architecture into the illusion of a permanent class condition—was more problematic. And however appropriate it might be for an artist to draw upon democracy as a source of artistic symbols, there was ultimately no way for Wright to absolve himself from the admittedly unjust charge that architecture was itself symbolic of the inequities democracy had ostensibly been designed to overcome.

Though presented with hell-fire rhetoric, Broadacre City offered a completely passive picture of the ideal American life, without any suggestion for how it might be created, as if on the assumption that things somehow take care of themselves. (And indeed Wright lived long enough to witness his trinity of individualism–technology–laissez-faire presiding over the transmogrification of suburban sprawl.)

Yet instead of devising or even advocating actions that might have resulted in practical plans for ordered decentralization, like Mumford or Clarence Stein, Wright remained in thrall to the inner harmonies of his personal vision. Instead of lending his authority to those with the aptitude to work for social change, he pushed himself to center stage and unveiled the Air House and the Pre-Fabs, magical solutions designed to transform social problems into artistic ones. But artistic illusion was insufficient to house the homeless or make the architect's services available, even in the form of Pre-Fabs, to other than the "upper middle third of the democratic strata" that comprised Wright's clientele.

To the Urbanist, the Modern architect's failure to engage in efforts toward significant social change suggested that the architect actually preferred the creative tension between the real and the ideal to changes that might have relaxed this tension and thus robbed his art of resonance: in an actual Utopia, of course, thousands would not have trooped through the doors of Wright's Usonian House. Without the aptitude and will to uphold the priorities of social intervention, Wright could offer the Usonian House as no more than a cut-rate artistic emblem, a souvenir for cultural ideals that his own actions had discounted. And, except as an exhibition, like the Usonian House, the city had neither time nor space for symbols requiring so much distance from daily life. Their proper place was in a museum; and Wright's objective of artistic autonomy reaches its logical conclusion in the Wright Room where, shrunk to the tax-deductible dimensions of the precious work of art, the great continental vision of America "thought-built" is comfortably installed within the building he contemptuously called "that Protestant barn"—there to be shared by all.

In the Wright Room we perceive the architect's individualism not as the quaint throwback it once appeared to European Modernists and American Depression-Era intellectuals, but as a preview of excesses to come in a period when idiosyncrasy became an established norm. Genius in art may need no justification, but to some observers the legacy of artistic autonomy inherited by the post-Modern generation has been but sporadically justified. To Fitch, for example, the Modern achievement of "a personal idiom of artistic expression" attained individually by Mies, Wright, and Le Corbusier was permitted by their successors to degenerate into "various rationales of personal freedom which often [were] puerile, subjective and anti-rational."

At its extreme, the trend transcended the occasional architecture-for-architecture's-sake outbursts of Ronchamp and the Guggenheim to produce an even purer form of architecture-for-art's sake, as in sketches and collages marketed by art dealers on the premise that a thing to hang on the wall had at least as valid a claim to "architecture" as the wall itself. But even more conservative structures often appeared designed to elicit the wrath of the collective superego, to provoke those who, like Mumford on the Guggenheim, were quick to condemn architects who claim the "privileges of the painter and sculptor without fully accepting the responsibilities of their own profession."

To Fitch, the architect's professional responsibility was primarily social, yet at the same time indivisible from his innate formal gifts. In his view, "the internal logic and consistency of their artistic and ideological development" made possible the Modern architects' great individual achievements. And in carrying this ideological development forward into the 1960s and 70s, Urbanism often seemed to have inherited the cultural momentum of the Modern Movement.

Whether Urbanism made comparable progress in the area of artistic development is another matter; often it seemed to harbor a strongly philistine reaction against the architectural application of modern art. Yet it would be difficult to locate an artistically innovative building built in New York during this period with anything near the impact created by the Urbanist's efforts to preserve the city's fabric from the impact of all new buildings, innovative and otherwise. It would be difficult, say, to locate a new building that focused public attention on the subject of architecture as intensely as did the loss of older buildings, such as Penn Station, a focus sustained by the Urbanist's efforts to prevent a recurrence of such destruction by educating the public on the merits of existing architecture. It would be hard to find a purely "architectural" solution to the problems of urban housing that had so rejuvenating an effect on the city's residential architecture as the "anti-architectural" ideas published by Jane Jacobs in 1961.

These are sweeping statements; yet they do not greatly overestimate the scope of Urbanism's impact on the built environment during this period, nor exaggerate the authority with which Urbanism rekindled a sense of urgency and promise that had been gradually ebbing from architectural thought and practice since the earliest days of the Modern pioneers. New York in these years of perpetual crisis became an "incentive zone" to architects whose belief in architecture as the traditional vessel of a culture's most enlightened ideals was increasingly ill served by the continuing "projection of architecture as a form of art."

On the other hand, it would be naïve to suppose that architecture could be purged from the pages of art magazines and art history textbooks by the somewhat puritanical reforms Urbanism sought to effect; indeed a book like the one you are reading at the moment could not hope to engage the attention of a reader unaccustomed to hearing architecture identified and analyzed as an art form. A building may stick out awkwardly when sandwiched by an art historian between a painting and a sculpture, but we have long since found it a digestible combination. To insist that an artist in any culturally accepted form of art follow the dictates of his audience calls for a reversal of more than a century of established cultural tradition. Yet this was essentially a condition Urbanism sought to impose on architects: that they should seek not to lead but rather to follow the consumer preferences of those who use their buildings, like self-effacing market researchers. Surely it is no more reasonable to compel an architect toward explicit goals and programs than to insist that a writer, say, should harness his imagination to a machine for cranking out social propaganda.

Since society has hardly granted architects the power to engineer society, why should they conduct their aesthetic affairs as though they possessed this responsibility? Indeed, a recurring theme in Urbanist polemic was the suggestion that the architect be discouraged from active participation in social decisions, on the grounds that his natural orientation toward aesthetics could only pollute a sphere of action where less ethereal considerations should prevail. Thus Jane Jacobs's contempt for the "Radiant Garden City" visionaries ironically mirrored Wright's contempt for the "mere 'artistic activity' " of painters and sculptors unwilling to acknowledge the autonomous architect's hegemony over their own forms. The dictum that "a city cannot be a work of art" carried with it the implication that the aesthetically oriented architect should have his license restricted to confecting pleasure villas in the suburbs or intellectual constructs in the classroom; that only those whose artistic notions had been purged by years of exposure to street crime and overturned trash cans could be entrusted with the design of the public environment; that architecture is ultimately too important a matter to be left to architects, at least to architects who suppose that art has any greater relevance to architecture's primary function than had cake to the diet of the French Revolutionary mob.

Yet it can well be argued that there is actually no architect more pragmatic than the Art Builder who, by his very willingness to accommodate his talents to the economic status quo, has in fact worked to establish the relationship of architecture to the social matrix on a footing far more solid than the Urbanist's self-appointed advocacy for the socially disadvantaged. An Art Building by Michael Graves, Emilio Ambasz, or Robert Stern may seem escapist, but since the escape is at least accessible in visual, sensual form (if only in the pages of art magazines), is it any more cloud-cuckoo than the advocacy architect's vain yearning for radical change to overcome the environmental oppression of the urban masses? In seeking to broaden the social responsibilities of his profession, the urbanist may have gained the environment but lost the building; and in what medium save the building has the architect ever been competent to express himself in a manner any segment of the public, large or small, rich or poor, can find useful?

Richardson's Law conveys the extent to which American architecture has traditionally been governed by opportunism; but to break the law in favor of a more elevated moral authority was to forfeit the only opportunity an architect might be granted for insinuating even severely compromised ideals into the public environment, and after more than a decade of experimenting with environmental politics many architects of the Post-Modern period returned to the medium of the building as though to an oasis from a desert of good intentions.

We may admire the architect who chooses to maintain a scrupulous responsibility toward the needs of society as a whole, yet we are aware that this responsibility is his choice (as, say, a martyr freely chooses martyrdom), and that he can equally well make some other choice. The socially committed architect appeases our conscience, but conscience is very often a bore. While we might hesitate to applaud aloud the architect who sneers openly at the Mobocracy, we delight in the freedom of the artist unwilling to cramp his style in the pursuit of obsolete Utopian ends. One isolated individual building may do nothing to solve social problems, yet we cannot dismiss the suspicion that the creation of such buildings may offer the highest social service to which an individual architect may realistically aspire.

As citizens in a democracy we may be uncomfortable with the distinction between the "higher" and "lower" forms of architecture (the "cultivated" and the "vernacular," to use John Kouwenhoven's terms). Still, given that the architect has no uncommon social power at his disposal, it is difficult to imagine another course that architecture's democratization might have taken other than in the hands of gifted individuals who, by the very virtue of their gifts, have inevitably defined architecture as an art even when this ran counter to their own sincere intentions.

But perhaps the most convincing defense of the architect's autonomy would point out that had the Modernist not set out to attain it, the Urbanist himself would not subsequently have been in a position to challenge it, and to propound so confidently his own views on what tasks an architect ought to perform. The rage of the advocacy architect against the injustices of the System, for example, sprang from the same Romantic intellectual tradition that inspired an architect like Wright to claim his autonomy as an artist by magnifying his defiance of conventional practice.

Jane Jacobs's attacks on the Corbusian principles of city planning owe a great debt to Le Corbusier's conviction that an architect might produce a practical set of plans for environmental change independent of official patronage—that, indeed, his independence guaranteed the superiority of his plan to anything official. Just as Le Corbusier took evident pride in the exclusion of his Voisin Plan from the 1925 Paris exposition of decorative arts, so, with the first sentence of *The Death and Life of Great American Cities*, Jacobs launched her own proposal with the clarion confidence of the Romantic outsider:

This book is an attack on current city planning and rebuilding. It is also, and mostly, an attempt to introduce new principles of city planning and rebuilding, different from and even opposite from those now taught in everything from schools of architecture and planning to the Sunday supplements and women's magazines. My attack is not based on quibbles about rebuilding methods or hair-splitting about fashions in design. It is an attack, rather, on the principles and aims that have shaped modern, orthodox city planning and rebuilding.

And when Jacobs proceeds to evoke the colorful, intricate choreography of everyday street scenes as though they had been lifted intact from early Jerome Robbins ballets, who can doubt that her theories of urban design have been refined from a profound artistic, not to say literary, sense of what it means to live in the modern American city? In an age that can voice the sentiment, through the artist Claes Oldenburg, that "I am for an art that grows up not knowing it is art at all," who would deny that the statement "a city cannot be a work of art" represents a highly sophisticated aesthetic proposition?

Like Modernism, in other words, Urbanism can already be interpreted as an aesthetic phenomenon, the excitement of the modern city a sensation comparable to the thrill that Modern architects experienced in the presence of the Machine. The Urbanist's repudiation of Modern orthodoxy was, perhaps, an aesthetic act, as each generation defines the art of its time in reaction to that of the preceding generation. Moreover, Urbanism proved as susceptible as Modernism to having its egalitarian impulses subordinated to the consumer interests of the upper middle class. Through the application of such concepts as "planned shrinkage," "brownstoning," "recycling," and "urban pioneering," the ideological impetus behind urbanism helped to generate a market for the luxury commodities of "urban lifestyles," just as the socialist rhetoric of early Modernism was transmogrified into the bronze and travertine showcases of the International Style. It took almost forty years to go from the first Bauhaus manifesto to the Four Seasons; it took only half that time to go from Jane Jacobs's apotheosis of her humble corner grocer to his replacement by Bonjour, Croissant, and all that implies.

In the end Urbanism may have been less successful in giving a physical than an emotional form to the social values it sought to represent: of all forms perhaps the most vulnerable to the ironic twist of events. The question of which was "right"—the Urbanist or the Art Builder—was more than a little academic, so nearly did they resemble two sides of the same late

Romantic coin. But did the coin have any value apart from calling heads or tails in academic bets, whiling away the time while waiting for the chance to build?

Stripped of ideological intent and semantic associations, architecture is neither an art nor a branch of social service but a profession. Most practicing architects have more in common with doctors and lawyers than with painters or politicians, as little interest in creating Art Buildings or fomenting social change as in probating wills or setting broken bones. The conflict articulated in the Post-Modern period represented extremes, reverse sides of the slim, shiny coin invested in the philosophical interests of a profession that often prides itself on its imperviousness to philosophical extremes. Even so, it seems pertinent to the history of the profession during this period to ask why "many of its more intelligent members" were drawn away from professional practice into conspicuous ideological conflict.

In part, the conspicuousness of the conflict arose from its contrast with the comparative homogeneity of the Modern socio-aesthetic mixture. The Modern architect anticipated a future in which the environment would be progressively recast to reflect the underlying unity of democracy's social and artistic goals. His buildings were showcase pavilions designed to preview this approaching fusion of values. The machine would be perceived as an art work, the art work as a machine, or the product of a machine. The worker's house would be beautiful; all other buildings would be compelled to measure up to the honest beauty of the worker's house.

The Post-Modern generation inhabited a world in which the Modern future could be looked back on and retroactively assessed as an art movement that had produced a limited number of exquisite artifacts as detached from the world of everyday reality as were other significant works of art. Considered in the light of its designers' original expectations, the Modern future was a shabby wreck at best, at worst an aborted totalitarian nightmare. The machine was noisy and smelly; the worker wanted sham antiques. Somewhere between Berlin in the 1930s and New York in the 70s the artist had lost his solidarity with the worker, the SoHo painter had begun litigation to evict the hat maker from his loft building, and the Bauhaus ideal of an environment of integrated social and artistic values seemed as far removed from reality as the price of a Photorealist canvas from the price of a tasseled, mass-produced lampshade.

Yet in the aftermath of the Modern objective, we are often inclined to regard the breakdown of social and artistic unity in the built environment as a major cultural failing, the visible symptom, as it were, of a civilization whose center has not held. Relieved though we may be that the antiseptic Modern future did not come to pass, we cannot consider ourselves entirely exempt from the application of Auden's criterion of "unity retained" as a primary cultural standard. We are often compelled at least to analyze our inability to retain this unity in the built environment, if not to formulate solutions to recover it. Where did Modernism go wrong? How can we restore the balance between our social and artistic goals? Faced with the opportunity to create a new building, we can try adding a wheelchair-access entry here, a Henry Moore sculpture over there, but the result scarcely brings us nearer the social and artistic synthesis we retain as the ideal of advanced culture.

Perhaps the fault lies with the ideal. For to say that Art Buildings and Urbanism were two sides of the same coin is not to suggest that the conflict between them was without significance. But rather than signifying a general cultural failing, the socio-aesthetic conflicts in Post-Modern architecture may represent the most constructive response possible to a particular cultural need: if the profession's ambivalence toward social and artistic goals originated in the expectations generated by Modernism, an examination of its origins may help to show that the socio-aesthetic conflicts of the Post-Modern period were an inevitable consequence of the need to reform these expectations, to revise our conception of the tasks that architects perform.

In hindsight we observe that the Modern architect saw himself as heir to two conflicting cultural traditions. In one role he saw himself as the democratic heir to the aristocratic patron's position as society's form giver, a medium through which the social order passed into an enduring physical form. In his second role he came to regard himself as an autonomous artist, subject only to the laws of art, a virtuoso creator of precious objects, an inspired progenitor of noble visions.

It should not be surprising that the Modern architect found it difficult to reconcile these two roles, for while the first role called for him to assume the patron's traditional responsibility for articulating and preserving a stable social order, the second demanded that he often act in outright opposition to established social conventions, in the manner typical of Romantic artists. The first role was that of Regent or Protector; the second, that of revolutionary storming the walls of stale convention.

And indeed it could be said that, as an art movement, Modernism succeeded in provisionally reconciling these opposed tendencies only to the extent that it presented itself as the opposition party to the prevailing conventions of the early twentieth century (as visualized by the Beaux Arts, for example), and preached the overthrow of that order in the Romantic's traditional rhetoric. Once Modernism had managed to establish itself as a mainstream of contemporary culture, it ceased to satisfy the

Romantic needs of the autonomous artist and shortly passed, via the International Style, from a manifestation of creative vitality to a moribund convention to be opposed by a succeeding generation.

In its early years, Modernism's creative ferment permitted architects to gloss over the conflict between the two cultural roles to which they aspired. The understanding was that such conflicts would be resolved in the future. Perhaps architects would learn to collaborate; perhaps technology would make it possible—bridges and factories suggested this might be so; perhaps war would make it necessary; perhaps the catalyst would be economic collapse. Perhaps in some mystic manner as yet untapped by the western mind, it would be possible to be a genius and not show it. Would the future dare deny the aspirations of those who worshipped it so devoutly? Meanwhile, there was a whole past of accumulated culture to be abolished, cornices to be pulled down, pitched roofs to be flattened, winding roads to be straightened, curtains, lampshades and upholstered sofas to be confiscated: before the advent of the Modern Art Building, the cataclysmic vision was the sole outlet in which the geometrically precise, neoclassical conceptions of Modernism could express their Romantic hearts.

In retrospect, however, it seems fair to grant that the Modern architect's ideal preference was to align themselves with the first tradition—to become a neutral medium through which the culture of democracy would pass into its appropriate environmental forms. But history denied them this option, at least on the scale to which they aspired, because in a sense the tradition was as obsolete as the ancien regime. Who was there to say what were the appropriate forms? Even if all architects in the world were able to gather together in congress and agree on an appropriate international style, what power on earth existed to underwrite the agreement?

Only the power of art. The Modern search for a comprehensive, unified "style"—in Sullivan's case, a rule that would admit "no exceptions"; in Wright's case, a philosophy of Organic Architecture; in Gropius's case, a design methodology that would preclude the need for virtuosic genius—represented the hope that architecture might continue to express the cultural power it had received from the patron along with the unifying imprint of his artistic taste. It expressed the somewhat magical belief that, should architects somehow contrive to articulate an authoritarian style, they would be rewarded by their culture with authoritarian power—transformed, of course, into acceptably democratic terms.

And so, in a sense, they were rewarded. But only to a very limited extent, and only within the realm of art, and even then only if they managed somehow to break free from the constraints of a unifying style and define for themselves, as geniuses, a discernibly individual point of view.

Both Gropius and Wright professed spiritual affinities with the architecture of Japan and medieval Europe—not surprisingly, cultures of a rigid social hierarchy—yet each of them pursued an individual paradigm that effectively precluded the attainment of unity that these cultures manifested in their buildings. Wright would not have granted Le Corbusier a permit to erect a complex of Cartesian towers in downtown Broadacre City; Le Corbusier's Radiant City reserved no wilderness areas suitable for Wright's endless suburban sprawl. Mies van der Rohe's steel and glass vocabulary entered "the vernacular" only to the extent of one's ignorance that the grammar was distinctly "Miesian," and its failure to satisfy architects working without benefit of that ignorance revealed that a truly impersonal vernacular was hardly Modernism's major objective.

What was that objective? To retain architecture's traditional cultural power in a culture increasingly reluctant to grant it. If the explicit aim of Modernism was to make architecture more expressive of democratic ideals, the overriding objective was to husband architecture's power in the course of this transition.

Architects of many persuasions were agreed that the great social advance of democracy over aristocracy demanded an architecture worthy of that greatness. What was troubling was that conscious efforts to express democracy's greatness seemed invariably to lead toward proposals that perpetuated autocratic values. In this respect, at least, the urban Utopias envisioned by Wright, Le Corbusier, and Tony Garnier were almost indistinguishable from the mock-imperial pomp of Washington, D.C., the White City, and the City Beautiful Movement, phenomena Modern architects universally deplored.

Democracy inspired scores of individual architects to contemplate vast visions of whole continents transformed into harmonious ensembles designed to rededicate the built environment to democratic ideals. The paradox was that in attempting to convey democracy's grandeur they proved unable to avoid evoking the values of cultures that democracy had ostensibly been undertaken to replace. Again and again it appeared that democracy in the built environment was expressed not by the degree of control architects were able to retain, but by the degree of autonomy they were compelled to surrender. Democracy in architecture fell somewhere between anarchy and totalitarianism. It expressed itself in windows and cornices that almost but not quite matched each other; in insensitively sited new buildings that suddenly ruined long-cherished views; in the restless cycle in which ideal building formulas were widely promoted, then swiftly abandoned.

For a time Greece offered the vocabulary of forms most appropriate to democracy; then the ideal source was Rome; then Romanesque. On Sundays architecture was content to be Gothic; during the week, the Italian town palazzo made a handsome club. One moment a bridge was raw engineering; the next, clad in architectural masonry; the following year, it reverted to structural steel but retained its status as "architecture." It was difficult to tell if that tall structure off in the distance was a smokestack or a church. Up close, it was impossible to tell which structure had tapped the greatest cultural power: the church, which was architecture, or the chimney, which was not. Towns that were planned for beauty were rarely if ever as impressive as towns that were planned for greed; nor could the fault be laid at the feet of their designers.

The effect of American architecture could be exhilarating, but by any existing standard of architectural greatness one was encouraged to conclude that the general effect of American democracy was to weaken the architect's power: to weaken his control over his own medium, and to weaken the power of the medium itself to represent in enduring, harmonious form the social and aesthetic values with which Americans sought to endow their culture.

There was, however, one area of activity in which the architect could continue to function more or less according to the traditional standards, one realm in which the architect could perpetuate the power he had enjoyed under the autocratic patron. This area was art. As Freud wrote,

In only a single field of our civilization has the omnipotence of thoughts been retained, and that is in the field of art. Only in art does it still happen that a man who is consumed by desires performs something resembling the accomplishment of those desires and that what he does produces emotional effects—thanks to artistic illusion—just as though it were something real. People speak with justice of the "magic of art" and compare artists to magicians. But the comparison is perhaps more significant than it claims to be. There can be no doubt that art did not begin as art for art's sake. It worked originally in the service of impulses which are for the most part extinct today. And among them we may suspect the presence of magical purposes.

The consuming desire of the Modern architect was that his work retain the power it had once derived from association with the actual omnipotence of the patron's thoughts, and this desire could find its fulfillment only in art. As the Modern Utopia demonstrated, the aesthetic choice became a kind of substitute for the decision of state. The Utopia was a magical instrument that enabled the architect to retain in the realm of art the power that, in the social sphere, had become as nearly extinct as the political apparatus that had once supported it.

To paraphrase Freud, Modern architecture did not begin as architecture-for-architecture's sake. Modern architects did not drift unaccountably into art, nor did they seek cynically to subordinate architecture's social function to their own glory as creative artists. Rather, they gravitated inevitably toward art because only in the sphere of art could the architect retain— as purely aesthetic concepts—the values of unity and stability with which architecture had traditionally expressed the patron's power.

Unfortunately, as Europeans were quick to appreciate, architecture in American democracy did not derive its power from unity and stability. It derived its power from diversity and change, from energy that perpetually broke through the restraints of unity and stability toward the exuberant state of multiplicity and flux. It is this energy that, before Wright, had defeated all attempts to arrive at a workable formula for an architecture appropriate to American civilization. If Wright's philosophy of Organic Architecture was more successful than earlier attempts, this was due, in part, to the fact that Organic Architecture was not itself a "workable formula," at least not one others could apply, but rather a formula singularly appropriate to Wright.

Diversity and change were two of the essential qualities of democratic culture to which Broadacre City was designed to give form. A "unity in diversity," a principal clause in the American social contract, was the Usonian motto. American culture was destined to attain its highest common denominator through each citizen's pursuit of his own individual sovereignty. Diversity meant a perpetual declaration of independence; free will; the rejection of the center outside the self. It meant faith that all lines do meet, or at least if permitted to run long enough form invariably harmonious patterns; that in individual liberty lies the only reliable basis for true social order. Additionally, in Wright's case, diversity meant eccentricity; free love as well as artistic freedom; and the belief that among the diverse cast of democratic characters stood a few individuals—prophets, avatars, members of the Jeffersonian aristoi—uniquely gifted to perceive the harmony of the whole and to lead by their original example those less gifted toward its earthly fulfillment.

Like the evolution of life on earth, diversity was predicated on change. Change implied the identification of American culture with the evolution of life itself, the natural progress of America toward the fulfillment of its cultural destiny in a New World, organic growth as a paradigm for ordering that progress. Change was almost always for the best. Change meant optimism; limitless possibilities for "going out" and "moving on"; mobility— social, physical, and psychological; the infinite perfectibility of man; progress, the spiral, the car; the Adventurer riding the crest of America's global prestige toward horizons that wouldn't stop until everyone reached a happy ending; housing starts; the electric maid; the atomic elevator; profit as an index of virtue; faith that the Creator smiled on America as he smiled on the human being, that because we were a good people we deserved to be a great one, that the finest measure of this greatness and proof of goodness would be the environment transformed for the benefit of all who would simply believe; man in possession of his earth; Eden regained; lay-away heaven.

Broadacre City was Wright's plan for the conceptual democratization of architecture. It proposed the visionary means by which the American architect could unite his social and artistic functions into a "harmony of the whole." Its strategic purpose was not so much to make architecture accessible to the masses as to guard architecture's cultural importance against the dilution that accessibility seemed to threaten. It argued, in fact, that democracy should not weaken but on the contrary should strengthen this importance; that if one could only stand back far enough one could view the entire American continent as a cathedral beside which Wright's 1926 steel behemoth loomed no larger than a glinting shard of glass.

The symbolism was transparent, the theory made sense: the city stood for centralized power and authority in the modern secular state, and decentralization stood for the breakup of that authority through the democratic process. To escape the crowded forest was not merely to flee from congestion, crime, and filth, but to repudiate the authoritarian values of Old World cultures in favor of democratic values.

In this allegorical tableau, Wright's autonomy as a creative artist—"the tree that escaped"—was a metaphor for the freedom that American democracy guaranteed all its citizens. But presented as a practical set of plans for environmental change, Broadacres preached the reverse: Wright employed his genius to will himself into the position of the repudiated autocrat. In his conception of the Architect as Legislator, and, above all, in his belief that a country might attain the harmonious proportions of a work of art, the artist and the despot simply changed places. Like many of those who could afford to move to the suburbs in the 1930s, 40s, and 50s, Wright left the city not to embrace democracy, but to escape it.

One of the major ironies of urbanization, of course, is that while decentralization has been on the whole far more chaotic than the most dedicated anarchist could possibly hope for, suburban culture has been far more thoroughly homogenized, and centrally determined, than that of the old central cities. One can hardly hold Wright responsible for the unprecedented concentration of influence and wealth in the hands of the industrial conglomerates that fashion, produce, and distribute the goods, services, manners, and morals of decentralized urban America. But Wright did fall prey to a similar irony, for while Broadacre City correctly anticipated decentralization as the viable form of the urban future, it presented an atavistic, wholly autocratic conception of architecture, the intellectual equivalent of ITT.

Wright sought a comprehensive, organically unified master plan that would allow an architect the maximum possible expression of diversity and change. Yet while extolling these virtues in theory, he failed to understand that in practice his master plan could only obstruct their free expression, for "unity" would invariably overrule "diversity" whenever "the harmony of the whole" was threatened by outbursts of spontaneity he had not himself foreseen and planned for. Like calculated spontaneity, Wright's "unity in diversity" emphasized the former at the expense of the latter. Those with a preference for the diversity of the central city risked being locked up in some provincial St. Mark's Tower.

As with diversity, so with change. The result of trying to design for change was static, lifeless, an endless monotony of landscape, an entropy of leveled affluence, the boredom of a continent under glass, as rigid in its attempt to integrate the man-made environment with nature as were Le Corbusier's attempts to keep the two apart. Like unified diversity, planned change was a concept that neutralized itself for no apparent purpose other than to establish the architect as a kind of deity who alone could sense the patterns of diversity, the objectives of change.

In the endless plans and models for Broadacre City, Wright experimented with pouring the "new" ideas of diversity and change into the "old" molds of unity and stability; but not even a mold the size of the globe—Broadacre's ultimate dimension—was sufficient to contain the ideas that he properly identified as American architecture's appropriate ideological foundation. The city did possess these values; and in leaving the city, Wright pursued not the new values but the old ones.

In the assumption that an architect could conceive a master plan for diversity and change, Broadacre City was Wright's application for a position that was no longer available—not to an architect, not to a democratically elected chief of state. It was the projection of a wish that architecture could make a smooth transition from aristocratic to democratic culture without sacrificing one iota of the power an aristocrat's architect could vicariously command.

Like the White City before and Disney World after, Broadacre City yearned for a period in which architects might indeed be granted the power to fuse the social and artistic values of their culture into a comparatively unified, comprehensive, and stable environment—in effect, to approximate a durable synthesis between their culture's art and life. But in a democracy, to Wright's chagrin, there was no authority who could beckon to the enlightened architect and decree: yes, this is the form I would like my culture to possess, now and into the future; these are the avenues down which I would like to observe my power radiate outward to the farthest end of my domain. Apart from Disney World and world's fairs, there was no market for unity, no cultural impulse sufficiently strong to implement the one keystone of insight that would cement the whole into harmony, no realistic expectation that intelligence or power together or separately could institute the kind of plan Wright wished to author.

Instead there were "special interests": car manufacturers who wanted interstate highways immediately; real estate speculators who wanted easy access to cheap land; war veterans returned from Europe with a government willing to provide them with the means to purchase houses; public relations consultants who advised their clients to build the world's tallest building; civic boosters who wanted their city to be the twentieth-century Athens, Rome, Paris, Vienna; social reformers clamoring for parks and sunlit streets.

The architect with a talent to express, and with access to the costly materials with which to express it, might expect to work for any of these groups; but the architect who wished to serve democracy could not expect to consolidate their conflicting interests into a harmonious unity. And the architect who sought the autonomy of the creative artist served yet another special interest group, a constituency of critics, curators, patrons, and intellectuals with class interests of their own.

An architect might compose forms and ideas from his culture into a project his culture might at some level accept as a work of art, but he could not delude himself indefinitely that the talent for such work was equivalent to, or a substitute for, a determination to deal directly with his culture's social issues. And an architect might persuasively argue that his profession should more aggressively pursue solutions to social problems, but he had no right to complain if his arguments secured him neither commissions nor a place in architectural history. Above all, perhaps, the architect had to confront the probability that his efforts to reconcile aesthetics and sociology in a unified form would succeed in inverse ratio to the scale of the project. Well might Wright boast that La Miniatura had exacted as much time and care as the world's largest cathedral, given that his reputation was substantially founded on his intuitive understanding that only the small private house (ideally the architect's own) could provide the American architect with the opportunity to create the socio-aesthetic synthesis the cathedral had symbolized.

Yet this exclusion from the public sphere—the traditional sphere of great architecture—was hardly something the self-annointed "greatest architect of all time" was prepared to accept without protest. And if the original 1935 set of Broadacres drawings was, as Hitchcock suggested, Wright's commemorative catalogue of the projects that went unbuilt during the lean middle years, the final 1958 set of drawings lamented the passing of a world, a kind of environment, that no architect in a democratic culture would ever be able to build no matter how many commissions he received in his long life. No matter that he was regarded as the greatest master in his field, that his name was a household word; he could not hope to impose the harmony of art upon the pluralistic whole without subverting the culture whose qualities he sought to express.

When Wright advised his young married clients to go out "ten times as far as you think you ought to go ... You will find you never can go far enough," perhaps he had in mind the tall power masts that had begun to march across his own Arizona ranch to provide electricity for the suburban developments spreading north from Phoenix. Very few of these potential southwestern Usonians proved to be clients, however, and in the mid-50s Wright sued the county in an unsuccessful attempt to have the eyesores removed.

But just as Wright could not escape urbanization, not even in the desert, so he could not escape Urbanism. Indeed, his own efforts to contain urbanization within the architect's strict control in Broadacre City could only accelerate the emergence of Urbanism by demonstrating the impracticality—indeed the irrelevance, of designing a city—a continent—the world—as though each represented a potential work of art. In reality, decentralization was to Wright himself nothing more than a source of personal irritation; and while he no more intended to contribute to Urbanism than an oyster hopes to produce a pearl, his aggressive ventures into the field of urban design proved the inadequacy of art to deal with the complex social issues brought about by urbanization.

That he came to understand and possibly regret his own role in the emergence of Urbanism may partly explain his motivation to design Mile-High Illinois, the 528-story skyscraper unveiled two years before his death. It is almost as though, on second thought, Wright wanted to take it all back, to recall all of Broadacre City and compress it into one single monument, a megastructure that possessed the monstrous scale of the megalopolis but delivered it into the hands of a single architect—like the steel and glass cathedral that inaugurated Wright's urban work. It was as though he had somehow finally sensed that there was no practical way to reconcile architecture to democracy without sacrificing his own artistic interests, no true way to cultivate diversity without relinquishing his absolute control over unity, no way he could ever retain control over "the harmony of the whole" except in the design of the individual building.

But however tall and futuristic, Mile-High Illinois was too little, too late. Urbanism could not be halted by Wright's recall, any more than urban problems would be solved by another generation's experiments with mega-structures and new towns. Just as it was impossible to reverse urbanization, so it was pointless to resist the Urbanist's demand that architecture return to the social matrix from which the Modernist had strayed.

Wright himself could not resist it. Unwilling as he may have been to carry out his threat to move to Taliesin the Third, neither would he re-linquish the pied-à-terre at the Plaza. The effectiveness with which Broad-acre City's autocratic form neutralized its democratic content never succeeded in resolving Wright's ambivalent conception of architecture. Drawn to the city again and again as a matrix of the social values he wished to adopt as the content of his art, he had each time to reject the city as a threat to the organic unity of his art's form. While the building must escape the crowded forest in order to come into its own, the architect himself must return to the city repeatedly, irresistibly attracted, as though aware that without the city as a source of nourishment, even as a source of discomfort, there could be no "tree" hardy enough to make the escape.

Wright's dilemma was at once a personal conflict and a reflection of the dualistic nature of the profession with which he had identified himself so completely as to become, in his culture's eyes, its very personification. His ambivalence toward New York was keyed to a duality he would never resolve: the social and artistic values that coexist in architecture could be neither synthesized nor divorced. They could not be permanently unified in stable harmony, any more than the Guggenheim Museum and the Usonian House could occupy the same site at the same time. One must invariably supplant the other in an endless round of competing priorities.

Wright's attempt to reconcile the conflict between his social and artistic objectives arrived at no final solution that other architects could use as a model. In retrospect, however, it served the significant purpose of pointing toward the cultural contradictions confronting the architects who would follow him. Even though Wright's Utopian solution to the socio-aesthetic conflict looked back with obvious yearning to the authoritarian means with which environmental unity had been ordered by great architecture in the past, his absorption by this conflict in his later years anticipted the fractured development of architecture in the Post-modern period.

One reason, perhaps, for the renewal of interest in Wright's work at a time when orthodox European Modernism was widely subject to revisionist scorn is that he probed far deeper than the Modernists into the conceptual problems raised by their common objective to recast architecture in a democratic image. He traveled farther because he traveled alone. Victor Hugo's predictions notwithstanding, Wright's career was never accommodated by so tidy a historical dialectic as that exploited by the Europeans in their campaign to establish an International Style. His Oak Park practice began too late and too brilliantly to permit him to stand (and fall) with Sullivan in the battle against Burnham and the American Renaissance. And while profound philosophical differences did separate Wright from the Europeans, he and they so little formed a true polarity that historians have found no difficulty in establishing Gropius, Mies, Le Corbusier, and Wright as the supreme Modern quartet.

Yet Wright's isolation from the Modern Movement spoke for more than the accidental timing of his birth; it spoke as well for the happenstance nature of his culture. It reflected his position in a culture with no strong tradition of legitimate central authority capable of ordering the environment by design, no tradition that could be called upon and directed to mold architecture systematically toward legibly democratic ends. While the mere fact of Wright's United States citizenship might lend at least shaky support to the contention that his work embodied ideas more purely democratic than those prevailing in contemporary Europe, by the same token his culture held out less hope that he or any other American architect or group of architects could ever decree a "democratic architecture" on the imperial scale of projects envisioned by the designers of democracies less pure.

Wright's advocacy of decentralization, like his antipathy toward New York, reflected the belief that centralized authority was incompatible with the cultural imperatives of democracy, a belief European Modernists did not share. Le Corbusier may have wished to remake the architecture of Paris, but it did not occur to him that Paris itself, in any form, was the problem. Le Corbusier's task was to realize the style of building appropriate to the age, as generations of European architects had done before him. But just as America had no Paris, no official center of culture, so Wright's society had never produced an official style with which it felt comfortable, nor had its architects enjoyed the security of knowing it their task to fashion one.

In the absence of a supporting school, shared ideology, historical movement, or authoritarian tradition, Wright's recourse was to absorb within himself the social and artistic objectives his culture expected him to achieve. To the disgust and delight of his critics, architecture and personality merged. The dualistic nature of his medium assumed the character of a perpetual identity crisis, an unceasing struggle between the "known radical" and the "cause conservative"; the Romantic genius and the County Architect; the Adventurer and the Cave Dweller; the bohemian rebel and the medium of pure mind through which the soul of American democracy would reveal its most enlightened values in architectural form. These dualisms anticipated an ambivalence in the American architect's cultural role that became increasingly visible as Modernism receded, dimming with its passage the equally authoritarian vision of the future with which it had equipped a generation of architects with a fused sense of social and artistic purpose.

With his flowing capes and Bunthorne haberdashery, Wright was intermittently an aesthete but never an aesthetician. Nor was he an ironist, a master of paradox, a mystic poet of sublime ambiguity, much less an introspective neurotic paralyzed by inner turmoils of psychic ambivalence. He was an architect who dealt masterfully with the concrete forms of building, an aggressive absolutist convinced beyond the shadow of occasional doubts of the cultural importance of his calling. It was only when he followed that calling away from the plastic form of the individual building toward his architectural vision of an entire civilization that his work became subject to paradox, irony, contradiction, ambiguity, and ambivalence. In the Prairie Houses, limiting himself to materials and methods he understood and could authoritatively command, Wright produced masterpieces accessible to all who might view them, an achievement clear and unambiguous, even in photographs. In Broadacre City, releasing his imagination in a torrent of ambiguous metaphor, he produced designs which even he was unable to identify as either pipe dream or plan.

Yet for anyone as determined as Wright to produce Great Architecture, this was an inevitable direction for his calling to take. In architecture, quantity is a quality. It was one of Wright's greatest achievements to recognize and so treat the private middle-class house as the natural unit of American democratic architecture; yet it is understandable that after Oak Park he never remained fully satisfied with this achievement: what child brainwashed in the nursery by prints of the great European cathedrals could fulfill his adult destiny in the American suburbs? However sincerely Wright might insist that more care, skill, and effort went into building La Miniatura than had been expended on either St. John the Divine or the Woolworth Building, La Miniatura was still La Miniatura, neither a cathedral nor a cathedral of commerce but a two-bedroom bungalow in Pasadena. The small-house problem might well be the noblest challenge to which the American architect might rise, but what would the noble architect who solved it have to his credit? A lot of small houses.

Great Architecture wasn't just big buildings, however; it was architecture with a public profile, a visible social function. By tradition, Great Architecture had served—or aspired to—the function of defining a civilization's social values and relationships through the harmonizing powers of art. But the issue Wright faced was whether his own civilization had not shattered that tradition permanently, or at least transformed its face past all recognition. In aristocratic cultures, Great Architecture was public architecture, to be shared by an entire, albeit a highly stratified, society; indeed part of its function was to articulate and stabilize the stratification. Yet while democracy might indeed make it possible for the wide spectrum of society to share more fully in "the good life," one of the good things of which it progressively deprived society—and its architects—was Great Architecture as it had been traditionally designed. In America, Great Architecture was increasingly privatized, limited to the few who could afford to build it, extended to the many in the form of fantasy: movies, television, art books, shelter magazines, and world's fairs.

Public Works: A Dangerous Trade was the title Robert Moses gave his autobiography, and public architecture presented the commissioner's distant cousin with dangers of his own. Where Moses faced threats to his political power, Wright risked the loss of artistic power, for to enter the public environment was to encounter threats to the hope that the harmony of the whole could ever be extended beyond the front doorstep of a Wright-designed house.

That the Wright-designed house had become the accepted vernacular helped little. As Mumford observed, Wright's pioneer inventions had been absorbed by his culture (which was flattering) to the extent that their author's name was no longer popularly linked to them (which was problematic). What was more disturbing was that the culture that had absorbed them utilized them for social and economic purposes over which art held no sway. As decentralization proceeded, Wright not only saw the open floor plan ruined by "inferior desecrators." He also saw the landscape desecrated by the exercise of the very principles—individual autonomy, enterprise, escape from the crowd—from which his vision had been inspired.

If in Oak Park his goal had been simply to build the perfect house, his greater mission now became to recall the promiscuous proliferation of his forms from the disorder of decentralization back to the order they had obeyed under his command as architect of the individual building. An irresistible manifest destiny of mind beckoned him to expand his vision away from the safe, ordered haven of the building in an apparent effort to encompass by the magical instrument of art the disordered developments of life. He expanded the scale of his art to keep pace with a society that had absorbed the inventions of his earlier years and applied them to uses incompatible with his artistic vision, with the harmony of the whole. He projected a world made safe for his houses and for the democracy of which those houses represented the ideal artistic incarnation. In theory each Wright-influenced house should have represented the gradual advance of his vision over the continent; in practice each suburban subdivision drew the continent ever farther from the vision, and in later years Wright often seemed to return to the design of the private house as though in retreat, seeking a refuge from the frustrations of failing to integrate the house with the society whose values the house purported to express.

Wright's attitude toward democratic civilization resembled that of the Modern Movement toward industrial technology. To the Modernists the Machine was analogous to an absolute monarch whom it was their duty, as respectful ministers, to enlighten. They recognized the Machine's power to determine the social values and relationships of their age, yet they aspired to do more than produce discrete works of art to celebrate its power and impact. They sought rather to harness its power and direct its impact toward appropriate social and artistic goals. And they found, in due course, that technology was not simply raw energy at their disposal, but a phenomenon with its own laws and patterns of development that could not be wrenched by artists into congruity with the laws and patterns of art. The ironies occasioned by their determination to do so were sometimes mirthful, sometimes cruel: "machines for living" unable to perform such basic functions of human habitat as keeping out the rain; "scientifically" configurated housing projects that invited record levels of crime and deviant social behavior.

Similarly, it was Wright's goal not merely to be inspired by democracy to produce architectural sonnets dedicated to its glory, like Fallingwater, but to devise epic forms capable of molding the raw social impulses of "the masses" into an entire environment worthy of its spirit and power. Like industrial technology, whose destructive power and creative potential Wright also recognized, democracy represented a social phenomenon that must destroy the forms of the past and lead to the creation of new forms. Wright placed himself at the fountainhead of this creative process. But what he learned from the middle years forward is that his society was unable to offer him the means to create forms on a scale comparable to those of aristocratic cultures, much less on the scale he deemed suitable to democracy's greatness. Rather, the social values of American democracy had bred a public architecture seemingly impervious to the power of art to give it form. Like technology, democracy had its own rules, and Wright's attempts to substitute the rules of art for the social values of democracy produced cruel ironies as the dream of ordered decentralization gave way rapidly and irrevocably to the eyesores of suburban sprawl.

In a sense, of course, Wright's "public buildings" were redundant: his private houses were designed to give the public what he considered its ideal form—each member severed from the mass and enshrined in individual sovereignty. The irony was that, in trying to give this form, in Broadacre City, the character of a truly public environment, Wright withdrew even farther into the private recesses of his imagination. Despite the handful of major public buildings he did manage to build, he entered the social sphere of Great Architecture chiefly within the fantasy projections of his own mind.

One such projection, Mile-High Illinois, is perhaps the project that best sums up Wright's attitude toward public architecture. Though the work was self-commissioned, by his widow's account Wright carried out the designs somewhat grudgingly, in reluctant recognition of society's unreformable impulse to gather together for "mental exercises" and "mutual assassinations." The result suggested a belated revenge on the city of Chicago for permitting the failure of Wright's greatest work of public architecture, Midway Gardens, more than forty years before. Notable as a monument to Wright's ego, the skyscraper was also a supreme gesture of his contempt: if people must gather together, he seemed to say, then at least let them take up the least possible amount of space on the earth's surface whenever they do so. Let them do it all in one place, all at one time. Let them be "pig-piled" up to a height where perhaps vertigo will cure this unwholesome desire for spontaneous human contact.

Like the chain of St. Mark's towers proposed for Broadacre City, Mile-High Illinois—sealed off, air pressured—was conceived as an awesome, Piranesi-like reformatory for those unwilling to wean themselves from the human contact characteristic of urban life. But the only way Wright could truly protect the harmony of the whole was by abolishing the public environment altogether. In Broadacre City the public environment was "everywhere and nowhere," that is to say nowhere—except possibly the highway, where people traveled in separate cars safely isolated from the risks of direct social contact. In Paris, Haussmann had laid down broad boulevards to facilitate the swift dispersal of angry mobs; in Broadacres, Wright decreed scenic highways so that the "mobocracy" would not be tempted to alight from their cars.

To what extent was Wright aware that the vision of decentralization had gone hopelessly sour, and to what extent was he prepared to admit it? Alvar Aalto recalled that in the 1950s, when he was living in the United

States, he accompanied Wright on a drive through the expanding suburbs of Boston. Wright smiled beatifically, extended a magisterial hand out over the passing landscape, and proudly exclaimed, "All this I have made possible."

"And you know," Aalto later commented, "I just couldn't see it." But what did Wright see in the emperor's new city? Did he imagine that what others saw as the mounting heap of "God's own junkyard" was actually the blossoming Broadacres of his dream—whistling in the dark as he drove through the blinking neon twilight of his vision? Or did he suppose he could bring the BosNyWash megalopolis to order by driving through it as on a royal progress, alighting from his Cherokee Red Lincoln Continental now and then to command a wayward Usonian to "turn that garbage off" and tune to Aaron Copland? Had he invested so much in the vision that he could allow no unsightly facts to mar it in his mind's eye, even as the gap between the vision and the fact grew wider?

No Modernist urban Utopia, certainly, was ever so closely emulated by reality on such a scale; yet the very resemblance of reality to the vision did not so much vindicate the vision as magnify reality's defects (and indict the architect for endorsing so tawdry a reality). How could Wright miss them? "All this I have made possible"—how could an intelligent person say such a thing and keep a straight face? It is as though Einstein had beamed over Hiroshima. Didn't the Adventurer in Wright want to roar with laughter at the thought that the greatest architect of all time had made possible the conversion of America's natural paradise to an asphalt continent of Holiday Inns, Tastee-Freeze stands, automobile graveyards, billboards, smog, tract housing, mortgaged and franchised coast to coast?

To a succeeding generation, it was not the reality but the vision that appeared defective. Architects came to admire the architecture of the highway precisely for its perfect innocence of high artistic aspirations, its blissful ignorance of Utopian intentions, above all, perhaps, for its ironic contrast with the inflated ideas they had been taught to regard, by such examples as Wright, as inseparable from their responsibilities as architects.

Wright himself showed no such sense of irony. Stalking the highways of America at midcentury, he was alternatively a wrathful Isaiah, fulminating against the Mobocracy for its perversion of his ideas, and a gaga Jehovah, pottering about the wasteland to which the American Adam of the twentieth century had been expelled, muttering aloud, at least to Alvar Aalto, that he had made it and it was good.

But if Wright saw no irony in the transmogrification of Broadacre City into postwar suburban sprawl, it was perhaps because Broadacres was not really about cities, not about suburbs, nor buildings, nor planning, nor highway beautification. It was primarily about the architect. It was a meditation on the condition of the architect in American democracy, on the transformations that democracy had worked upon his cultural role, on the values he was given to express, on the avenues along which he might (and might no longer) proceed to express them. It was about the unprecedented position in which he was placed by the recurring conflict between his culture's social and artistic values as represented in its public environment.

Like Wright's capital city of the future, the American architect was himself everywhere and nowhere. Neither an autonomous artist nor an anonymous civil engineer, neither a statesman nor a decorator, neither an accountant nor a philosopher, the architect was expected to perform the tasks of these and other specialists, and to give them a united, harmonious form besides. His cultural position was ambiguous at best, his professional condition subject to recurring conflicts between the social and artistic functions into which the tasks he performed could be roughly divided.

It was occasionally noted that Wright tended to treat his clients as though they were his guests; it might be more accurate to say that he treated them as his subjects. He had dislodged the patron from his traditional position of authority and in his place substituted the authority of his own genius. And when he turned his attention from the individual building to the public environment in which the traditional patron had erected his greatest works, he found his genius powerless to create architecture, and so in its place he created the architect. In place of the means to create buildings, he found only the means to create a platform from which to criticize, from the lofty detachment of the artist of genius, the society it had been the traditional architect's duty to mold and to serve. In place of public architecture, he created the public persona of the architect. Succeed as he might in becoming "the greatest architect of all time," he must confront the likelihood that *his* time could give him no real work to perform in the public sphere of traditional Great Architecture save that of publicly performing the role of the "greatest architect of all time."

If the establishment of the architect as a quasi-autonomous artist had been the manifest concern of Wright's "first career," in the second he was drawn to examine the consequences of that objective, the cultural consequences of his alienation from the social matrix that had traditionally endowed Great Architecture with the physical forms of social cohesion that his individual buildings might allude to symbolically but could not tangibly provide. He found that the architect might well carry a "harmony of the whole" around in his head, as might a religious, a political, or an industrial leader, but that he stood no better chance than they of imposing this harmony upon the whole of his culture. Indeed, he had stacked his own odds against himself: his claim to artistic autonomy compelled him to regard his own inner harmony as unresolvably dissonant with that of the society he surveyed.

"In the view initiated by romantic sensibility," Susan Sontag observed, ". . . art becomes a statement of self-awareness—an awareness that presupposes a disharmony between the self of the artist and the community. Indeed, the artist's effort is measured by the size of its rupture with the collective voice (of 'reason')." To Wright, the Romantic sensibility and the spirit of American democracy were one and the same. Yet he apparently never paused to reflect on the extent to which his "rupture" from the community, provoked by his Romantic impulses as an artist, had disqualified him as a mouthpiece for the collective voice. He never quite grasped, that is to say, the fact that his conception of democracy harbored so profound a contradiction between its social and artistic objectives, nor that this contradiction in turn had radically altered the architect's cultural role as an interpreter of these objectives to his society. The *lack* of self-awareness was itself ironic, for no one had contributed more than Wright to the shaping of this role, and no one performed it more brilliantly.

Utopianism is an art of the impossible that sometimes discloses possibilities unobserved by those who practice it. Broadacre City was a "statement of awareness" by an architect only partially aware of the possibilities suggested by his own proposal. Broadacres's everywhere/nowhere ambiguities revealed what Wright's thundering self-righteous absolutism could at best only temporarily conceal; the cultural insecurity of the architect in a period of cultural flux, a time when it was less constructive for him to deliver final answers than to ask searching questions about what tasks his society might reasonably expect him to perform. Wright's urban theories, so instrumental in the years of his personal transition from Oak Park through depression to international fame, represented in addition his major effort to adjust to a profound transition in the architect's cultural role.

In Broadacre City one encounters Wright making a heroic effort to maintain the formal connection between the social and artistic programs of public architecture, striving to heal, or at least to span, the breach that Romanticism had opened up between them. One sees a passionate Romantic engaged in the futile attempt to solve the very problem Romanticism had caused. But the historical significance of Wright's urban theories is not that they failed to resolve the conflict between architecture's social and artistic goals, but that they exposed it. One implication of his efforts was that the socio-aesthetic conflict was not a problem to be solved, at least not by the individual architect of genius, but was rather a condition every

American architect had to live with. And perhaps the ultimate implication was not that these goals *couldn't* be harmoniously reconciled in the public environment, but that they *shouldn't* be: that the public environment was the open forum that democracy had set aside for the open airing of its major cultural conflicts, not for the harmonious resolution that only an individual building might provisionally attain.

Imagine a sequence of American urban design that would begin, say, with L'Enfant's plans for the city of Washington (1791) and end with Robert Venturi's statement that "Main Street is almost all right." About halfway along this imaginary continuum, make a mark indicating the Chicago Columbian Exposition of 1893. Imagine, in other words, an approach to urban design that begins with an imported plan for a permanent imperial city, to be executed in classical forms and durable marbles, that continues through the physical representation of such a city in materials designed to last no more than a season, and ends, say, on Hennepin Avenue in downtown Minneapolis: a six-block stretch of stripper bars and porno bookstores for which Venturi's firm designed, in 1981, a unifying border of tall metal "trees."

In the plans for Washington, L'Enfant projects a vision of American culture following European precedent, in which social and artistic values shall be progressively united in firm, ordered vistas, radiating outward from the distinctly legible and legitimate center. In the White City realized by Burnham, the vision of marble permanence is an illusion crafted in plaster, the whole a unified, artistic vision set apart from everyday life by admission turnstiles. On Hennepin Avenue, the architect retains a dim, ironic memory of environmental unity in a series of metal, treelike shapes, hung with metal discs designed to reflect the neon signs of a raw slice of American life at its tawdriest.

On an imaginary line drawn to connect these three points in the history of American urban design, Wright's work in the field of theoretical urban planning would fall at the three-quarter mark. It signaled the advent of a period when the American architect began with understandable reluctance to surrender a power that in truth had never been his own, a vicarious power to give enduring environmental form to a stable unity between the social and artistic values of his culture. It corresponded to a moment when architects began, like Wright himself, to experiment with their own innate capacity to explore the contrasts between these values. Where it had formerly been the architect's supreme cultural task to cement the unity between these values in visible, public form, it now became his task—whether he performed it willingly or not, knowingly or not—to illuminate, to comment upon, even to aggravate the conflicts and discrepancies among them.

Wright's example showed that while the former task was beyond the power of individual genius, the latter was a task no other individual specialist in his culture was better equipped to undertake.

It is the intellectual transformation of the architect's public cultural role, rather than the physical transformation of the American landscape, with which Wright's urban designs were chiefly, if unintentionally, concerned. In the very process of trying to reactivate the architect's traditional role as form giver to the public environment, Wright was in fact undertaking, indeed inventing, a wholly different role for the architect to perform. The lesson of Broadacre City was not that the American environment could not be improved through better design and planning, nor was the lesson that it could be. The lesson, rather, was that the individual architect served a function altogether different, in the wider cultural context of the public environment, from the design skills he was called upon to exercise in individual buildings. In the Wright Room all is order, grace, and under glass. Outside are traffic, litter, stained and incompetent buildings, sky, people in the street, a city: the twentieth-century Adventurer's territory. It was here that Wright began to exercise, eccentrically, the skills that a succeeding generation of architects would expand and recognize as a legitimate, indeed an integral, part of their cultural position.

"All this I have made possible." But in fact Wright did not live to see the transformation he had helped to make possible in the architect's role, a transformation he might for that matter have found even more appalling than the sight of suburban sprawl. His urban work helped make possible an American architect open to the rhetorical function his profession had long played in American culture, an architect less disposed to serve society as its established or would-be form giver than to conduct an ongoing public inquiry into the relationships between his society and its forms, to catalyze by buildings, projects, and published opinions a continuous, dynamic, rarely harmonious, often rancorous dialogue on the socio-aesthetic procedures through which environmental forms evolve.

He made possible an architect receptive to the possibility that the most enlightened forms of architecture could not provide American society with the stable, uniform environments dreamed of by Burnham, Wright, and other nineteenth- and early-twentieth-century architects and planners, but could offer only fragments, shards, provisional constructs and metaphors, flashes of insight and poetry, wit and anger that at best might serve to enlighten society on the diverse and dynamic culture that lay outside unity's grasp. Not least, Wright helped make possible the emergence of an architect who, precisely by rejecting the static environments projected by these designers, and thereby acknowledging the limitations of his art, helped to move its practice toward a more faithful expression of the democratic ideals to which their Utopian plans had been consecrated.

To suggest that American architecture had lost the capacity to provide unity and stability is not to say that it had ceased to perform its traditional function of seeking and articulating cultural order. It is to say, rather, that order in our culture had ceased to be identified exclusively with these values, could not be fully grasped by seeking to represent them, and that architecture continued to perform its traditional function by reinforcing the values of diversity and change.

Certainly it was not by virtue of its unity and stability that New York became the capital of the American Century, but by the city's boundless capacity to instruct us in the American virtues of diversity and change. The city's architecture became emblematic of modernity not by reconciling art and life in an enduring, harmonious form, but by signifying the emergence of a radically different kind of cultural order in its dynamic display of artistic visions and materialist dreams struggling in the streets, its power and imagination rising to the skies in breathtaking competition. Neon overlaid facade on facade; lights at night made new building forms unimaginable by day; window dressers ruled the city's public spaces with an authority few architects could hope to match.

Some have always recoiled from the spectacle as from the chaos of Babel; but others have been as provoked by its beauty as by that of the primal American landscape, sensing in the city's endless process of provisional order and ad hoc growth not the random bombardment of raw energy upon the senses, but the enlightenment of values indispensable to the definition of American experience. At the apogee of its cultural influence, New York's function was not to create a permanent, even a livable, city but to represent in visible, physical form the order of diversity and change underlying American culture. The skyline threw up a milestone announcing to the world the distance of this order from that of earlier civilizations, where change and diversity were apt to occur more as symptoms of a culture breaking down in poverty and neglect.

While cultures in other times and places had defined order by synthesizing social and artistic values in environments of comparatively stable harmony, the city had shown that our compelling need was to explore, illuminate, and comprehend the dynamic interplay among them. And architecture— at once an academically certified art form and, in Sullivan's phrase, "a social manifestation"—emerged as the most useful instrument that our culture possessed for undertaking the exploration.

Through the architect's medium, we have been invited to watch art intersect with life each time we open the door to a building, watch a building going up or coming down, or just walk past a building in the street. Though his medium, we have been granted the unique privilege to interpret an act of art as a political statement. We have been able to obtain a precise cost accounting of our ideals, to determine the exact distance between life as it is and life as it should be, down to the last cubic inch. We have been given the solid evidence on which to judge at any moment which of our ideals have found a marketplace, which are pending, which have lost their meaning, and which have only temporarily misplaced it. We have been able to witness for ourselves how markedly an ideal realized differs from its drawing-board projection, and to appreciate how tedious and dangerous life as it should be can be at times, how very unwelcome the harmonies of art can be when we are simply not in the mood. We have been able to discover how one man's harmony is another's bruised shins, another's stuffed-up sinuses, another's profit, another's prison; why it is essential that art stay out of life when it is not wanted.

In a Utopia, in a more static time, or in hindsight from a distant future, architects may indeed appear to forge a stable unity between the art and life of their culture. In our time, however, as a living language, American architecture has spoken more eloquently of the difference between them.

N O T E S

INTRODUCTION

2
"with Wright": Morton White and Lucia White, *The Intellectual versus the City*, rev. ed. (New York, 1977), pp. 209, 190.

2
"generous park system," "thanks to an architect": Frank Lloyd Wright, *The Future of Architecture* (New York, 1953; reprint, 1970), pp. 289–290.

2
"worm's eye view": Frank Lloyd Wright, *A Testament* (New York, 1957), p. 229.

2
"Streams": Frank Lloyd Wright, *The Living City* (New York, 1958; reprint, 1970), p. 59. Originally published in 1958, *The Living City* is a revised version of *The Disappearing City* (New York, 1932), later revised as *When Democracy Builds* (Chicago, 1945).

3
"by way of the atom bomb": *Living City*, p. 58.

6
"Truth Against the World": Frank Lloyd Wright, *An Autobiography*, 2nd rev. ed. (New York, 1977), p. 36. Wright's autobiography was first published in 1932; revised editions appeared in 1943 and 1977. In the notes that follow, pages cited refer to the 1977 edition unless otherwise noted.

6
"irrational," "surprising and fantastic": Nikolaus Pevsner, *Pioneers of Modern Architecture*, 3rd rev. ed. (Harmondsworth, 1957), p. 217.

7
"Romance—the Free Philosophy": *Testament*, p. 62.

7
"no mere license": Frank Lloyd Wright, "In the Cause of Architecture," in *Frank Lloyd Wright: Writings and Buildings*, ed. Edgar Kaufmann, Jr., and Ben Raeburn (New York, 1960), p. 183.

7
"Follow the zigs and zags": William Barrett, *The Truants: Adventures among the Intellectuals* (New York, 1982), p. 193.

7
Wright on Hugo: *Testament*, p. 17. For a brilliant discussion of Hugo's ideas on architecture (and Wright's distortion of "Hugo's prophecy"), see Neil Levine, "The Book and the Building: Hugo's Theory of Architecture and Labrouste's Bibliothèque Ste.-Geneviève," in *The Beaux Arts*, ed. Robin Middleton (Cambridge, Mass., 1982), pp. 138–173.

8
"of architecture": dustjacket of Frank Lloyd Wright, *An American Architecture*, ed. Edgar Kaufmann, Jr. (New York, 1955).

8
"refusing to design": Robert Twombly, "Wright's Price Tower Sold," *Express* (Spring 1981), p. 19.

8
variations on St. Mark's Project: see Arthur Drexler, *The Drawings of Frank Lloyd Wright* (New York, 1962), pls. 122, 175–178.

8
"an idea that had to wait": Frank Lloyd Wright: *The Story of the Tower: The Tree That Escaped the Crowded Forest* (New York, 1956), p. 18.

8
Wright on the architect's self, tools, opportunities: Frank Lloyd Wright, "The Sovereignty of the Individual," in *Writings and Buildings*, p. 99.

10
"In conclusion": Henry-Russell Hitchcock, "Frank Lloyd Wright," in *Encyclopedia of Modern Architecture*, ed. Wolfgang Pehnt (New York, 1964), p. 324.

■ 1910–1925: TOWARD THE WRONG PLACE AND TIME

14
"a developing structural art": letter to W. H. Wilson, Aug. 17, 1915. Quoted by Godfrey Rubens, intro. to William Lethaby, *Architecture, Mysticism and Myth* (London, 1974), p. xvii.

15
Wright's anti-urban epithets: *Future*, pp. 181–189 passim; *Living City*, pp. 59–60 passim.

17
Guggenheim would survive nuclear attack: Lewis Mumford, "What Wright Hath Wrought," *The Highway and the City* (New York, 1963), p. 129.

18
"even more abstract": Autobiography, p. 453.

19
"history is essential": Vincent Scully, American Architecture and Urbanism (New York, 1969), p. 257.

20
"no man can quite": "Art," in Ralph Waldo Emerson: Essays and Journals, ed. Lewis Mumford (New York, 1968), p. 236.

21
"Wright's long life's work": Vincent Scully, Frank Lloyd Wright (New York, 1960), p. 11.

22
"the real America": Future, p. 282.

23
"New York had": F. Scott Fitzgerald, "My Lost City," in The Crack-Up, ed. Edmund Wilson (New York, 1956; Harmondsworth, 1965), p. 22.

23
"The steamers": Paul Rosenfeld, Port of New York (New York, 1924; reprint, Urbana, Ill., 1966), p. 291.

24
"roam the streets": Autobiography (1943 ed.), p. 276.

24
infant in drawer: Finis Farr, Frank Lloyd Wright (New York, 1961), p. 199 (interview with Olgivanna Lloyd Wright).

25
"a sort of religious": Henry-Russell Hitchcock, In the Nature of Materials: The Buildings of Frank Lloyd Wright, 1887–1941 (New York, 1941), p. 82.

25
"After 1910": ibid., p. 59.

26
"a man disciplined": "Sovereignty," in Writings and Buildings, p. 99.

26
"This absorbing": Autobiography (1932 ed.), p. 165.

27
"Victor Hugo": Testament, p. 17.

28
"a proud and soaring thing": Louis Sullivan, "The Tall Office Building Artistically Considered," reprinted in Kindergarten Chats and Other Writings (New York, 1947), p. 206.

28
"so broad": Louis Sullivan, The Autobiography of an Idea (New York, 1926), p. 221.

28
"We are at that dramatic moment": Sullivan, Kindergarten Chats; quoted in Lewis Mumford, The Brown Decades, 2nd ed. (New York, 1971), p. 72.

28
"Sullivan was the first": Mumford, *Brown Decades*, p. 74.

31
Wright on collectors: *Testament*, p. 207.

31
"last great Chicago work": Hitchcock, *Materials*, p. 62.

32
"a synthesis of all the Arts": *American Architecture*, p. 60.

35
"Not a chastened Taliesin": *Autobiography*, p. 214.

35
"Something was coming clearer": *Autobiography* (1943 ed.), p. 190.

37
"help Japan": Frank Lloyd Wright and Baker Brownell, Architecture and Modern Life (New York, 1938); excerpted in *Writings and Buildings*, p. 199.

37
"nothing more or less": *Autobiography* (1932 ed.), p. 241.

37
"that house": *ibid.*, p. 245.

38
"For once in a lifetime": *Modern Life*; excerpted in *Writings and Buildings*, pp. 205–207.

38
"transition building": *Modern Life*; excerpted in *ibid.*, p. 206.

38
"The New Imperial": *Modern Life*; excerpted in *ibid.*, p. 207.

39
"Are really good buildings": *Modern Life*; excerpted in *ibid.*, p. 206.

39
"a monumental dead end": Robert C. Twombly, *Frank Lloyd Wright: An Interpretive Biography* (New York, 1973), p. 142. This biography is the Baedeker to Wright's career. I here record my debt to Mr. Twombly for his guidance and companionship in the course of my own somewhat idiosyncratic tour. My fear of getting lost in the dense conceptual thickets of Broadacre City was considerably mitigated by having Mr. Twombly's book at hand to steer me back to the major highways of Wright's life and work.

39
"mere 'artistic activity' ": "In the Cause of Architecture," in *Writings and Buildings*, p. 193.

41
"I suspect tragedy": *The Letters of F. Scott Fitzgerald*, ed. Andrew Turnbull (New York, 1963), p. 179.

41
"see with my own eyes": Alexander Woollcott, "The Prodigal Father," in *While Rome Burns* (New York, 1934), p. 176.

41
"The truth is probably": Wolcott Gibbs, "Big Nemo," in *More in Sorrow* (New York, 1958), p. 84.

41
"[If] I were suffered to apply the word 'genius' to only one living American, I would have to save it . . . for Frank Lloyd Wright": Woollcott, p. 179.

42
"witless and vindictive": *ibid.*, p. 173.

42
Woollcott's last byline: *Atlantic Monthly*, March 1943; quoted in Richard H. Goldstone, *Thornton Wilder: An Intimate Portrait* (New York, 1975), p. 171.

42
"When a Samson": Woollcott, p. 173.

44
"half a dozen": Fitzgerald, *The Crack-Up*, p. 25.

44
"We thought we were apart": *ibid.*

44
"But you see": A. Crawford, "Ten Letters from Frank Lloyd Wright to Charles Robert Ashbee," *Architectural History* 13 (1970), p. 67.

■ 1926–1959: TWO CITIES

46
"In democratic communities": Alexis de Tocqueville, *Democracy in America*, trans. Henry Reeve and Francis Bowen, ed. Phillips Bradley (New York, 1945), 2:82–83.

47
"I would go back to town": the passage appears in this form in *Autobiography* (1943 ed.), p. 276. For Wright's reference to the 1926 New York visit, see p. 313 of the 1977 edition: "During the months that followed the Minneapolis debacle in the 'Northern Baptist Belt,' we were in New York. Sister Maginel took us in."

47
"Architecture and eloquence": Ralph Waldo Emerson, "Thoughts on Art"; in *American Art 1700–1960*, ed. John W. McCoubrey (Englewood Cliffs, N.J., 1965), p. 73.

47
"perhaps the tradition": Rosenfeld, pp. 294–295.

48
"The new races": José Clemente Orozco, "New World, New Races, and New Art"; reprinted in *Artists on Art*, ed. Robert J. Goldwater and Marco Treves (New York, 1958), p. 479.

48
German professor [Kuno Franke]: *Testament*, pp. 131–132.

48
"it was the towers of Manhattan": Rosenfeld, p. 288.

49
William Norman Guthrie: "In an effort to make the church attractive to progressive parishioners, Dr. Guthrie worked out a ritual based on the theory of the essential unity of all religions, which included Greek folk dancing, American Indian chants, and many other things which the conservative element in the diocese heatedly declared to have no place in an Episcopalian church" (The WPA Guide to New York City, New York, 1939; reprint, New York, 1982). Edgar Tafel says that Martha Graham (whose first group, Martha Graham and Trio, debuted in New York in 1926) had been invited by Guthrie to choreograph the "ritual" (conversation with the author).

50
"The purpose of the cathedral": Glass Architecture by Paul Scheerbart and Alpine Architecture by Bruno Taut, ed. Dennis Sharp, trans. Shirley Palmer (London, 1972), p. 124.

50
Marinetti on pasta: Elizabeth David, Italian Food (Harmondsworth, 1969), pp. 93–95.

50
inspiration for Metropolis: Fritz Lang, Metropolis (London, 1973), p. 6.

50
"The face of the earth": Sharp, p. 46.

50
"Imagine a city": Frank Lloyd Wright, "The Nature of Materials," Architectural Record (April 1928), in Writings and Buildings, pp. 226–227. The parallel between Scheerbart and Wright is drawn by Sharp in his introductory essay, pp. 27–28.

51
"the whole of glass architecture": Sharp, p. 61.

51
"the free churches of America": ibid.

51
"so many ideas": ibid., p. 71.

51
"I dream": "The Nature," in Writings and Buildings, p. 227.

51
"to resist": Sharp, p. 45.

51
"crystal symbol . . . one day rise": Walter Gropius, first Bauhaus manifesto (Weimar, 1919); quoted in Peter Gay, Weimar Culture: The Outsider as Insider (New York, 1968), p. 98.

52
"Like a cluster": Luigi Barzini, O, America, When You and I Were Young (New York, 1977), p. 24.

52
"grove of churches": Colette, "Maiden Voyage of the Normandie," in Places, ed. Margaret Crosland, trans. David le Vay (New York, 1971), p. 58.

52
"American architecture": *Testament*, p. 101.

52
"It seems": Rosenfeld, p. 292.

53
"If this power": "The Art and Craft of the Machine," Wright's 1930 version of a speech originally delivered in 1901, in *Future*, p. 91.

53
"With me": Sullivan, letter to Claude Bragdon; quoted in Bragdon, *More Lives Than One* (New York, 1938), p. 159, and in John Kouwenhoven, *The Arts in Modern American Civilization* (New York, 1967), p. 74.

54
Henry James on church-owned real estate: *The American Scene*, ed. Leon Edel (Bloomington, Ind., 1968), pp. 94–95.

54
"Why does the Church": *Living City*, p. 200.

54
"The failure to see God": *Future*, p. 71.

55
"a new expression": Fitzgerald, *The Crack-Up*, p. 29.

55
"We have to get people": *Future*, p. 314.

56
"Architecture is dethroned": "The Art and Craft of the Machine" (1901 version), in *Writings and Buildings*, p. 58.

56
"the press was to become": Edmund Wilson, *To the Finland Station*, rev. ed. (New York, 1972), p. 17.

56
"cathedrals suffered execution": Lorenz Eitner, "Revolutionary Vandalism," in *Neoclassicism and Romanticism* (Englewood Cliffs, N.J., 1970), p. 140.

56
"the architect cannot bury": *Future*, p. 236.

56
"We go occasionally": *ibid.*, p. 298.

59
"Not only do I intend": quoted in Winthrop Sargeant, "Frank Lloyd Wright," *Life*, (Aug. 12, 1946), p. 85.

59
"I've found out": *Autobiography*, p. 154.

60
"He could design": Norris Kelly Smith, *Frank Lloyd Wright: A Study in Architectural Content* (Englewood Cliffs, N.J., 1966), pp. 83–84. A dazzling study, memorable not

only for its acute insight into Wright's thought but as a model for the type of architectural criticism suggested by the Sullivan quotation at the opening of my book. Lewis Mumford's *New Yorker* articles on Wright, though on a smaller scale, are attuned with equal brilliance to the conception of architecture as "a social manifestation."

60
"cottage for level ground": *Living City*, p. 70.

61
"everywhere and nowhere": *Future*, p. 298.

61
"In 1935": Sargeant, p. 94.

61
"brings into coherent relationship: Hitchcock, *Materials*, p. 88.

61
"the ultimate importance": Smith, p. 170.

63
"Incentive Zoning" was a term coined in the 1960s by the New York City Department of City Planning to describe a legal process that enabled the city to influence architectural forms without strictly dictating them to architects. In terming New York City Frank Lloyd Wright's incentive zone, I mean not only to indicate the impact of New York upon his later work, but also to suggest the significance of that work to the increasing influence of urbanism upon architecture at the present time.

63
"entirely in accord": Scully, *Architecture and Urbanism*, p. 161.

63
"So that those": *Story of the Tower*, p. 17.

63
"An idea that had to wait": *ibid.*, p. 18.

64
"Now the skyscraper": *ibid.*

64
"Broadway Creed": *Autobiography*, p. 487.

65
"a coarse, dark vein": Lewis Mumford, "A Phoenix Too Infrequent," in *From the Ground Up* (New York, 1956), p. 90.

65
"our greatest nineteenth-century architect": Philip Johnson, "100 Years, Frank Lloyd Wright and Us," in Johnson, *Writings* (New York, 1979), pp. 192–193.

65
"To sum up": Pevsner, *Pioneers*, pp. 192–193.

65
"Choice": Gertrude Stein, "American Cities and How They Differ from Each Other"; excerpted in *Gertrude Stein's America*, ed. Gilbert A. Harrison (New York, 1965), p. 54.

67
Wright on Sullivan as a "sentimentalist": *Autobiography*, p. 130.

68
"to cross a new frontier": James Marston Fitch, *Walter Gropius* (New York, 1960), p. 25.

69
Mies and the nineteenth-century box: *Testament*, p. 203; also cited in Twombly, p. 276.

69
"man-eating skyscrapers": *Autobiography*, p. 341.

72
"Wright's introduction": Smith, pp. 154–155.

72
"from the ancient patterns": *ibid.*, p. 158.

73
"was considered": Twombly, p. 165.

73
"we make out": William Butler Yeats, "Per Amica Silentia Lunae"; quoted in Edmund Wilson, *Axel's Castle* (New York, 1931), p. 44.

73
Wright threatens move to New York: *New York Times*, Nov. 10, 12, 1954.

74
"I know": Woollcott, p. 178.

74
Wright's letterhead: Edgar Tafel, *Apprentice to Genius: Years with Frank Lloyd Wright* (New York, 1979), p. 98. Tafel's memoir of life as a Taliesin apprentice is the best documentary record of Wright at the critical turning poing between the middle years and the second "Golden Age." It is also, in my view, the most convincing portrait of Wright drawn to human scale.

75
"every architectural episode": *ibid.*, p. 64. In this connection, Smith writes: "To many persons the villain of the depression story seemed to be the city of New York. Possibly the strain of anti-urbanism that enters Wright's thinking at this time was shaped in part by this common feeling" (p. 115).

75
"civilization be measured": W. H. Auden, "The Greeks and Us," in *Forewords and Afterwords* (New York, 1973), p. 9.

76
"ne plus ultra": *Living City*, p. 58.

76
"it is in the aggregation": Montgomery Schuyler, "The Skyline of New York," *Harper's Weekly* (March 20, 1897); quoted in John Kouwenhoven, *The Columbia Historical Portrait of New York*, 2nd ed. (New York, 1972), p. 394.

76
four-year-old daughter: "Daddy," said she, "they could have made it [the Empire State Building] higher—couldn't they? . . . Then why didn't they?": *Autobiography*, pp. 340–341.

77
obsolescence of the modern city: *Autobiography*, p. 343; *Future*, p. 182.

77
"By way of": *Living City*, p. 35.

77
"It is as desirable": *Future*, p. 236.

78
Wright designs a continent: Sybil Moholy-Nagy, paraphrased in Scully, *Frank Lloyd Wright*, p. 12.

78
St. Mark's model in Broadacre City exhibition: see especially installation photographs of the exhibition in *Taliesin* magazine (October 1940), p. 38, and in *Architectural Forum* (January 1938), p. 19. Wright was editor of *Taliesin* and guest editor of *Architectural Forum*.

79
Frank Lloyd Wright and Iovanna Wright, *Architecture: Man in Possession of His Earth* (New York, 1962).

79
"the agent of state": Frank Lloyd Wright, "Broadacre City: A New Community Plan," *Architectural Record* (April 1935), p. 246.

79
"in other words": Smith, p. 152.

80
Schapiro on Broadacre City: Meyer Schapiro, "Architect's Utopia," *Partisan Review* (March 1938), p. 43; a point raised by Smith, p. 154.

80
"has never faced": Mumford, "Phoenix," p. 88. In his *Urban Utopias in the Twentieth Century* (New York, 1977), Robert Fishman describes Wright's one attempt at "cooperative" planning: "In 1940 a group in Detroit sponsoring a plan to resettle auto workers on the land asked him to design a group of homesteads for twenty-five families. . . . Each house was surrounded by its own farmland. The workers were to continue part-time employment at a factory 20 miles away, while they gradually brought more and more of the land under cultivation. . . . Construction was never actually begun on this 'working model' of Broadacre City. . . . He succinctly summarized the affair in his title for the published plans: 'Berm Houses for Cooperative Workers. Failed for Lack of Cooperation' " (Fishman, pp. 147–148). The title also summarizes Wright's own negative attitude toward "any form of collectivism"; see Frank Lloyd Wright, *The Natural House* (New York, 1954), p. 186.

81
"had nothing whatever": Smith, pp. 149, 152. Smith is referring to Edmund Wilson's discussion of the "contagious examples" set, it was hoped, by nineteenth-century American Utopian communities (*Finland Station*, p. 102).

81
"In human terms": *Living City*, p. 59.

81
"Night is but": *Living City*, p. 245.

82
Broad Acre: Frank Lloyd Wright, "On Broad Acre Ranch," *The Weekly Home News* (Spring Green, Wis., Apr. 18, 1929); cited by Twombly, p. 176.

83
"There is only one solution": *Natural House*, p. 140.

83
"to his own 'Usonian' ": Mumford, "Phoenix," p. 91.

83
origins of Monopoly: Calvin Trillin, "Monopoly and History," *The New Yorker* (Feb. 13, 1978), pp. 90–96.

84
"a bicycle shed": Nikolaus Pevsner, *An Outline of European Architecture*, 7th ed. (Harmondsworth, 1963), p. 15.

85
"Here I am": quoted in Twombly, p. 223.

85
"After all everybody": Gertrude Stein, *Paris France* (New York, 1940), p. 2.

86
Landlord's Game: Trillin, p. 93.

86
Arthur and the Round Table: Smith, pp. 119–120.

87
"I am not fond": *Autobiography*, p. 593.

89
"the first truly": *Natural House*, p. 115.

89
"cream colored masonite": Norval White and Eliot Willensky, *AIA Guide to New York City* (New York, 1967), p. 386. A judgment considerably softened if not reversed in subsequent editions of the *Guide*.

89
"I would rather solve": *Natural House*, p. 79.

90
"we shall solve": Henry Ford, "The Exodus from the City," in *Ford Ideals* (Dearborn, 1922), pp. 425–428; quoted in White, *Intellectual versus City*, p. 201.

90
"the house of moderate cost": *Natural House*, p. 79.

91
cultivated and vernacular traditions: Kouwenhoven, *Arts in Modern American Civilization*, pp. 43–74.

91
"you can never get": *Natural House*, p. 186.

92
"today we have": *Future*, p. 85.

92
"No wonder": *ibid.*, p. 141.

92
Mrs. Plasterbilt, etc.: *Natural House*, p. 18.

92
"To put it bluntly": Smith, p. 9.

92
"embarrassed": *Natural House*, p. 197.

92
"very wealthy people": *ibid.*

92
"the upper middle third": *ibid.*

93
traffic problem: *Living City*, p. 85.

93
"What would you say": *Future*, p. 30.

94
"all my life": *Natural House*, pp. 172–173.

94
"the boards in the ceiling": *ibid.*, p. 175.

94
"it has been said": *ibid.*, p. 38.

94
"the world's greatest," "of infinite variety," "the principles": dustjackets of *Natural House* and *American Architecture*.

96
"the universal modern art": *Future*, p. 70.

96
"thousands of New Yorkers": *Natural House*, p. 118.

97
"To say the house": *ibid.*, pp. 115–116.

97
"of infinite variety": *ibid.*, p. 116.

97
"the scientific art": *American Architecture*, p. 44.

98
" So go far": *Natural House*, p. 139.

99
"inferior desecrators": quoted in Twombly, p. 278.

99
"a bedlam": Olgivanna Lloyd Wright, *Our House* (New York, 1959), p. 287. As the material in this chapter shows, Olgivanna Wright's books illuminate more fully than her husband's his connection to New York in the 1940s and 50s. I have relied on them not only for her accounts of life at Taliesin the Third, but even more for the portrait they paint of Wright as a social being: his behavior with friends, neighbors, relatives, apprentices, fellow architects, the rich and famous, the press, and clients. In my account of Wright's ambivalent relationship to "the community," I have concentrated on the conflicts that precipitated the creative crisis of the middle years. By contrast, Mrs. Wright's books show how successfully, and with what humor, he learned to live with these conflicts after he had put his disasters behind him. Indeed, despite (or perhaps because of) the somewhat cloying tone of reverence, her books suggest the great extent of her own contribution to Wright's "rehabilitation." My essay is about Wright's debt to New York, but in my view his debt to Olgivanna Wright remains another "unwritten chapter" in the story of his later years.

99
"established themselves": *ibid.*

99
"The Taliesin atmosphere": Olgivanna Lloyd Wright, *The Shining Brow* (New York, 1960), p. 174.

99
"William Short": *ibid.*

99
"For the last twenty years": *Our House*, p. 287.

101
"style centers": *Future*, p. 120.

101
"sensitive, unspoiled students": *ibid.*

101
"Architecture is limited": Adrian Stokes, "The Luxury and Necessity of Painting," in *The Image in Form*, ed. Richard Wollheim (New York, 1972), p. 81.

102
"The Fellowship": Frank Lloyd Wright, "An Extension of the Work in Architecture at Taliesin to Include Apprentices in Residence," Taliesin Fellowship announcement brochure, reprinted in *Autobiography*, p. 420.

102
"for any city": Norma Evenson, *Paris: A Century of Change, 1878–1978* (New Haven, 1979), p. 361. While Evenson's study provides a more direct approach to Le Corbusier's urban Utopian vision than to Wright's, it is of universal interest in documenting the complex symbiosis between architecture and planning with which both architects were concerned. Also, because even American ideas of urbanism were shaped to a considerable degree by Le Corbusier's absorption in the very French concept of "urbanisme," I found the book invaluable in trying to relate and contrast Wright's ideas to contemporary thought in the third part, "1960–1980: About Town and the Building."

102
"I'll think as I act as I am": *Autobiography*, p. 405.

102
"the inspirational leadership": "An Extension," in *Autobiography*, p. 419.

103
"The masses of men": Frederick Schuman, "Liberalism and Communism Reconsidered," *Southern Review* (Autumn 1936), pp. 335–336; quoted in Richard H. Pells, *Radical Visions and American Dreams* (New York, 1973), p. 323. Smith writes that the Depression was the great "public event that completed [Wright's] reorientation" toward the social and philosophical direction his work took in later years (pp. 113–114). Pells's study provides a superb synthesis of the Depression's impact on culture and social thought.

104
"leaders in thought": "An Extension," in *Autobiography*, p. 418.

104
Stein and Toklas regret: *Our House*, p. 244.

105
"The Big City": "An Extension," in *Autobiography*, p. 419.

105
"nature is the source": *Kindergarten Chats*, p. 149.

106
"At times Mr. Wright": *Our House*, p. 287.

106
"Robert Moses is struggling": *Natural House*, p. 139.

106
"he simply": *Our House*, p. 245.

107
"To many such": *Future*, p. 192.

108
"the modern theater": *Natural House*, p. 79.

108
"The Broadway Creed": *Autobiography*, p. 487.

110
"Go back far enough": *Living City*, pp. 23–24.

110
"were in fact": Fishman, p. 157.

110
"Both human divergencies": *Living City*, p. 24.

110
"Turn that off!" Olgivanna Lloyd Wright, *Frank Lloyd Wright: His Life—His Work—His Words* (New York, 1966), pp. 135–136.

111
Guggenheim protest: *New York Times*, Dec. 22, 1956.

111
"condemned in architecture": Twombly, p. 258.

111
"you may go": Mumford, "Wright Hath Wrought," p. 128.

111
"I am sufficiently familiar": quoted in Twombly, p. 258.

112
art historians: but Frank O'Hara grasped at the Guggenheim's 1961 exhibition of the New York School that "the thing is that with this show the Guggenheim became part of New York" (*Art Chronicles*, New York, 1975, p. 5).

112
"the grandeur": Robert Rosenblum, "The Primal American Scene," in *The Natural Paradise: Painting in America 1800–1950*, ed. Kynaston McShine (New York, 1976), p. 15.

112
Abstract Expressionism's rise between 1943 and 1959: *ibid.*

113
"what they now call": "Frank Lloyd Wright Talks of His Art," *New York Times Magazine* (Oct. 4, 1953); excerpted in *American Architecture*, p. 223.

113
"My concern": quoted in McShine, p. 109. The artists' statements in this chapter are found in the section "Toward the Abstract Sublime: A Selection of Twentieth-Century Artists' Texts," pp. 107–129.

113
"the latest sense": "Wright Talks"; excerpted in *American Architecture*, p. 122.

113
"I am breaching": quoted in McShine, p. 110.

113
"rather walk": quoted in *ibid.*, p. 117.

114
"I take SPACE": Charles Olson, *Call Me Ishmael* (New York, 1947); quoted in Olson, *Selected Writings*, ed. Robert Creeley (New York, 1966), p. 2.

114
"Michelangelo": *Future*, p. 250.

114
"Corbusier": quoted in Twombly, p. 276.

114
"were unable to rise": Frank Lloyd Wright, "Recollections: The United States 1893–1920," *Architect's Journal* (London) (July 1926); excerpted in *American Architecture*, p. 60.

115
"What is it": *Architecture and Modern Life*, p. 275.

115
"Abstract art": quoted in McShine, p. 127.

115
"To us art": quoted in *ibid.*, p. 125.

116
"the fact": quoted in *ibid.*, p. 120.

116
"I do not paint": quoted in *ibid.*, p. 109.

116
"I am Nature": quoted in *ibid.*, p. 120.

116
"dream of open space" and comparison of Guggenheim to a Pollock: Scully, *Architecture and Urbanism*, p. 176.

116
"There was a reviewer": quoted in McShine, p. 125.

116
"Maybe the world": quoted in *ibid.*, p. 120.

116
"My imagination": quoted in *ibid.*

117
"The cult of space": quoted in *ibid.*, p. 125.

117
"claimed the privileges": Mumford, "Wright Hath Wrought," p. 137.

117
"absurdities as a museum": *ibid.*, p. 138.

118
"I know how flagrantly": Woollcott, p. 178.

■ 1960–1980: ABOUT TOWN AND THE BUILDING

143
"an imitation of Le Corbusier": Jane Jacobs, *The Death and Life of Great American Cities* (New York, 1961), p. 23.

143
"urbanism": *Random House Dictionary* (New York, 1967), p. 1572. But we can probably date our contemporary "meaning" of Urbanism, such as it is, to 1922 and the following exchange, recounted in Fishman, p. 188: "Le Corbusier has recounted the origin of his first plan for an ideal city, the 'Contemporary City for Three Million People.' In 1922 he was asked by the organizers of the Salon d'Automne to prepare an exhibition on urbanism. 'What do you mean by urbanism?' Le Corbusier asked the salon's director. 'Well, it's a sort of street art,' the man replied, 'for stores, signs, and the like; it includes such things as the ornamental glass knobs on railings.' 'Fine,' said Le Corbusier, 'I shall design a great fountain and behind it place a city for three million people.' "

145
Mumford traces technology to prehistoric man in his *The Myth of the Machine* (New York, 1967).

146
"skinny glass boxes": quoted in Twombly, p. 276.

146
"Any city of *futurism*": *Autobiography*, p. 344.

149
"Americans have": Robert H. Walker, *The Reform Spirit in America* (New York, 1976), p. 15.

149
"For Sullivan": Smith, p. 16.

150
"architecture or revolution": Le Corbusier, *Towards a New Architecture*, trans. Frederick Etchells (London, 1927), p. 267.

152
"the Machine": "Sovereignty," in *Writings and Buildings*, p. 93.

153
"the knowing, accurate and magnificent": Le Corbusier, *Looking at City Planning*, trans. Eleanor Levieux (New York, 1971), p. 18.

154
"the term architecture": Pevsner, *European Architecture*, p. 15.

154
"had an almost": Mumford, "The Fujiyama of Architecture," in *From the Ground Up*, p. 75.

155
"Wright's exhibition": *ibid*.

156
"The two characteristics": W. H. Auden, "The Poet and the City," in *The Dyer's Hand* (New York, 1968), pp. 83–84.

156
"We have been": quoted in Morrison Heckscher and Elizabeth G. Miller, *An Architect and His Client* (New York, 1973), unpaged.

157
"Everyone knew": Kenneth Clark, address delivered at Pritzker Prize Ceremony, May 1981; excerpted in *Express* (Summer 1981), p. 7.

157
"the buildings": Smith, pp. 7–8.

158
"all history disproves": quoted in John Jacobus, *Philip Johnson* (New York, 1962), p. 113.

159
"many of its": Kenneth Frampton, *Modern Architecture: A Critical History* (New York, 1980), p. 280.

159
"the great drawback": interview with Franzen, *Architectural Forum* (May 1963), p. 144; quoted in James Marston Fitch, *American Building: The Historical Forces That Shaped It*, rev. ed. (New York, 1973), p. 278.

159
"Mies didn't give": quoted in Peter Blake, "Philip Johnson Knows Too Much," *New York* (May 15, 1978), p. 58.

159
"the most disturbing aspect": Fitch, *American Building*, p. 282.

160
Mumford's opinion of skyscrapers: Mumford, *Brown Decades*, pp. 69–70.

161
"even Frank Lloyd Wright": Fitch, *American Building*, p. 219.

162
"A *city*": Jacobs, p. 372.

162
"soft cop": Robert Goodman, *After the Planners* (New York, 1971), p. 13. A classic of the *Zeitgeist*, perhaps the most passionate expression of the radical social thought that fueled urbanism in the late 1960s and early 70s and that perpetuated the rift between the "Urbanist" and the architect.

163
statistics on economic inequality: see Richard Parker, *The Myth of the Middle Class* (New York, 1972), esp. pp. 51–91.

163
Wright on Jefferson's "aristoi": *Testament*, p. 62.

164
"Protestant barn": Farr, p. 263. A short-list of classic Wright insults, including his memorable description of Mies van der Rohe's Seagram Building as "a whiskey bottle on a card table."

164
"a personal idiom": Fitch, *American Building*, pp. 280, 278.

165
"the internal logic": *ibid.*, p. 280.

168
"This book": Jacobs, p. 3.

168
"I am for an art": quoted in Barbara Rose, *Claes Oldenburg* (New York, 1969), p. 190.

173
"In only a single field": *Totem and Taboo*, in *The Basic Writings of Sigmund Freud*, ed. A. A. Brill (New York, 1938), p. 877.

178
commemorative catalogue of unbuilt projects: Hitchcock, *Materials*, p. 76.

178
"ten times as far": *Natural House*, pp. 140–141.

178
Wright sues over power masts: Twombly, p. 263.

184
"mental exercises," "mutual assassinations": Olgivanna Lloyd Wright, *The Roots of Life* (New York, 1963), p. 236. Regarding the idea of Mile-High Illinois as a "second thought," Wright stated: "If I were to do Broadacre City again the major change would be the Mile-High Building, which would absorb and justify and legitimize

the gregarious instinct of humanity, and the necessity for getting together surrounding an Idea, which would be the sky-city—and it would mop up what now remains of urbanism, and leave us free to do Broadacre City" (quoted in *ibid.*, p. 235).

184
Wright's outing with Aalto: Anthony C. Antonaides, "The Truth about Architects," *Express* (Summer 1981), pp. 10–11; also *Humor in Architecture*, forthcoming.

185
Peter Blake, *God's Own Junkyard* (New York, 1964).

187
"In the view": Susan Sontag, "Approaching Artaud," in *Under the Sign of Saturn* (New York, 1980), p. 16.

188
"Main Street": Robert Venturi, *Complexity and Contradiction in Architecture*, 2nd ed. (New York, 1977), p. 104.

188
plan for Hennepin Avenue Entertainment Centrum, by Venturi, Roche and Scott Brown: "News Report," *Progressive Architecture* (July 1981), pp. 31–34.

ILLUSTRATIONS

122
Steel cathedral: "It consisted of": Fishman, p. 141.

126
Broadacre City: "Typical street view": *Living*, pp. 138–139.

139
Key Project: "The last project": dustjacket of Drexler.

ILLUSTRATION SOURCES

Permission to reproduce the following drawings by Frank Lloyd Wright from the collection of The Frank Lloyd Wright Foundation is courtesy The Frank Lloyd Wright Memorial Foundation.

122
Project: Steel Cathedral including Minor Cathedrals for a Million People, New York City, N.Y. 1926. Elevation. Pencil and red and green pencil on tracing paper, 26 3/8 × 28 3/4″. Photograph courtesy The Museum of Modern Art, New York.

123
Project: Steel Cathedral, New York City, New York. 1926. Plan. Pencil and colored pencils on tracing paper mounted to board, 23 5/8 × 31 1/2″. Photograph courtesy The Museum of Modern Art, New York.

124
Project: St. Mark's Apartment Tower, St. Mark's-in-the-Bouwerie, New York City, N.Y. 1929. Perspective. Pencil and colored pencils on tracing paper, 28 1/4 × 10 1/8″. Photograph courtesy The Museum of Modern Art, New York.

125
Project: St. Mark's Apartment Tower, St. Mark's-in-the-Bouwerie, New York City, N.Y. 1929. Aerial perspective. Pencil on tracing paper, 19 3/4 × 15″. Photograph courtesy The Museum of Modern Art, New York.

126
Broadacre City: Typical Street View at Civic Center. 1958. Photograph courtesy The Frank Lloyd Wright Memorial Foundation.

136
Solomon R. Guggenheim Museum, New York City, New York. 1943. Elevation. Pencil

and colored pencils on opaque buff paper, 20 1/8 × 24 1/4″. Photograph courtesy The Museum of Modern Art, New York.

137
Solomon R. Guggenheim Museum, New York City, New York. 1943. Elevation. Pencil and colored pencils on opaque cream-colored paper, 20 1/4 × 24 1/2″. Photograph courtesy The Museum of Modern Art, New York.

138
Solomon R. Guggenheim Museum, New York City, New York. 1943–59. Elevation and section. Pencil and colored pencils on tracing paper, 26 3/4 × 30 3/4″. Photograph courtesy The Museum of Modern Art, New York.

139
Project: Manhattan Sports Pavilion, New York City, New York. 1956. Aerial perspective. Brown ink, pencil and colored pencils on tracing paper, 26 × 57 1/2″. Photograph courtesy The Museum of Modern Art, New York.

139
Frank Lloyd Wright/Taliesin Associated Architects. "Key Project" Apartment and Hotel Towers and Gardens, Ellis Island, New York Harbor. 1959–61. Aerial perspective. Pencils, inks, and gold paint on tracing paper, 33 7/8 × 51 1/8″. Photograph courtesy The Museum of Modern Art, New York.